Management Education for the World

A Vision for Business Schools Serving People and Planet

Katrin Muff
Business School Lausanne, Switzerland

Thomas Dyllick
University of St. Gallen, Switzerland

Mark Drewell
The Globally Responsible Leadership Initiative Foundation, Belgium

John North
University of Pretoria, South Africa

Paul Shrivastava
Concordia University, Canada

Jonas Haertle
PRME Secretariat, UN Global Compact Office, United Nations

In Association with the GRLI Foundation

Edward Elgar
Cheltenham, UK • Northampton, MA, USA

D1042815

Published by
Edward Elgar Publishing Limited
The Lypiatts
15 Lansdown Road
Cheltenham
Glos GL50 2JA
UK

Edward Elgar Publishing, Inc.
William Pratt House
9 Dewey Court
Northampton
Massachusetts 01060
USA

Paperback edition reprinted 2014

A catalogue record for this book
is available from the British Library

Library of Congress Control Number: 2013931295

The book is available electronically in the ElgarOnline.com
Business Subject Collection, E-ISBN 978 1 78254 764 8

ISBN 978 1 78254 762 4 (cased)
     978 1 78254 763 1 (paperback)

Typeset by Servis Filmsetting Ltd, Stockport, Cheshire
Printed in Great Britain by Berforts Information Press Ltd

Contents

Figures

Tables

About the authors*

Katrin Muff (DBA) has been Dean of Business School Lausanne (BSL), Switzerland, since 2008 (www.bsl-lausanne.ch). She obtained both her doctorate and her MBA from BSL. Under her leadership, the school has expanded its vision from a focus on entrepreneurship to also embrace responsibility and sustainability into a three-pillar vision for both education and applied research. She previously worked for Schindler in Switzerland and Australia, for Alcoa in business development, for M&A in Switzerland and the United States, and as General Manager of their first Russian manufacturing plant in Moscow. After her position as Director, Strategic Planning EMEA of IAMS Pet Food (a division of Procter & Gamble, in the Netherlands), she co-founded Yupango, a coaching consultancy dedicated to developing start-up companies and training management teams.

Thomas Dyllick (Dr. oec. HSG) is a Professor of Sustainability Management, and Managing Director of the Institute for Economy and the Environment, at University of St. Gallen, Switzerland (www.iwoe. unisg.ch). He currently serves as University Delegate for Responsibility and Sustainability (www.sustainability.unisg.ch). He was vice-president in charge of teaching and quality development from 2003 to 2011, and dean of the University of St. Gallen's Management Department between 2001 and 2003. He is the author of several books and many publications in the fields of corporate sustainability, sustainable development, and management education; he serves on a number of boards.

Mark Drewell MA (OXON), FRSA is the CEO of the Globally Responsible Leadership Initiative, a worldwide partnership of companies and business schools taking action to develop the next generation of globally responsible leaders (www.grli.org). Born in the UK, he studied Philosophy, Politics and Economics at Oxford University and spent 20 years working in South Africa with the international, diversified, industrial company Barloworld Limited – where he headed Corporate Affairs, Investor Relations and

---

* For further correspondence with the authors and 50+20 please write to 50plus20@grli.org.

Group Marketing and led the company's move into sustainability. His contributions to society include having chaired the boards of The World's Children's Prize for the Rights of the Child and the Endangered Wildlife Trust. He is a frequent public speaker.

John North is a next generation integrational entrepreneur, operating across the boundaries of society, business and academia. An MBA graduate, who created 2 online businesses during his undergraduate degree, he worked as an international strategy consultant advising Fortune 500 companies and was the founding head of Accenture's sustainability practice in Ireland. His passion to make a difference in his home country brought him back to South Africa in 2009, where he combines local work as the senior advisor to the Albert Luthuli Centre for Responsible Leadership, University of Pretoria (www.up.ac.za/crl) and an international role as Project Head of the Brussels-based, UN-backed Globally Responsible Leadership Initiative. In the latter role he is focussed on a series of implementation projects of the 50+20 Agenda of management education in service of society (50plus20.org).

Paul Shrivastava (PhD) is the David O'Brien Distinguished Professor of Sustainable Enterprise at the John Molson School of Business, Concordia University, Montreal (johnmolson.concordia.ca/sustainable). He also serves as Senior Advisor on sustainability at Bucknell University and the Indian Institute of Management-Shillong, India. In addition, he serves on the Board of Trustees of DeSales University, Allentown, Pennsylvania. He also leads the International Research Chair in Art and Sustainable Enterprise at ICN Business School, Nancy, France. In these roles he combines scientific and artistic approaches to sustainable development.

Jonas Haertle is Head of the Principles for Responsible Management Education (PRME) secretariat of the United Nations Global Compact Office (www.unprme.org). Previously, he was the coordinator of the UN Global Compact's Local Networks in Latin America, Africa and the Middle East. Prior to joining the United Nations, Jonas worked as a research analyst for the German public broadcasting service Norddeutscher Rundfunk. He holds a master's degree in European Studies from Hamburg University, Germany. As a Fulbright scholar, he also attained an MSc degree in Global Affairs from Rutgers University in the USA.

* For further correspondence with the authors and 50+20 please write to 50plus20@grli.org.

Preamble

A V-tactile nano-fiche transcript, Brazzaville, 5 June 2112

WELCOME TO THE YEAR 2112

Let us tell you a story that began a century ago – in the year 2012 – when globally responsible leadership had just started to emerge. It was an amazing time. After 200 years of intensive development, society had all the economic and technical capabilities necessary to enable 7 billion people to live on the planet. However, they had not focused on living *well*; more than a billion people were starving at that time.

Not only that, but they also held with the peculiar idea that you could design and maintain a system which delivered perpetual growth on a finite Earth. In hindsight it seems a laughable concept, but in 2012 most people actually *believed* in that system. Every country on Earth (except Bhutan) had, if you like, a national goal of growing gross domestic product. At the time it seemed a perfectly logical approach, given how they believed in the fundamental idea that tangible products make you happy.

They expressed the equally odd idea that the primary function of businesses was to make its shareholders as wealthy as possible. People didn't yet understand that the things that make human beings happy and life worthwhile largely involve less tangible aspects, like love, being part of a community, the quality of their relationships, meaningful work, service, and living in an unspoiled, natural environment.

Interestingly, during this tumultuous period a group of people emerged who held a different view. They were working towards the idea of globally responsible leaders. Globally responsible leadership was really built around very simple questions, such as *What kind of world do you want to live in?* and *What kind of world should we create with the extraordinary technical and economic capabilities that we have mastered?* These people had realized that pursuing perpetual growth for its own sake was not ecologically possible, or even sensible from the perspective of human progress and well-being.

The business world further witnessed a new movement around globally responsible leadership. The movement was built on the idea that we need entrepreneurs – people who could create new initiatives to build the kind of society that we have in 2112; but also statesmen, people who would lead on behalf of society using the resources of their own organizations in service of the common good; and thirdly, above all else, *leaders*. Leadership in the new context was defined as being about sense-*making*, about understanding the real context in which a leader was working. It was also about sense-*giving*, providing clarity about what everybody in the organization was working for. The early twenty-first century saw the emergence of a new type of leadership, a more inclusive and holistic approach where people started to organize more organically. Movements like Occupy and Indignés were early expressions of such new ways of organic organizations.

The crisis in the early twenty-first century was centered on an unsustainable economic system and their collective failure to create a world worth living in for all the people on the planet. At that time they expected the population to reach 9 billion people worldwide. During this period their priorities began to shift, culminating in the birth of globally responsible leadership. With this agenda of global responsibility, people started to explore the fundamental questions of *purpose,* and the purpose of the role of business in particular. In 2012 the common business mantra was all about short-term profit. Despite this collective folly, no chief executive of a great company went to their grave fondly recalling how they had doubled the earnings every year for 10 years. Profit does not feature in the legacy of any leader. Neverthless, that was how their system determined the fate, failure and success of organizations.

Something new emerged from this crisis of purpose: the idea of purpose-driven organizations that joined the dots between what society needed from a social and environmental perspective; and what their organization was doing – not only the incremental aspects. If you read the history books you'll find something called corporate social responsibility which, as a famous academic jokingly described it at the time, was basically about putting lipstick on a bulldog. The trouble with corporate social responsibility concerned a misdirected mindset, in that "we should try to produce our products with less energy and waste" without ever asking whether the products were *needed* at all.

During this transition, global society, leaders and organizations explored the notion of purpose, their *raison d'être*, repeatedly asking themselves the deeper question: *What kind of world do I want to create?* An increasing number of companies and even business schools saw themselves as stakeholders in the creation of a very different kind of world, a sustainable world where people lived well. *All of them.* Such concepts took them into the landscape of different behaviors, of being entrepreneurs, leaders, statesmen and, critically, of living true to their values. This is something that we in the twenty-second century tend to take for granted, namely that the journey of responsible leadership always starts with an *inner* journey. If you don't look at yourself you can't effectively consider the potential of your own organization. If you don't know who you are, how can you lead others?

Since the second half of the twentieth century, people in management education and business schools in particular focused on creating diligent administrators, capable managers and, in the political sphere, lobbyists pursuing largely self-interested goals. At some level they wanted to create leaders with the courage, awareness and the inner wisdom to do the right thing, make the right call, to say *yes* to what is right and *no* to that which makes no sense. But, more often than not, people in management education were equally trapped, just like the business organizations they trained, the policy makers and pretty much society at large. Everybody was caught in the twentieth century paradigm of perpetual growth, shop-until-you-drop, and short-term profit maximization.

A small group of people tried to do something about it. They imagined a world where management education was made available to everybody, not only to the elite. They wanted to develop leaders across all kinds of organizations who would contribute to the well-being of those they connected with, and develop solutions that would improve the planet's fragile state. The leaders we have been celebrating over the past decades emerged from this movement, the creators of the learning circle which they called the *collaboratory*. It may well be difficult to imagine, but back in 2012 it was unusual to have students and researchers meet with design engineers, environmental scientists, students and business leaders to work out new solutions. In 2012 the dominant way was the so-called *sage on the stage* – a professor lecturing several hundred students in an antiquated lecture theater. They believed that the role of the teacher was merely knowledge transfer, as if the man (and it usually was a man) standing on the podium had *the* answer: magically attained knowledge of some eternal truth. It was during those heady days that the shift from teaching to *learning* commenced.

The emergence of the Internet brought with it a range of distinctly bizarre products and services. For example, students consulted media-issued rankings on business schools that did *not* take into account what students would *learn* or contribute to society upon graduation. Instead, these rankings measured how much more students could *earn* after graduation, or how many articles from the researchers at a given school were published in specialized journals that were distributed to very few readers – and generally had no requirement for societal value whatsoever.

In the decades before the European and U.S. governments went bankrupt their ministries of education would pay a great deal of money to educational institutions which maintained this perplexing model, rather than pick the best places to fund against any measure of societal *value*. As often as not they simply supported the institutions that had been in existence the longest. Students had to borrow money to pay for their education, money that they were supposed to pay back after graduation. To make matters worse, many graduates failed to find jobs at all. By the mid twenty-first century youth unemployment touched 50 percent in most developed countries. In the United States, student loans grew so bloated that they surpassed the accumulated debt of all households. After the presidential elections in 2016, mounting student debt resulted in a revolution that helped to break the U.S. dollar, which until then had still been the leading world currency. In the decade that followed the higher education system simply collapsed, together with the government. Nobody could afford to pay for education anymore, while those in the emerging nations who needed education most still had extremely limited access.

This period of economic and social turmoil gave rise to a new system.

The upheaval must have been quite something – a time of fundamental change throughout the world. What finally emerged from the shambles were several related initiatives that provided learning to all those who needed it. The collaboratory movement resulted in 'pop-up' business schools emerging all over the world. These schools were built around the idea that all stakeholders within a system need to come together to resolve the most pressing issues of this world, and that subject experts had to make sense of the contribution of their fields based on the needs of a given issue. The simple truth was that any given problem always requires the involvement of many different fields of expertise. Research scholars developed new ways to contribute to these issues, collaborating with many people outside their functional disciplines. *Trans*disciplinary research was still a new frontier.

The year 2012 was also the twentieth anniversary of the famous 1992 Rio Earth Summit. How we wish *we* had been present to witness the birth of this transformation! Consider transporting *yourself* back to 2012. *Imagine* what it was like. Think through how *you* would react, and what *you* would have done to create a society which is globally responsible, a future for the kind of world which, a hundred years later, we now can enjoy – a world where everyone lives well, where social inequality is a thing of the past, and where we live in balance with the natural world.

We hope you enjoyed this short history lesson. Now we invite you to further explore the concept of global responsibility and how it evolved. Let us begin the journey.

OUR JOURNEY – A PROCESS OF CO-CREATION

> Never doubt that a small group of thoughtful, committed citizens can change the world; indeed, it's the only thing that ever has.
>
> Margaret Mead

50+20 is a collaborative initiative between the Globally Responsible Leadership Initiative (GRLI), the World Business School Council of Sustainable Business (WBSCSB), and the Principles of Responsible Management Education (PRME). The initiative reflects the concerns of many students, parents, entrepreneurs, and scholars across the world. Our point of departure is a shared belief that the time is ripe for critical reflection on the role that business and management education plays in society, today and particularly tomorrow.

The manner in which our initiative was born and developed reflects how we believe global issues can be addressed and resolved. 50+20 is a collaborative effort between three organizations, all actively trying to determine how to change management education for the better. Rather than embarking on competitive projects, we traveled to meet each other, to sit together and hammer out the problems. Before long we decided to join forces and work on a common vision. Its sounds easy with hindsight, but the road was not always smooth and the collaboration not always evident. Yet again, this is a realistic reflection of how collaboration works in the real world: improvised and (more often than not) imperfectly orchestrated. This is the world. This is life. But it's a start.

Parallel Initiatives

50+20 emerged from two parallel initiatives. The World Business School Council of Sustainable Business (WBSCSB) initiated 50+20 as part of an initiative that was born in a supplementary event at the Academy of Management in Montreal in August 2010. Thirty-five leading sustainability scholars and a few business school deans from around the globe met to talk about breaking the silos in business and management education. Some of these deans gathered in a corner and decided it was about time that business schools engaged in the public debate on sustainable development and reflected on what contribution management education could make to create a better world.

Meanwhile, the Globally Responsible Leadership Initiative (GRLI), a global partnership of leaders from companies and business schools, had launched project SB21: a blueprint for the business school of the twenty-first century. The initial meetings of WBSCSB and GRLI sparked a great amount of passion, drive and enthusiasm – chemistry and synchronicity at its best. The Principles of Responsible Management Education (U.N. backed PRME) in New York was a natural third partner, given their ambition to sign up as many business schools and management-related academic institutions as possible, and to inspire them to provide more responsible management education, research and thought leadership. In January 2011, the three organizations signed a joint agreement of collaboration; projects SB21 and 50+20 were merged into one with the team members elegantly complementing one another in terms of know-how, skills, global make-up and competences.

Several common themes quickly arose from the partnership. The need to move from incremental to "deep" sustainability recognizes that the mainstream approach to the triple bottom line of environmental, social and economic problems was inadequate to address the global challenges of social justice and environmental sustainability. We recognized that the voice of business schools needed to be heard in the public debate on sustainable development. We saw the need for a *transdisciplinary* approach to bridge different fields, as well as the willingness to question the underlying assumptions of our dominant economic and business thinking. Such issues include responsible leadership, the required metamorphosis of business organizations from maximizing short-term profit to becoming servants of society – and what it takes to develop leaders who are able to embrace such a challenge.

The goals of the PRME signatories and its six principles (as detailed in the Box below) served as a common starting point.

With this background, 50+20 grew into a collaborative initiative that sought to develop new ways and opportunities for management education to transform and reinvent itself. We asked critical questions about the state of the world, the emerging societal issues, the dominant economic logic, the purpose of business, the crucial role of leadership, and the challenges facing management education. We embarked on a process of internal and external dialogue to clarify where and how the boundaries and contours of a new vision for management education must be drawn. As part of this discussion we had to clarify questions concerning stakeholders, authorship and applicability of the vision.

As the stakeholders of this vision include society (future generations included) and the natural environment, we designed a broad consultation process. We commissioned surveys and held meetings with critical stakeholders in order to assure an inclusive "outside-in" approach that informed the "inside-out" visioning process, managed by a core team of 50+20 participants.

Our analysis of the current state of affairs in management education

THE PRME PRINCIPLES

As institutions of higher education involved in the development of current and future managers we declare our willingness to progress in the implementation, within our institution, of the following Principles, starting with those that are more relevant to our capacities and mission. We will report on progress to all our stakeholders and exchange effective practices related to these principles with other academic institutions:

Principle 1 – Purpose: We will develop the capabilities of students to be future generators of sustainable value for business and society at large and to work for an inclusive and sustainable global economy.

Principle 2 – Values: We will incorporate into our academic activities and curricula the values of global social responsibility as portrayed in international initiatives, such as the United Nations Global Compact.

Principle 3 – Methods: We will create educational frameworks, materials, processes and environments that enable effective learning experiences for responsible leadership.

Principle 4 – Research: We will engage in conceptual and empirical research that advances our understanding about the role, dynamics, and impact of corporations in the creation of sustainable social, environmental and economic value.

Principle 5 – Partnership: We will interact with managers of business corporations to extend our knowledge of their challenges in meeting social and environmental responsibilities and to explore jointly effective approaches to meeting these challenges.

Principle 6 – Dialogue: We will facilitate and support dialogue and debate among educators, business, government, consumers, media, civil society organizations and other interested groups and stakeholders on critical issues related to global social responsibility and sustainability. We understand that our own organizational practices should serve as an example of the values and attitudes we convey to our students.

concluded that, in general, there is a very narrow perspective on its societal mandate and in its definition of societal "value-add". We encountered a great deal of lip service being paid to the teaching of ethics and sustainability when measured against a yardstick of what the world really *needs*.

We accept that our vision to recast management education in a different, more hopeful role will be met with resistance by some established stakeholders in both business and management education. It is therefore important to recognize the moral courage required by the current guard of business school deans and professors to drive change. To re-envision (and by implication put into question) a system that one represents is never easy.

A Collaborative Effort

Envisioning profound changes in management education raises the issue of authorship. The 50+20 process included a number of thought leaders outside the field of management education, including students, philosophers, business leaders, leadership consultants, corporate educators, pedagogical, andragogical and sustainability experts, activists, and artists. All participants made important contributions to the visioning process alongside the core of forward-thinking business school deans, management and leadership educators.

The vision itself was written as an evolving, collaborative process where contributors created a process of continuous integration and exchanges. Our work method reflects the way we envision the functioning of a collaboratory – a concept that rests at the heart of the vision.

An international group of stakeholders in management education met in a number of retreats, working on progressively evolving elements of the vision. At every meeting at least 50 percent of the participants were first-timers, ensuring an inclusive and open approach with fresh perspectives. We further used professional facilitation processes that served different purposes during these retreats:

- The **New York Retreat** focused on visioning what needs to happen in management education to ensure that we contribute to a world worth living in (26 participants, including business school deans, directors and professors, artists, consultants, innovation and educational experts and thought leaders).
- A **Global Stakeholder Survey** clarified expectations and inspired the vision (140 participants from 36 countries, including management scholars, students, business professionals, NGOs and not-for-profit

employees, educational experts and coaches, artists, opinion leaders and concerned citizens).

- The **St. Gallen Retreat** discussed first drafts the visioning team had put together (35 participants, including (in addition to New York) students and representatives of student organizations, NGOs and not-for-profit organizations).
- The **Stuttgart GRLI General Assembly** served to critically evaluate the work's preliminary vision and scope (40 international participants, including thought leaders in responsible leadership from business and academia).
- The **Global Challenge: Future Student Competition** demonstrated how concerned and engaged young adults viewed the future of management education, helping sharpen our vision (1091 students from 79 countries).
- The **Munich WBCSD Conference** tested the preliminary vision and gathered feedback from the business community on the vision (15 participants, including corporate sustainability directors from around the globe).
- The **Lausanne Retreat** was a steering committee and editorial session, assessing the results of an intense collaborative vision writing exercise involving 22 writers and opinion leaders over a period of two months. It was the first time the vision took on a clearly recognizable shape (seven participants from three continents).
- The **Brussels Retreat** created alignment behind the vision and evaluated actions to engage different stakeholders (25 participants from New York, St. Gallen and Stuttgart Retreats took part).

Between the retreats, the main writers wrote and re-wrote the vision and the chapters leading up to it. Each iteration offered new perspectives, highlighted unresolved issues and added more clarity. Critical questions were debated over and over again: *Are we too radical? Are we radical enough? Are we preaching to the converted? What about those who are not in agreement with our assumptions, or those who are still attached to the dominant economic theories?*

In parallel to the vision development, we conducted a global process of harvesting and selecting emerging benchmarks. To date, we have collected more than 80 examples which are displayed for public comments on our website. This process will continue as the 50+20 initiative grows – and we welcome contributions from all parts of the globe.

There are a number of fundamental assumptions which can be summarized into the following key paradigm shifts we believe are necessary in order to reach our goal:

1. **The civic organization: a new environmental, societal and economic paradigm**
    In order to create a world where all citizens live well and within the limits of the planet, we need a different kind of society with a different economic framework that is celebrated for its contribution to society and the world.
2. **Globally responsible leaders: a new leadership paradigm**
    In order to lead business and society to collaborate in the challenges related to creating a world worth living in, we need a new type of leader who can lead organizations through this challenging transformation process.
3. **From business school to management education: a new educational paradigm**
    In order to develop leaders able to lead this transformation, we need to re-define the framework of education that currently educates leaders. The new landscape needs to include all stakeholders who contribute to management education, research and related public interaction.

Given that the very foundations of business and management education are critically examined, the application of the vision concerns business, management and leadership education in general. The stakeholders in this landscape include not only business schools, leadership and executive development programs, corporate universities, but also think tanks, business consultancies and vocational training centers. Likewise, the prospective students addressed in this work not only include current and future business leaders, but also emerging entrepreneurs among the 4 billion people at the "bottom of the pyramid" who present the biggest opportunity for making global societal progress.

The 50+20 vision proposes a framework of a number of different roles to be played by management education. It also highlights key responsibilities for stakeholders in the larger community of management education. The expectation is that different stakeholders adopt this vision in different ways. Some stakeholders may choose to focus only on one element. Others may choose a selection of ideas, while some may embrace the entire vision. We anticipate institutions joining forces to create collaboratories on a regional level, while others may choose to share emerging research practices, develop faculty training and re-training programs, or co-create new educational solutions. Whichever avenue is taken, all such stakeholders will be part of a growing global movement that cares strongly about creating a world worth living in.

THE CONTEXT OF OUR WORK

50+20 is a movement among a growing number of management education providers that critically questions what and how they teach and conduct research. This movement has produced a *work* – in the same sense that one would refer to a piece of music or a cathedral as a work – combining technical and artistic, creative and inspirational dimensions. At the core of this work is a vision of management education that does not aim to be the best in the world, but the best *for* the world.

We took the opportunity to entirely re-envision the field of management education. Whilst every attempt has been made to start with a blank canvas, we recognized the need to take into account the changing global, environmental and business contexts. We have also attempted to draw a picture of the larger community of stakeholders in the landscape of management education. In order to describe the context and background of our vision, some clarifying remarks are needed.

In the 1950s, the Ford and Carnegie Foundations sponsored two reports to promote scientific rigor and academic legitimacy of higher business education in the U.S. Since then, no other initiative has come close to the impact these reports have had in influencing the priorities in management and business education during the past 50 years, worldwide. The majority of business schools, and to a lesser degree management education efforts at large, continue to function in line with an agenda that was set in the late 1950s by these reports and the actions that followed from them. Their widespread adoption is an Industrial Age success story.

Resetting The Management Education Agenda

Over 50 years have passed since the agenda for management education has been set. The RIO+20 United Nations Conference on Sustainable Development (June 2012) marked the twentieth anniversary of the 1992 Rio Earth summit: 20 years have passed since governments were urged to rethink economic development and find ways to halt the destruction of irreplaceable natural resources. It is at this juncture in history where the 50+20 project takes action to reset the management education agenda for the coming 20 years and beyond.

Modern management emerged as a response to the challenges faced by organizations who sought to take advantage of the opportunities afforded by the Industrial Age. The focus of management as an academic subject throughout the twentieth century dealt with issues framed around efficiency, productivity and economic returns. While the development of management as a profession has enabled modern organizations to grow in size, scope, and complexity, it is severely challenged to come up with adequate responses to the world today – one where natural resources are limited, wealth is poorly distributed and there is a shortage of effective societal leadership. This 50-year-old legacy needs to be addressed.

In 1992 the United Nations Earth Summit in Rio marked a turning point in how governments and business approached economic development. The need to find ways to halt the destruction of nature and pollution of the planet gained the center stage. In an attempt to embrace social, environmental and economic issues, the term *sustainability*, popularized by the Brundtland Report in 1987, was introduced to equip growth with the notion of sustainable development.

Twenty years later, in June 2012, the world reconvened again in Rio to seek new answers to the sustainable development challenges of the twenty-first century. The global agenda is moving towards the three sustainability pillars of social justice, environmental boundaries and economic innovation. This re-framing includes a questioning of the logic of growth as a goal unto itself. Public discourse is beginning to explore the possibility that sustainable development is an inadequate framework. The need to identify and find solutions to human progress beyond economic growth with a social and environmental spin is increasingly apparent in this context, given how management education is out of step with the scale and nature of the challenges we face.

Our work is premised on the view that the world needs a mindful, sustainable approach to the planet's finite resources. We recognize that many societies, both rich and poor when measured in traditional economic terms, are stressed to the point of fracture by shifting demographics, poverty and the rapidity of change itself. We observe a growing global community seeking *purpose* rather than *consumption*. The growth of the cultural creatives[1] provides hard evidence of an emergent large-scale new "level of consciousness" spreading throughout the world. As Tim M. Macartney asks so pertinently "What kind of society is it that would not place the Children's Fire at the very center of its institutions of power?"

> In their Earth Wisdom teachings, the elders of the Native Americans talk of The Children's Fire. This fire is a reminder of the promise: "No law, no action of any kind, shall be taken that will harm the children."
> Tim 'Mac' Macartney "The Children's Fire"

In this context, the role and fundamental purpose of business is under scrutiny. The pursuit of profit as an end in itself appears at best a poor contribution to society and, at worst, a primary driver in the perpetuation of a failed system. The call is out to expand our understanding of the purpose of business beyond mere profit-making to sharply defined, value-added contributions to society and the world. Business leaders are being called upon to reconcile an array of competing priorities and to lead responsibly in a time of runaway uncertainty and complexity.

We believe the time is ripe to reinstate the Children's Fire into our society, and our work seeks to contribute to this effort. We believe that a world where everybody lives well and within the limits of the planet is a possible and a desirable goal. To create such a world requires new approaches to how we think about the economy, business, leadership and education, let alone how we actually organize and act and achieve it.

The vision we propose represents not only an incremental shift but a radically new perspective of what management education for the future could look like. We acknowledge that many of the elements may feel familiar. They already exist piecemeal and in partial form in various places around the world. On the whole, our approach to management education and its implementation requires nothing less than a fundamental transformation of the existing model. A transformation is not a revolution, in that it does not seek to overthrow that which is currently in place, but rather to build on it, preserving what was good in the previous model. The deepest purpose of such a management education framework is to create and hold the space for an entirely new world of business to emerge. The world needs engaged, reflective and responsible entrepreneurs, managers and leaders in all sectors and in all regions of the world. We believe it is the responsibility of management education to provide such leadership. We call it *responsible leadership for a sustainable world*.

The vision is intended for those with a deep awareness and understanding of the global challenges we face, who possess a sense of urgency to bring about change and an unwavering belief that we all "own" the responsibility to create such change. We hope that our goals resonate with you, and that you also feel inspired to take action, in your own life and work. Imagine what we could collectively achieve if we act *now*.

NOTE

1. Ray/Sherry (2000).

PART I

The challenge

1. Imagine a world worth living in

> Globalization today is not working for many of the world's poor. It is
> not working for the environment. It is not working for the stability of the
> global economy.
>
> Joseph Stiglitz *Globalization and its Discontents*

AN UNSUSTAINABLE DEVELOPMENT MODEL

Our global society stands at a junction in a road. We can either continue
playing the economic game of musical chairs, avoiding responsibility when
and where we can, while hoping others will lose the game in our stead. This
is a dangerous path that will lead toward a disrupted, chaotic world – far
more so than it is today.

The alternative is to attempt something fundamentally different, namely
to focus on the well-being of all of us – and indeed of all living things –
while respecting the limits of the planet.

In some respects our society is better off today than it was in 1972,
when the Club of Rome published its *Limits to Growth* report that made
us aware of the world's finite capacity to support us. Forty years later, we
find that fewer of us live in poverty. More children are attending school,
of which increasing numbers are girls. Such improvements have been
achieved despite a growing world population, which is finally showing
signs of slowing – but therein lies a problem. Slower population growth
does not equate to population stabilization; we still expect the world
to grow increasingly overcrowded. Barring any disasters, the overall
population will reach about 9 billion by 2040.

The current global development model is unsustainable, not only environmentally but also socially and economically. We know that our collective actions (or inactions) are triggering tipping points as environmental
thresholds are breached, risking irreversible damage to both ecosystems
and human communities. Our collective failure to adopt sustainable
development condemns up to 3 billion people on Earth to a life of
poverty. In addition, the economic crises we are facing today did not start
in 2008; their origins are deeply buried in economic assumptions that no
longer hold water. These crises highlight the urgency to fundamentally

rethink and rebuild the economic system, to make it work for the long term in favor of sustainable development, for adequate employment and social justice. The current situation is succinctly described by Tom Friedman[1] as Mother Nature and Father Greed hitting the wall at the same time.

A New Paradigm For Economic Growth

In 1987, the Brundtland Report brought the concept of sustainable development to the international public policy agenda as a new paradigm for the three pillars of economic growth, social equality and environmental sustainability. The Report argued that sustainable development could be achieved by an integrated policy framework embracing all three pillars.

Today, leading thinkers suggest that the economy must be considered as a subset of society. While sustainable development remains a generally accepted concept, it has not succeeded in becoming a practical reality for governments or business. To date, sustainable development has suffered from a failure of political will and serious business engagement. As the signs of multiple crises (climate, resources, food, water, poverty, migration, democratic uprising, and unemployment and finance) escalate, an overall approach to incremental improvement has fallen well short of meeting the world's social and environmental challenges.

Sustainable development is fundamentally about understanding and acting on interconnections that link society, the natural environment and the economy. It is about seeing the whole picture, such as critical relationships between food, water, land and energy, but also between poverty, low levels of education and lack of democratic governance. Sustainable development is also about ensuring that our actions today are consistent with a future that is worth living in, for our children and indeed all of the 9 billion global citizens expected to populate the planet by the middle of this century. The challenge is summarized by the UN Secretary-General's High Level Panel on Global Sustainability:[2]

> But what, then, is to be done if we are to make a real difference for the world's people and the planet? We must grasp the dimensions of the challenge. We must recognize that the drivers of that challenge include unsustainable lifestyles, production and consumption patterns and the impact of population growth. As the global population grows from 7 billion to almost 9 billion by 2040, and the number of middle-class consumers increases by 3 billion over the next 20 years, the demand for resources will rise exponentially. By 2030 the world will need at least 50 percent more food, 45 percent more energy and 30 percent more water – all at a time when environmental boundaries are throwing up new limits to supply. This is true not least for climate change, which affects all aspects of human and planetary health.

In this chapter we look at the social, environmental and economic challenges of sustainable development, before developing elements of a vision for a sustainable world.

SOCIAL CHALLENGES

Based on the Millennium Development Goals (MDG), the world's leaders made a promise in 2000 to halve the number of people living in absolute poverty by 2015 compared with 1990. In 1990, 46 percent of the world's population lived in absolute poverty. By 2005 that number had fallen to 27 percent, and is projected to fall below 15 percent in 2015. Good progress has been made in particular in China and India, while poverty in sub-Saharan Africa is still significantly above the MDG. Despite these efforts, eliminating poverty remains a major task, as more than a billion people still live in poverty. With regard to hunger, global food production has kept pace with the growing population, but *access* to food is a different matter. In recent years, hunger has risen in conjunction with food prices, with an increase of 20 million undernourished people since 2000.

Progress has been made in education worldwide, with an additional 52 million children enrolled in primary schools. But globally, poverty still kept 67 million children out of school in 2009 which means the MDG of giving all children a full primary education by 2015 will not be reached. Worse still, 215 million children are working for businesses instead of attending school. About 68 percent of secondary school-age children were enrolled in 2009, 9 percent more than in 1999. Gender parity in secondary school enrollment has improved globally, from 76 girls per 100 boys in 1991 to 95 per 100 in 2008. Women have seen substantial improvements in rights, education, and health and labor opportunities over the past 20 years. Whilst disparities still persist, clear improvements have been made.[3]

The world's population currently stands at about 7 billion. While the global population growth rate has slowed markedly since its peak in the 1960s, we expect an additional billion people in the next 15 years. Current estimates suggest that the global population will reach nearly 9 billion by 2040 and could exceed 10 billion in 2100.[4] Population growth rates remain high in many low-income countries; among them some of the world's most fragile states with poor natural resource endowments. In comparison, populations are stable or even shrinking in more developed countries. This means that developing countries are challenged to greatly enlarge their capacity for education, training and job creation if they want to prevent frustration and social unrest among their younger population. More developed countries face a very different situation: they have to prepare for life-long education and old-age employment, while young talent will become increasingly scarce.

Today, over half the world's population live in cities, highlighting a growing urban population. Over the next two decades, the urban population is projected to grow by another 1.4 billion, from 3.5 billion in 2010 to 4.9 billion in 2030. Most growth is anticipated to occur in medium-sized cities within developing countries. The global urbanization trend integrates newcomers into consumer markets and provides access to middle-class lifestyles. The creation of necessary infrastructure, educational and employment opportunities for these new middle classes puts great demands not only on governments and the economy, but also on resources and ecosystems.[5]

ENVIRONMENTAL CHALLENGES

Since the publication of *Limits to Growth* in 1972,[6] scientists across the world have drawn an ever clearer picture of the fact that the natural world does not have the capacity to sustain human population growth and economic activity. It has become very clear that we have not only used up available capacity but have started to overuse it systematically. In order to assess the overall state of the natural world, three major scientific analyses (The Ecological Footprint (EFP), the Millennium Ecosystem Assessment (MEA) and the Planetary Boundaries Approach (PBA)) have been presented. All analyses produced equally disturbing results.

According to the calculations based on humanity's EFP, we are using 135 percent of the resources that planet Earth generated in 2011. In other words, the global community currently uses the bio-capacity of 1.35 planets to satisfy current global demand. This 35 percent overshoot indicates that we are using natural capital faster than it can replenish itself – for example, in the form of shrinking forests, species loss, resource depletion, and by accumulating waste such as carbon dioxide in the atmosphere and the oceans.

The EFP measures humanity's demand on the biosphere for biologically productive land and sea required to provide the resources we use and to absorb our waste.[7] Footprints are different from nation to nation, depending on the size of the population and the level of consumption. We would need three planets if global consumption reached European levels and *five* planets to attain the level of the United States. We need to remember that not only the footprint but also the available bio-capacity differs between nations. Significant ecological reserves are available in countries like Canada, Australia, Finland and Russia, but also in South America and parts of Africa. On the other hand, European and Arab countries, China, India, Japan and the USA don't offer significant ecological reserves, resulting in the current overall global ecological deficit.

The real question is: *what would the rapid rise of BRICS countries and others copying Western lifestyles and consumption levels mean for humanity's EFP?* The answer is that we would need the bio-capacity of two planets by 2030 and four to five planets by 2050 to satisfy the needs of a consumer-oriented world. As we only have one planet to share, we may have to anticipate that competition and conflicts for the planet and its resources will increase substantially, unless we manage to fundamentally change the economic system.[8]

While the arguments continue in some quarters, most of us are finally (albeit reluctantly) reaching a collective understanding that our actions are triggering a series of tipping points as multiple environmental thresholds are breached, risking irreversible damage to both ecosystems and society. Some say it is too late to make meaningful changes, while others deny the reality of such reports.

The 2004 Millennium Ecosystem Assessment (MEA) is the largest assessment ever undertaken on ecosystem health. It was commissioned by the UN and prepared by 1360 experts from 95 countries, and represented a consensus of the world's scientists on the rate and scale of ecosystem changes and consequences for 24 *ecosystem services.* Ecosystem services are services provided by nature in the form of provisioning services (like wood, crops, water or genetic resources), regulating services (such as water purification, climate or erosion regulation) and cultural services (including educational or recreational values of nature). The findings make it clear that humans have radically altered global ecosystems over the last 50 years. While the changes have brought economic gains, these were achieved at growing ecological costs that threaten the achievement of the Millennium Development Goals. The results are sobering: 60 percent of the ecosystem services analysed have degraded during the past 50 years. Most of the services provided by nature for free have become not only costly, but increasingly scarce.

Last but not least, a group of scientists led by Johan Rockström from the Stockholm Resilience Centre[9] propose a framework of planetary boundaries designed to define a "safe operating space for humanity", based on current scientific research. It indicates that human actions have gradually become the main driver of global environmental change since the Industrial Revolution. The scientists assert that once human activity has passed certain thresholds or tipping points, defined as *planetary boundaries*, we run a considerable risk of irreversible and abrupt environmental change.

The Planetary Boundaries Report identifies a total of nine critical earth system processes and their boundaries: climate change, rate of biodiversity loss, nitrogen and phosphorus flows into the biosphere and oceans, global freshwater use, change in land use, ocean acidification, atmospheric aerosol loading and chemical pollution. Based on their initial estimates, the scientists conclude that human activity appears to have already transgressed the boundaries associated in three areas: climate change, rate of biodiversity loss and changes to the global nitrogen cycle. Further, we are approaching boundary limits in four more areas: the global phosphorous cycle, global freshwater usage, ocean acidification and global change in land use. The scientists suggest that these boundaries are strongly interlinked; crossing one boundary may shift others and even cause them to be overstepped. The positive news is that, with regard to ozone depletion, we have actually reversed the trend and secured a safe operating space – at least for now – demonstrating that we are capable of achieving progress when we decide to act. Changing or halting the other trends will require significant changes in policy at global, regional and national levels and will require every global citizen to become co-responsible for this world.

ECONOMIC CHALLENGES

We need a new economic model of natural capital, economics of pollution, of labor markets and employment, of human and social capital. We need economics that integrate both the real economy and financial markets which have been allowed to lead a life for themselves.[10] Only then may the economic system regain its constructive role as a true engine of a sustainable economic development.

The economic challenges for a sustainable world did not start with the 2008 economic crisis, nor did they end a year later. Getting the economy "back on track" in its twentieth century form is not a solution to the fundamental problems underlying the current economic crises and the failure of global governance. Working towards a sustainable economy is a massive challenge that needs the contributions of many stakeholders, in particular those of governments, society, business, science and education.

In a highly interconnected global economy no nation is immune to events originating elsewhere. The national debt crises, rooted primarily in the OECD economies, are forcing massive reductions in public spending, with far-reaching effects for every economy. Also, we are still in a fundamental financial crisis, highlighted through massively volatile asset prices, large unresolved accumulations of bad debts and no rules in place to prevent future derailments. Some 200 million people across the world are formally unemployed. Many of them are young. Approximately 1.5 billion people endure "vulnerable employment" with little job security and few, if any, employment rights. We are also in the midst of a growth crisis, as seen in anemic growth rates in multiple countries. This is mirrored in politics in many countries as a fundamental governance crisis, with national governments seemingly unable to identify and implement adequate collective action to address the economic challenges. On the one hand we are witnessing increased calls for global governance and reconnecting back to the original pioneering spirit of the United Nations,[11] and an emergence of local "tribalism" on the other.

The major systemic financial failure is at the top of the list of the 2012 analysis of global risks by the World Economic Forum, which examines events with the highest potential impact over the coming decade. Severe income disparity tops the list in terms of the highest perceived likelihood of occurrence. The major concern, however, is related to the interconnection between different categories of risk, creating particular constellations of global risks that may result in a dystopia – a world full of hardship and devoid of hope. The interplay between fiscal, demographic and societal risks could result in a world where a large youthful population is exposed to chronic, high levels of unemployment, while concurrently the largest population of retirees in history becomes dependent upon already heavily indebted governments, further threatening social and political stability. Another such risk constellation concerns our safeguards: the capacity to manage systems that underpin our prosperity and safety in a highly interconnected world. The constellation of risks arising from emerging technologies, financial interdependencies, resource depletion and climate change exposes the brittle nature of existing safeguards, including the policies, norms, regulations or institutions which are designed to manage vital resources, ensure orderly markets and public safety.[12]

More fundamentally, the challenges of sustainable development question our economic model of consumption based on quantitative growth. What until recently was only voiced by those considered radical has reached the conservative mainstream: our economic model is broken and needs to be fundamentally transformed. Now, calls for the reform of capitalism abound; the McKinsey global managing director is calling on business leaders to rebuild capitalism for the long term,[13] while Porter and Kramer are popularizing the idea of creating shared value, which involves creating economic value in a way that also creates value for society. Similarly, the 2012 World Economic Forum in Davos addressed "the great transformation".

Old Assumptions, New Thinking

Our current economic model is based on many assumptions made during the nineteenth century, when physical capital was scarce and natural capital abundant. *These assumptions are no longer valid today.* The current model addresses neither the real issues of today's world, nor does it measure the things that really matter to people. Economic progress is dependent on quantitative growth, resulting in the creation of unintended negative consequences – often termed externalities. These externalities include the destruction of nature and resource use, climate change, widening inequalities between and within countries, health and social problems, and global unemployment.

We must ask ourselves to what extent we are producing real economic *value*, given the one-sided concentration on material growth and success which, for example, consistently fails to increase happiness among wealthy nations. What about ecological and social externalities, which are neither accurately measured nor integrated into our common measures of economic progress? Major risks are exempted from economic responsibilities, with governments and society at large having to step in as lenders (for the banking system) or risk-takers (for technical risks like nuclear energy) as a last resort. We don't seem to be able to create economic growth which does not deplete social and natural capital. Furthermore, we systematically devalue long-term objectives and capital stocks by discounting their future value for purely financial reasons. Yet, these are the priorities we should value most.

VISION FOR A SUSTAINABLE WORLD

The World Business Council for Sustainable Development (WBCSD) proposes a vision for the decades to come. Their *Vision 2050* states that by the year 2050 some 9 billion people will live well, and within the limits of the planet.

We may imagine a reality where economic growth has been decoupled from ecosystem destruction and material consumption, and has been reconnected with societal well-being. Imagine all societal stakeholders working towards the global common good – the greatest possible good for the greatest possible number of individuals. Imagine a society that has redefined the notion of prosperity and successful lifestyles, as well as the basis of profit and loss, progress and value creation. Imagine a world in a peaceful state, caring about environmental impacts, as well as personal and societal well-being[14] – and respecting differences in culture, thought and behavior. Imagine global citizens translating these differences into sources for personal growth and enrichment. All of these factors together become what future economists may call a *sustainable economy*.

We – that is *all of us*: governments, citizens, parents, corporations, activists, NGOs and educators will need to contribute to realize that vision. Such a transformation requires that management educators understand what kinds of leaders are needed to drive a new economic reality, how business needs to change in order to become a positive force in achieving such a vision, and how we can engage to influence this transformation.

NOTES

1. Cited in Gilding (2011: 87).
2. UN Secretary General (2012: 12ff).
3. UN Secretary-General (2012: 17–21).
4. UN Secretary-General (2012: 25).
5. UN Secretary-General (2012: 29).
6. Meadows et al. (1972).
7. WWF et al. (2010): www.footprintnetwork.org.
8. Gilding (2011: 50–53).
9. Rockström et al. (2010).
10. Jackson (2011); Johnson (2011).
11. "Apple Inc. has assembled a collective call for a global governance", *Le Temps*, 7 March 2012.
12. World Economic Forum (2012: 10–11).
13. Barton (2011).
14. WBCSD (2010: 6).

2. Imagine business contributing to society

Imagine a world where business is celebrated for its contribution to society.

Nick Main, Deloitte

Some thought leaders suggest that we should prepare ourselves for persistent economic turmoil, a future where instability is the norm rather than the exception. Governments have their own problems as they grapple with runaway national debt, forcing extensive reductions in public spending which further produce detrimental effects on the global economy. Meanwhile we struggle with a fundamental financial crisis characterized by rising unemployment, unresolved accumulations of bad debts – and no credible safeguards to prevent future debacles. No wonder then that many of us consider the business world as being disconnected from overall society, unwilling or unable to direct its productive capacities to more constructive uses.

We not only need a sustainable economy, but also *sustainable business*. Many stakeholders characterize the purpose of business as making unrestrained profits and maximizing personal income amongst managers and shareholders. Consider how current levels of unemployment and social inequality are rising to unknown heights, the exploitation of natural resources and the impact of climate change which has passed critical levels. Financial markets are driving economies and societies to a near meltdown, exposing the helplessness of our political governance. Business faces the choice of either reforming capitalism, or letting capitalism be reformed *for* them. It is not unreasonable to anticipate drastic political changes as a result of the public pressure, driven by people who have lost their trust in business serving a positive purpose in society.[1] Business currently represents part of the problems the world is facing, instead of being a part of the solution. The source of this disconnect lies in the model of business that has been used to legitimize narrow and selfish interests. The number of multinational corporations (MNCs) doubled in just the past 15 years and the number of their foreign operations and affiliates nearly tripled. Today, 200 corporations account for 23 percent of the world's GDP, and 51 of the top 100 economies in the world are corporations.[2]

These dynamics indicate that business is no longer in touch with society's challenges and needs – if indeed it ever was.

Few alternatives have been discussed to address the growing disconnect between business and society. Individual employees are increasingly choosing a different route when working for organizations that contribute to the world's problems rather than resolving them. They become so-called free agents, self-employed, independent one-person businesses. Before the Industrial Revolution, 80 percent of people were self employed. It was only in the past century that corporations started employing the majority of the available workforce, with the rate of self employment hitting rock bottom in the late 1980s, where 90 percent of people worked for corporations.

Since then, something has shifted. In an unprecedented change, individuals turned their backs on the corporation and returned to self employment. In the first decade of the twenty-first century, more than 40 percent of employees are self employed again.[3] This emerging trend offers a new perspective to our concerns about employment and the so-called unemployment.

DISCONNECTED BUSINESS – THE FRIEDMANIAN FALLACY

If we want a sustainable economy we first need to take a closer look at the *purpose* of business.

In 1970, Nobel prize-winning economist Milton Friedman published a famous article: "The social responsibility of business is to increase its profits" in *The New York Times Magazine*. For decades the article served as the dogmatic backbone to legitimize a narrow concept of the purpose of business: "There is one and only one social responsibility of business – to use its resources and engage in activities designed to increase its profits so long as it stays within the rules of the game."[4] Friedman goes on to explain that in a free-enterprise and private-property system, a corporate executive is an employee of the owners of the business with direct responsibility to his employers. That responsibility involves conducting business in accordance with the owner's desires, which generally consists of making as much money as possible while conforming to the basic rules of the society. If a corporate executive announces social responsibilities as a businessperson, the statement should be seen either as pure rhetoric, or that they are acting in some way that is *not* in the interest of their employers. According to Friedman, if owners wish to perform an act of social responsibility it is up to them to do this on their own, and not up to their employees who may only do this on their own behalf, and at their own cost.

This message was reinforced by the shareholder value concept, originally developed by Alfred Rappaport.[5] Taking Friedman's belief that management should first and foremost consider the interest of shareholders in their decisions, he developed a method to evaluate the shareholder value of different strategic decisions based on the estimation of future cash flow streams. His method has become very popular and widely used (or abused) by companies and business analysts alike. Although the pursuit of short-term profit maximization was not his intention,[6] the way the shareholder value concept was interpreted and applied in practice became synonymous with short-term value maximization in the shareholders' and managers' own interests. In the context of "quarterly capitalism" and the extensive use of stock options to align the interests of managers and shareholders, Friedman's message became identified as the doctrine of "greed is good".[7]

The Friedmanian doctrine – coupled with the shareholder value concept and stock option plans – has proven to be a powerful argument in favor of legitimizing ever-increasing profits and private income of shareholders and managers alike. In this paradigm prison, the business of business is profit. Other interpretations were decried by Friedman as being socialist and ineffective. Yet, fundamental questions always remained: *Why should business be directly responsible only to the owners or shareholders? Why not to employees, to customers or to society in general, as many others have suggested? What gives owners such crucial importance for business? And who are the owners in times of dispersed investor capitalism?*

Let us examine these owners of businesses. Who are they, exactly? As capitalism developed from entrepreneurial capitalism toward managerial capitalism and into the current form of investor capitalism, ownership has largely been replaced by *investment*. Until the Second World War, owners were identical to managers, a situation still found in many family businesses today, with no differences in interest between these two groups. Businesses were managed according to the long-term interests of the owners and their families. Responsibility was direct and personal, with the owner-manager often playing an important role in their local communities. A key issue was the separation of the rights of ownership (profit) from the responsibilities of ownership across the global economic system through the universal adoption of a system of limited liability, which commenced at the end of the nineteenth century.

With the rise of employed managers, a new class of professional administrators took over the management function in business, pushing *entrepreneurial* capitalism into *managerial* capitalism. This development was first analysed by Berle and Means in 1932 in their famous study on how legal ownership became separated from effective corporate control in the United States. During the 1970s and 1980s we witnessed the arrival of a new era with the rise of investor capitalism that fundamentally changed the context again.[8] Since then, institutional investors took over the role of owners, mostly managing their holdings for short-term profit, while owners are being downgraded to the status of financial investors. Ownership in times of investor capitalism has lost its former meaning, of owners who take on a *long-term* perspective, who accept risk and responsibility for the business as a whole.

With ownership being replaced by investment it is more accurate to treat most current shareholders as investors. Given that the average holding period for U.S. equities has reduced from seven years in the 1970s to seven months today, we may even want to call them speculators. Worse still, "hyper speed" traders – some of whom hold stocks for only a few seconds – now account for 70 percent of all U.S. equities trading.[9] Although the situation may be different in other parts of the world, the trend towards short-termism is spreading globally. The fact is that investors are mostly involved for the money and hold none of the pride and sense of responsibility owners used to show. If investors are not satisfied with the returns or find a more promising investment, they give up their ownership without a second thought. Businesses are under increasing pressure to meet investors' expectations, in order to maintain their share price and ensure access to new capital. Yet, to turn shareholders' expectations into a business purpose makes no sense at all.

Other business concepts have been explored in the past. Peter Drucker, who has been called the man who invented the concept of management, developed a very different, much broader concept of the purpose of business. For Drucker, profits may be the *result* of management but they are not its *purpose*. Profit is the price a business has to pay to the owners to stay in business but it cannot serve as a guiding principle of business management. For Drucker, the purpose of business must lie outside the business itself. In fact it must lie within society, given that business is an element of society just like any other institution.

Drucker defined the dimensions of management as threefold: economic performance, making work productive and the workers successful, and considering the impact on society.[10] Every social institution exists for a specific purpose. In the case of the business enterprise the specific purpose is economic performance, which is intimately tied to supplying goods and services to customers in an economical manner. The second task of management is to make work productive and the worker successful. As business has only one true resource – people – management performs by making human resources productive. Drucker's third dimension is managing the social impacts and the social responsibilities of business: "None of our institutions exists by itself and as end in itself. Everyone is an organ of society and exists for the sake of society. 'Free enterprise' cannot be justi-fied as being good for business. It can be justified only as being good for society."[11] In comparing the three dimensions Drucker makes it clear that it is impossible to separate these functions, each of which has a primacy of its own. Managing these dimensions must be conducted simultaneously, and within the same managerial action.

RECONNECTING BUSINESS TO SOCIETY

Reconnecting business to society has become a major challenge for management. Business is not just seen as failing to contribute to solving society's problems; worse, it is seen as *profiting at the cost of society*. Managers are viewed as self-interested stakeholders who neither display the responsibility nor the leadership expected from them as powerful members of a privileged elite. In order to restore business's standing as being good for society and worthy of the public's trust, business must be fundamentally transformed. We must not only rethink the ways we govern, manage and lead corporations, but also how we view business's value and role in society.

Many different approaches to reconnect business and society have been attempted in the past: corporate social responsibility, corporate citizen-ship, business ethics, social entrepreneurship, fair trade, conscious capital-ism[12] or corporate sustainability. Whilst they vary in focus, all approaches share the same goal: to bring business and society back together. In addition, several initiatives have been launched to engage business in putting these ideas into practice, including UN Global Compact, Globally Responsible Leadership Initiative (GRLI), World Business Council for Sustainable Development (WBCSD), CSR Europe, the Academy of Business and Society (EABIS), and The Caux Principles, to name a few.

With their 2011 article in *Harvard Business Review*, Michael Porter and Mark Kramer introduced the shared value approach into the mainstream. Nestlé, for example, began examining *creating shared value* (CSV) in 2006 and started reporting on it in 2008. In 2003, Jed Emerson introduced the concept of *blended value* that combines a company's generation of revenue with the generation of social value.[13] Around the same time, Philippe de Woot was calling for social responsibility within the firm and developed a thoughtful model of the corporation deeply rooted in humanistic thought, redefining leadership functions as entrepreneurship, leadership and states-manship. We shall examine CSV in more detail, given that Porter and Kramer may have contributed significantly to reaching the tipping point in this domain.

Creating Shared Value (CSV)

According to Porter and Kramer, the purpose of the corporation must be redefined as creating shared value, not only profit. The principle of shared value involves building economic value in a way that also creates value for society by addressing its needs and challenges. The starting point for business planning is society and its problems, not business itself. The goal of business is therefore to develop economic solutions for societal problems. This concept led Porter and Kramer to distinguish between false and true kinds of profits. Their approach seeks to lead companies to focus on profits that create societal benefits rather than diminishing them.

Shared value management is a positive step towards reconnecting company success with social progress. Doing something good for society while doing business is not conceived as social responsibility or philanthropy, but is a different way to achieve economic success; it is not seen as marginal to what companies do but is placed in the *center* of their activities. Shared value management reconnects company success and community progress in ways that have been lost in an age of narrow management approaches and short-term thinking, representing a more sophisticated form of capitalism imbued with a social purpose. Such a purpose arises not out of charity, but from a deeper understanding of creating *economic value* via *social value*.

In recent years no other concept has enthused corporate executives as much as CSV. Replacing responsibility with value took away the moral pressure that Corporate Social Responsibility (CSR) implied. Yet, there are critical voices that challenge CSV, calling it a "bandage on cancer",[14] as carefully dressed-up green washing. Indeed, as long as the concept does not create the disruptive effect that we need to break out of our existing paradigm, CSV might well risk suffering a similarly unhappy fate as CSR.

Creating shared value is criticized for co-opting weaker stakeholders rather than truly sharing value. For "shared value" to have real meaning (and not merely a new name for corporate social responsibility) the sharing must be equal, fair and relevant for everybody concerned. CSV needs to effectively distribute organizational benefits and profits amongst employees, communities, customers, business associates and other stakeholders. Sharing can be institutionalized through shared ownership, shared governance, open sharing of information (transparency), and shared responsibilities. The fundamental underlying issue that needs to be addressed is no less than a redistribution of wealth. Wealth needs to move from the minority to the overwhelming majority who have little or nothing. As long as all stakeholders are not treated as equal partners, CSV will not trigger the drastic shift we need to redefine the status quo of wealth. Thus, we need new business models that encourage participation for different stakeholders in co-owning companies and co-creating value collectively. The approach of creating shared value cuts across traditional disciplines, connecting economic questions and social concerns, as well as managers in the private and the public sectors.

Few managers have the necessary understanding of social and environmental issues to grasp these new challenges. Further, few public sector leaders have the managerial training and entrepreneurial mindset needed to design and implement shared value models. Most business schools still teach a very narrow view of capitalism, even though more and more of their graduates hunger for a greater sense of purpose.

A growing number of graduates are drawn to social entrepreneurship. The business school curricula will need to broaden in a number of areas to support even a shared value approach, let alone any deeper notion of reconnecting business to the creation of societal value. For example, the global middle class is expected to grow by an additional three billion to nearly five billion people over the next 20 years. The efficient use and stewardship of all forms of resources and values will have to define the next generation thinking on value chains. Marketing will have to move beyond persuasion and demand creation to reflect upon the consequences of consumption. It also has to think deeper on how to responsibly serve the neglected billions at the bottom of the wealth pyramid. Finance will need to rethink how capital markets can actually support long-term thinking and true value creation in companies, and not only benefit financial market participants. Operations and supply chain management will need to move to multi-criteria objective functions, balancing efficiency concerns with ecological and social impacts of operations. Finally, accounting will need to extend its tools and techniques to account for the environmental and social performance of companies, thereby broadening financial transparency and building true accountability.[15]

ENTREPRENEURSHIP, LEADERSHIP AND STATESMANSHIP

It is not only imperative to change the role of business, but also to develop the *functions* of corporate leaders as main stakeholders in the coming evolution. Philippe de Woot makes a case for globally responsible leaders: those who will be able to give back ethical and political dimensions to economic activity. According to de Woot, this requires a re-examination of the *raison d'être* (the deeper purpose) of business and a rebalancing of the key roles of businessmen.

The re-examined *raison d'être* of a corporation places its creative role within the wider perspective of the common good, without which it has no political or moral legitimacy. In that sense, no business exists for its own ends but serves a broader general interest which opens up the question of *meaning*. The corporation's activities have to be viewed within the broader context of human progress. The starting point for reframing business is to relegate economics to its appropriate status as a subset of a larger system and not the center of it. This framing is a dramatic change from our current system where economics dominates society and consequently imposes a limited vision of progress.

Other forms of progress in the cultural, social, political, spiritual and educational areas have intrinsic value. For example, human beings across all societies resonate with six dimensions of the human condition, irrespective of the amount of economic activity present in that society. These are: the quality of their personal relationships, being in or part of a community, doing meaningful work (paid or otherwise), learning something new (and not for the purpose of being more productive units of labor), service to others, and their degree of connectedness to nature. Even if economic progress is beneficial to some other forms of progress, it cannot act as a substitute for these human factors. Therefore, the performance of companies can only be fully aligned with societal needs if their function is defined and designed within a much wider understanding and assessment of progress. In this broad agenda containing cultural, social, political, spiritual and educational aspects, the economy can only be an enabler, not a replacement.

Through its constant innovation in the economic and technical domain, business plays a Promethean role. The Greek myth of Prometheus reflects that of the entrepreneur; he anticipates the progress that fire would bring to mortals. He takes the risk of stealing the secret of fire from the gods; and he has the energy to do it and to convince man to use it. He possesses all the rare characteristics that Schumpeter attributes to the modern businessmen.

All civilizations have marveled at this near-divine ability to *create*. Consider the hero blacksmith in Africa, the bronze masters in China, the inventors of the Mediterranean and the Middle East. Even Karl Marx was impressed by this uniquely human ability: "In the course of barely secular class domination, the capitalist bourgeoisie has accomplished wonders far surpassing Egyptian pyramids, Roman aqueducts and Gothic cathedrals".[16] Reviewed in this light, it is a deep tragedy that Friedmanian ideology, financial speculation and greed have come to dominate the real economy which has traditionally been the domain where material progress is created. Giving business a Promethean role represents the source of social legitimacy of any effective economic system.

The entrepreneur is a fundamentally creative entity. It is thus important to refocus business on its creative ability, rather than reduce it to a mere profit-making machine. To serve the global common good and address the challenges of our time, creativity needs to be repurposed. De Woot suggests that the specific function of economic and technical creativity needs to be transformed into progress for humankind. The way to do this is to address basic questions: *What kind of world do we want to build together with the extraordinary economic and technical resources at our disposal?*, or, *What for, how and for whom do we use our economic and technical creativity?* Such changes demand profound reflection and go well beyond many superficial CSR activities.

Answers to all these questions can only really be ethical or political in nature. We are therefore faced with the challenge to give back to economic and entrepreneurial creativity its ethical and political dimensions. De Woot suggests that business only becomes responsible when it transforms its culture by adopting new values and engages in the political debate with a broad array of stakeholders in a globalizing world.

In order to develop the corporate culture for the twenty-first century, de Woot proposes revisiting and rebalancing the three key roles of business-men as entrepreneurship, leadership and statesmanship.

Entrepreneurship

The challenge for entrepreneurship is to return to economic creativity and innovation. The core of entrepreneurial action is creativity in a real world of goods and services, as opposed to the logic of financial speculation. It is mainly through its entrepreneurial capacity that a company can serve the common good and face the challenges ahead. Defining the *raison d'être* of the business firm in terms of entrepreneurial progress will influence the strategies, the structures and the managerial behavior of the organization – as well as its specific contribution to the common good. It links the entrepreneur and businessperson to the collective responsibility of putting science and technology at the service of meaningful human development. Empowered by this mindset, companies can more easily direct their creative abilities toward the great challenges of our times: climate and resources, poverty and inequality, universal education to name a few, facilitating a better use of the creativity of economic stakeholders and their extraordinary entrepreneurial ability.

Leadership

The challenge for leadership is a return to ethics and human develop-ment. Management is no longer enough. If ethics are to be put back at the heart of economic activity, we need leaders and not only managers or administrators. Leadership is the art of directing the human dimension of the company: developing, motivating, empowering employees and giving sense to their work through values that are meaningful to them. Leadership rests on moral authority – and it is through this authority that values are disseminated throughout a company. Ethics gives meaning to a corporation's actions; it guides its decisions and their implementation. In a more positive way, ethics also gives sense to economic progress in a global and long-term perspective and makes it serve true development of a work-force. In order to do this we need a new type of leader as the "sense maker" and as an "architect of the corporate conscience". Such responsible leaders thereby commit to an ethical approach.

Statesmanship

The challenge for statesmanship is a return to the common good and to politics. Statesmanship implies the grounding of actions in a system of values which recognize societal interdependence and long-term sustainable development. It means participating actively in the definition of the common good and integrating it into the business activities. Given the capacity of business to attract some of the most energetic and able people in society, failing to actively participate in this task robs society of critical human resources. Business is exposed to political developments, yet its activities also have an impact on politics and the common good. Either way, business leaders need the capacity to think and act like statesmen. The crucial question is: how do such leaders use their political influence – as lobbyists in their own interest, or as *true statesmen* for the common good?

VISION FOR SUSTAINABLE BUSINESS

Imagine a world where business is celebrated for its contribution to society. The ability of business to contribute to the transformation towards a better world represents the core vision for sustainable business. In such a world, the interests of business and society are united. This vision includes an understanding of business as a societal institution with tasks and responsibilities beyond economic performance. It includes responsibility for the social impacts of business activities and, more importantly, the contribution to solving societal problems. The vision of sustainable business entails creating shared value with and for societal stakeholders, while focusing on the right *kinds* of profits.

Sustainable business is about managing for the long term and to address global responsibilities. For business leaders it involves fluency in three different key roles: entrepreneurship, leadership and statesmanship. It also means that an organization is well aware of its own limitations with regard to competence and political legitimacy. Sustainable business therefore supports and contributes the establishment of necessary framework conditions that help bring about a sustainable economy.

Implementing this vision may involve the following scenarios:

Imagine that effective measures are taken to limit the gap in income between top management income and the lowest income in the company, and that earnings are not dependent on share performance but on a comprehensive view of value generation, including economic, social and environmental values.

Imagine companies that no longer publish quarterly earnings, encouraging investors and executives to take a long-term perspective. Instead, they align compensation structures for executives with a long-term contribution of the business to society.

Imagine business strategy systematically addressing the twin challenges of international development: (a) reducing the ecological footprint of developed countries to sustainable levels, and (b) fostering a new kind of economic progress in emerging countries which has a positive environmental impact.

Imagine how business, the economy and the world would look if we think and act *long term*.

NOTES

1. Barton (2011: 86).
2. Mirvis/de Jongh (2010: 19).
3. Pink (2002) and Morgan (2006).
4. Friedman (1970).
5. Rappaport (1986).
6. In fact in his most recent book, Rappaport (2011) develops a new concept to save capitalism from short-termism.
7. Barton (2011).
8. Khurana (2007: 297–326); Khurana/Penrice (2011: 7).
9. Barton (2011: 87).
10. Drucker (1979: 36–46).
11. Drucker (1979: 42).
12. Conscious capitalism was developed by Raj Sisodia, see: www.consciouscapitalism.org.
13. Emerson (2003).
14. Denning (2011).
15. Porter/Kramer (2011: 77).
16. Marx (1848).

3. Imagine leaders who act for the world

> The main ethical question for our time is to choose what kind of a world we want to build together with the immense resources we have at our disposal.
> The Globally Responsible Leadership Initiative (2008)

THE LEADERSHIP VACUUM

We need globally responsible leadership in order to manage the transformation and build a new society. The concept of leadership not only concerns individual traits but represents an adaptive process that encompasses multiple levels of society and knowledge. Responsible leadership for a sustainable world is a culture of responsibility, a collective phenomenon that occurs within a global context.

Responsible leadership begins (but does not end) with individuals. Globally responsible leaders will need more cognitive sophistication to cope with the complexity of multi-dimensional responsibilities on a global level – as well as reflective awareness, critical thinking, multicultural and societal wisdom and the moral depth to weigh competing choices. These new dimensions complement existing traits, such as entrepreneurship and leadership competencies.

Many leading business schools claim that their mission is to educate leaders who will advance the well-being of society. For example, Harvard Business School's formal mission statement is "to educate leaders who make a difference in the world". MIT's Sloan School of Management aims to "develop principled, innovative leaders who improve the world". ESADE's key mission is to train individuals to become highly competent professionals who are fully aware of their social responsibility; while the School of Economics and Management at Tsinghua University's mission states that it strives "to advance and cultivate leaders for China and the world".

Yet, the reality remains that education and research in the area of leadership lies at the periphery rather than at the center of most business schools that profess to educate the leaders of the future.[1] There are many signs of such academic neglect: leadership as optional rather than core courses, and leadership courses being taught by external part-time rather than full-time or tenured faculty members. Only a few papers on leadership are published in the most prominent academic journals, and there are virtually no doctoral courses on the subject.

The demand for leadership education and development is often met by specialized institutions, such as the Center for Creative Leadership (CCL), as well as a variety of consultants and training organizations outside the formal management education space occupied by business schools. The demand for insights into leadership has also been met by popular writers. Business school academics turned best-selling authors have either been denied tenure, or have broken ranks with their more traditional colleagues. Many leadership bestsellers have been written by consultants, journalists and practicing leaders with a desire to share their wisdom or secure their legacies. Whilst some of the literature may be perceived to lack intellectual rigor, we should remind ourselves that there is no sanctioned body of leadership research that enables business practice to shift from trying to be the best *in* the world to becoming the best *for* the world.

Nohria and Khurana critically ponder: "Will students really take the mission statements of the universities they join seriously? Will they trust that these are institutions where one can learn to develop leadership? Or will they view universities as places where one obtains credentials and connections, some knowledge, but not lessons about leadership? Will leadership largely be perceived as a means of getting ahead, of gaining power, rather than of being understood as a serious professional with social responsibilities?"

Reaching Across Boundaries

The challenges for leadership and leadership development in business and society are increasing with the size, interconnectedness, complexity and diversity of business organizations in a globalized world. With business organizations increasingly interacting with all kinds of different institutions, today's most pressing challenges span boundaries – and so too must leadership. Based on the findings of a recent study[2] these boundaries exist in five different dimensions, ranging from vertical boundaries in organizations to horizontal boundaries across functions and units in organizations; from stakeholder boundaries with external partners and interest groups to demographic boundaries including gender, race, education and ideology; and to geographic boundaries across locations, cultures, regions and markets.

Although 86 percent of the senior executives surveyed agreed that it is extremely important that they collaborate across boundaries in their current leadership roles, only 7 percent of them believed they were very effective at doing so. The most important boundary dimensions were horizontal boundaries (71 percent) followed by geographic boundaries (26 percent) and demographic and stakeholder boundaries (17 percent). Vertical boundaries inside organizations (the classic hierarchical relationship) by contrast were the least frequently cited dimension (7 percent). These results suggest that leadership is concerned with boundaries outside of the organization to an increasingly large degree, suggesting that such executives are less effective in their management functions.

Social scientists have helped enrich our understanding of developmental aspects of a leader. Many concepts, however, point towards an achievable ideal state in the presumption that a human being could reach a perfect end point and be complete. A few scientists are more holistic and inclusive in their approach, recognizing that our nature is not static but emergent, dynamic, an open system. Graves[3] uses systems theory to explain both the individual and society as an inclusive bio-psycho-social coping system employed to solve existential problems. He provides a framework that allows us to examine leaders, organizations and societies and understand from which value perspective (meme) they consider a certain issue or situation. Understanding these different states and recognizing that leaders and their organizations can and will shift backwards and forwards between these states, provides an effective foundation for leader and leadership development.

Leadership challenges arise not only from complex and dynamic global markets, but also from societal challenges. Making business and the economy sustainable requires active engagement from corporate leaders, who can guide their own organizations through the global changes we collectively face. The financial and economic crises have shown that the ideal of a self-regulated system of self-serving stakeholders has led to failure on a global level, with long-term implications for economic development and human well-being.

East is East, West is West

From a Western perspective, a lack of both responsibility and leadership lies at the heart of our economic failures. Developing advanced leadership attributes requires profound changes in individual mindsets and behaviors, as well as in corporate culture. Some work is being conducted in this field; the Globally Responsible Leadership Initiative (GRLI) and the UN Principles for Responsible Management Education (PRME)[4] are two global initiatives founded by international organizations, whose common goal is to engage business schools and business organizations on a global level in the development and support of globally responsible leaders.

Different perspectives and reflection emerge when consulting Eastern literature. According to Julien, the Chinese traditional philosophy does not have a word for "action". Action is not something conducted by an "actor"; but happens within a flow of quiet transformations, within circumstances, conditions, with the individual simply being present in the potential of situations that occur.[5] Action occurs as a result of such circumstances and potential. Experienced masters know how to shape the flow of events by paying attention to synchronicities.[6] Zen philosophy further attests to such a person-free view of leadership which can be described as a non-egotist approach to making things happen, with process engagement replacing personal intervention. The Vedic tradition also builds on an understanding that change is facilitated in the more subtle, invisible realms, through connivance with circumstances. As a result, there are a number of Eastern cultures that do not possess a theory of "agency" or "leader", as seen in Western philosophy.

It is not surprising that the typical Chinese and Indian hero possesses very different attributes from a Western hero. The same comparison could be made with other Asian cultures and ancient philosophies from other parts of the world. India has its own rich heritage; and so do the countless indigenous people who display a strong relationship between themselves and their environment that is instinctively and fundamentally inclusive and holistic. We see great opportunities to enrich our Western understanding of leadership through an immersion in such other cultures and philosophies. This of course by no means suggests that the economies in these countries operate in accordance with such traditional thoughts or philosophies. Sadly, it has been observed that business leaders in non-Western cultures are no better or more responsible than their Western counterparts.

CLARIFYING LEADERSHIP REQUIREMENTS

How will we develop globally responsible leadership? Without a strong development framework, our efforts to progress toward more responsible leadership will remain limited, constrained, episodic – and more often as not marginalized in commerce and trade. In order to develop globally responsible leadership we must re-think our entire management education framework, which will require participation from all players who contribute to the field.

Globally responsible leadership is a response to both existing gaps in leadership theory and practical challenges facing leaders. The Globally Responsible Leadership Initiative (GRLI) defines globally responsible leadership as "the global exercise of ethical, values-based leadership in the pursuit of economic and societal progress and sustainable development. It is based on a fundamental understanding of the interconnectedness of the world and a recognition of the need for economic and societal and environmental advancement."[7]

As such, "global" qualifies the word "responsible" indicating that a leader (or acts of leadership) need to embrace the best interest of the planet and all living beings, reflecting a globally inclusive outlook. In our definition, "global" does not qualify the word "leader", as in "global leadership" which is something different and probably not applicable to our work. Globally responsible leadership has nothing to do with advancing the trend of globalization, which Ghemawat suggests is overstated in terms of reach and impact.[8] Our concept does not seek to advance a bid to establish the regime of globalization or an attempt to control the periphery from the centre, retaining the hegemony of industrialized West. What we wish to introduce is the thought of a local leader with a global perspective.

More recently, GRLI added that "Responsible leadership implies the grounding of actions in a system of values which recognize societal interdependence and long-term sustainable development. If the firm wishes to lend meaning to its actions and wants to give a purpose to economic progress by aligning it to societal progress, ethics are essential to enlighten tough choices and guide behavior. The main ethical question for our time is to choose what kind of world we want to build together with the immense resources we have at our disposal."[9]

Responsible leadership addresses the concern of a wider stakeholder base and asks for what and to whom leaders are responsible.[10] Responsible leadership differs from traditional leadership concepts in three significant ways:

1. It broadens the view from traditional leader-subordinate relationship to a leader-stakeholder relationship, shifting the focus of responsibility from the corporation or its shareholders to different stakeholders such as workers, clients, suppliers, the environment, future generations and society as a whole. The level of regard for others (equating to stakeholder inclusion) may of course vary with the nature of the leadership task and the organization involved.
2. Responsible leadership aims to generate value for other stakeholders and the society as a whole that goes beyond the value generated for the leader or the leader's organization. Responsible leaders are therefore individuals who reconcile their personal interests or those of

their organization within the context of a wider societal responsibility. They build and cultivate relationships with stakeholders to create shared value, taking into account the potential, long-term impact and indirect consequences of their actions. The concept of responsible leadership is related to the professionalism project presented by Khurana, who sees the need for a code of professional ethics for managers and leaders linking their work to "higher aims" and not just to "hired hands".[11]

3. The relationship between leaders and stakeholders is value based and driven by ethical principles. These values are oriented towards the creation of economic and societal progress and sustainable development. As the demands of these areas are varied and often conflicting, there will be situations where the choices will be difficult and controversial. Addressing ethical conflicts in a transparent and fair way will therefore be a crucial factor.

In addition, "globally" responsible leadership embraces further aspects. It refers to leadership in a global context, with the principles and practices of responsible management exercised everywhere, in all parts of an organization and in all its areas of activities. Globally responsible leadership also refers to leadership decisions taken with situational and regionally different demands and the needs of stakeholders in mind. Solutions will differ depending on the cultural, political and economic context.

When taking a more holistic or global perspective on responsible leadership the emphasis shifts from single leaders and their institutions and stakeholders to the exercise of collective responsibility. The idea of leading-in-partnership and its corollaries of co-determination and co-creation represent an emerging frame for responsible leadership. The classic pyramid framework[12] proposes four classes of responsibility for business in society: economic, legal, ethical and "discretionary" responsibilities.

Mirvis and de Jongh[13] suggest that these responsibilities should be considered as interactive and interdependent, providing a dynamic web of simultaneous interactions and considerations rather than the widely accepted linear approach. Such an understanding provides a systemic and holistic perspective, allowing responsible leaders to see linkages between economic, political, ecological, and moral factors and then incorporate them into deliberations and choices on value creation. Equally important is the introspective input that comes from "facing your maker" and carefully considering the purpose of your business and what you are supposed to do. This necessarily has personal, transpersonal, and spiritual components, representing a reflective practice which points leaders toward cultivating a much greater awareness, both internally and externally.

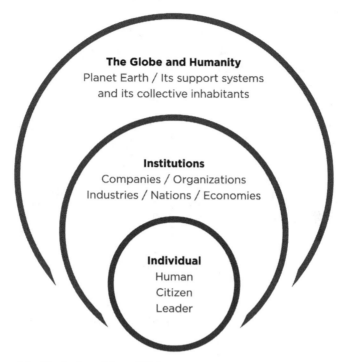

The Globe and Humanity
Planet Earth / Its support systems
and its collective inhabitants

Institutions
Companies / Organizations
Industries / Nations / Economies

Individual
Human
Citizen
Leader

Source: John North adapted from GRLI.

Figure 3.1 Responsible leadership – Me, We, All of Us

As a result, responsible leadership is a function of the individual leader (the "Me"), of responsible organizations (the "We"), and of responsible business in the larger ecosystem of investors, consumers, competitors, regulators, and other interests (the "Us") that provide a context for and also have to act responsibly to legitimize and sustain responsible business leadership. They present a holistic view of responsible leadership where Me, We, and all of Us are in conversation, seeking and moving toward alignment and otherwise engaging in or fostering honest and fair competition and cooperation. Such responsible leaders reflect a sincere commitment to a leadership *for* the world (see Figure 3.1).

Mirvis and de Jongh (2010) propose three different frames of responsible business leadership: a traditional modernist, a contemporary relational, and a holistic frame emerging on the horizon (see Table 3.1). Each frame is related to different characteristics in the economic, socio-political, eco-logical and moral spheres. The more we move from a modernist frame to a

Table 3.1   Responsible leadership frames

	Traditional (Modernist)	**Contemporary (Relational)**	**Horizon (Holistic)**
Economic Sphere	Profit Maximization	Value Creation	Total Wealth Creation
Socio-Political Sphere	Legal Compliance	Legitimacy	Partnership
	Shareholders	Stakeholders	Integrative Social Contract
Ecological Sphere	Externalities	Impacts	Sustainability
Moral Sphere	Minimize Harms	"Balance Interests", Harms / Goods	Do Good Repair and Enrich

Source: Mirvis and de Jongh (2010).

relational and holistic frame, the more developed and demanding become the responsibilities of leadership. In reality, responsible leadership consists of dynamic interactions between the different frames thereby creating an operational field that is shaped by responsible leadership in action.

THE CHALLENGE OF DEVELOPING RESPONSIBLE LEADERS

How can responsible leadership and leaders be developed? The age-old question of whether leaders are born or made has been answered in favor of the latter, with a few qualifications. Leadership cannot be taught in the same manner as in other fields. Teaching leadership through lectures, case studies, videos about great leaders and written examinations does not work. Leadership classes using such an approach may well develop the skill to *talk* about leading, but not the *skill to exercise* leadership. In other words, students of leadership are just as likely to improve their capacity to exercise leadership by reading books and watching podcasts by leadership gurus as they are likely to improve their physical condition by watching fitness videos and athletics competitions.[14]

Leadership cannot be taught, but it can be *learned*. Given the right conditions, virtually anyone can develop their capacity to lead more effectively. Such leadership development takes time and work. Anyone who wants to run a marathon in under three hours must spend many months in training. Equally, students and executives who want to develop their capacity to lead must get their hands dirty and actually *lead*.

Whether those who develop their capacity to exercise leadership do so in a responsible way depends on how they understand and integrate their responsibilities as a leader. The responsible exercise of leadership is not the result of putting someone in a particular job, investing them with formal authority, or supplying a book of ethical rules to follow. Recent studies show that developing the capacity to lead responsibly includes three different steps: learning theories and concepts, practicing, and reflecting.[15] Knowledge of ethical theories and concepts is at best a starting point. However, responsible behavior is less about knowledge of ethics than a question of practical experience. Leadership is acquired from the experience of learning to lead, follow, participate and co-create. Such experiences must not only matter to the learner; they must be personally challenging and carefully reflected upon.

It is crucially important that leadership behavior is practiced in a context where responsibility is demanded. Mary Gentile speaks of the necessity to practice ethical decision making and "build muscle" in order to produce the capability to be ethical when faced with challenging situations in real life.[16] Whilst this can to a certain extent be achieved by role playing, a more effective approach for individuals exercising leadership is to work with organizations that have a broader social purpose, giving them the opportunity to understand the wider moral context in which they live and work. Otherwise, they risk being captured by the narrow, short-term goals that dominate many profit-driven businesses. Introducing new factors and different perspectives will lead to better, longer-term, more responsible decisions. Without such external awareness managers and leaders can, in effect, become hostages to the limited organizational vision and produce harm to the environment they operate in, often without even being aware of it.

The core elements that make an experience a significant learning event include managing difficult relationships, playing for high stakes, or confronting adversity. In order to effectively use experiences for learning, management education should cover a variety of domains and provide novel challenges that teach different aspects of leadership.[17] Equally important is the framework of a safe environment where mistakes can be made and experiences critically discussed and analysed. For example: *What have we learned from the practical exercises? Where did we encounter problems or meet resistance? Such questions typically hide important learning points. How did we resolve these challenges? What helped us resolve them?* Meaningful behavioral learning occurs most easily as a result of a strongly felt need and a deep personal commitment. Challenging experiences and subsequent reflection can lead to significant development in leadership ability.

Most fundamentally, leader development is personal development. Psychologist Howard Gardner[18] has studied key figures in politics, business, social movements, academia, and the arts. His research shows how formative experiences shape the beliefs and practices of leaders in almost every culture. He argues that these experiences make up a leader's identity and that leadership is autobiographical. Great leaders differentiate themselves with an inherent sense of positive purpose which is developed over the course of a lifetime. The ability to reflect on one's own life, to write one's story and then write it again, looking for a red thread when looking back and finding, losing and re-finding one's place in this world is invaluable for a leader to feel a sense of being grounded, and of belonging.

Know Thyself

Before students or managers can embark on developing their leadership abilities they must take a look at themselves. They need to identify their inner core, or higher self which can effectively guide them through turbulent times. An integration of body, mind, heart and soul is an important pathway to strengthening such an inner connection. While most students find it easy to connect to their inner place of stillness and meaning, only those who train in self reflection can develop a solid connection to their core that can resist fear, pressure and uncertainty. Guiding students through their personal development requires a facilitator with the personal experience of such a connection – as well as possessing the skills to hold the space for students to discover and explore their inner selves in their own time, and in their own way.

Does responsible leadership require "great men and women" in order to succeed? From the moral realm, we could make a case that integrity is a cardinal foundation of great leadership. In the broader realms of responsible leadership, North suggests we replace competencies with four critical cornerstones which map back to the moral virtues of Aristotle and Plato:[19]

- *Critical reflection:* the capacity to reflect the "whole" when taking action and to reflect on the self and situation when doing so.
- *Practical wisdom:* the ability to draw on timeless knowledge and insights and to exercise good judgment when making decisions.
- *Moral courage:* the strength of character to defy convention and the drive to translate responsible decisions into action.
- *Global inclusion:* the capacity to engage and lead others for the common good.

Graves reminds us of the danger of looking for ideal or perfect states of human existence. His work highlights the emergence within humans of new bio-psycho-social systems that are created by interplay of external conditions with neurology. His eight-stage hierarchy of human development proposes a framework that guarantees neither timeliness nor direction. According to Graves, human beings and societies as a whole can both progress and regress, depending on circumstances and internal states. His framework includes the two basic notions of human beings either trying to make the environment adapt to the self, or the human adapting the self to the external conditions. He calls these "express self" and "deny self" systems, whose rhythmic motions add a cyclic aspect to his theory.

While it exceeds the context of this work to provide a detailed overview of Graves' theory, we would like to include the importance of the notion that a human being (and a society) as a whole is an open, dynamic and emerging system that is in constant interplay between an inner state of consciousness and an external environment. Recognizing the dynamic perspective of a leader rather than seeking to push or pull them towards a desirable end state represents a significant stepping stone to a new paradigm of leadership and human development.

TOWARDS GLOBALLY RESPONSIBLE LEADERS

The concept of leadership not only concerns individual traits but represents an adaptive process that encompasses multiple levels of society and knowledge. Responsible leadership for a sustainable world is a culture of responsibility, a collective phenomenon that occurs within a global context. For decades the study of leadership focused on identifying the distinguishing "traits" of leaders. We consider a number of critical qualities and competencies as important:

- A global, holistic, long-term and visionary perspective;
- Clarity, focus and intensity of commitment;
- Highly motivated to do good; to do the right thing (ethical thinking translated into action);
- Highly evolved capacity for creative, critical, holistic, ethical and systemic thinking and decision-making;
- Ability to navigate through uncertainty, ambiguity, setbacks, challenges and problems;
- Action and results oriented. Self-starter with a high need for achievement;

- Patience (with respect to staying on course) and *im*patience (with respect to being driven to achieve results as fast as possible);
- Highly skilled in learning by doing, adaptive, making and learning from mistakes quickly and inexpensively;
- Integrative, skilled at spanning across boundaries; and
- Skillful in determining root causes and critical success factors, and focusing on what is most important.

Creating lists is easy, but developing leaders based on these components is quite another matter. Responsible leadership can easily share the same fate as traditional leadership, drowning in a never-ending list of attributes. Yet, there are some specific features of responsible leadership that deserve to be highlighted. To date, most studies emphasize the importance of various forms of intelligence for leading responsibly: emotional, social, cultural, and spiritual intelligence, as well as systematic thinking. Furthermore, ego maturity, fortitude, patience, and pro-social and pro-environmental sensibilities also feature.[20]

Responsible leadership begins (but does not end) with individuals. Globally responsible leaders will need more cognitive sophistication to cope with the complexity of multi-dimensional responsibilities on a global level – as well as reflective awareness, critical thinking, multi-cultural and societal wisdom and the moral depth to weigh competing choices. These new dimensions complement existing known traits such as entrepreneurship and leadership competencies.

Mirvis and de Jongh (2010) refer to a study by the Hay Group discussing leadership competencies of CSR professionals. Their study highlights personal maturity, optimistic commitment, peripheral vision, visionary thinking, a systems perspective, collaborative networking, strategic influence and the capacity to drive change as key leadership attributes in this arena. Mirvis and de Jongh highlight a study of 10 companies where leaders in firms displaying advanced stages of sustainability were far more likely to question assumptions about their business than their counterparts in less advanced firms, further showing greater inclination to make creative connections between their own strategy and the interests of society, and apply a "both / and" mindset to paradoxes and conflicts.

Responsible leaders often embody dualities which may reflect the capacity to *hold tension*, an inherent quality in any great leader. Quinn (2004) describes these polarities as eight creative states that can be reached when the positive oppositions are successfully integrated (see Table 3.2).[21] He also shows what happens when these states are disintegrated, describing states of destructive leadership that are all too familiar.

What do these competencies, cornerstones, polarities and creative states

Table 3.2 Eight creative states of leadership

Eight creative states	Underlying polarities
1. Responsible freedom	Self disciplined and responsible AND spontaneous and expressive
2. Tough love	Assertive and bold AND compassionate and concerned
3. Reflective action	Mindful and reflective AND active and energetic
4. Authentic engagement	Engaged and involved AND principled and integrated
5. Appreciative inquiry	Optimistic and constructive AND realistic and questioning
6. Grounded vision	Grounded and factual AND visionary and hopeful
7. Adaptive confidence	Adaptive and flexible AND confident and secure
8. Detached interdependence	Independent and strong AND humble and open

Source: Robert Quinn (2004).

have in common? How can we condense them into a comprehensive profile that describes the challenge of globally responsible leadership? We suggest one particular dimension emerging as an underlying core enabler: the need for a shift in consciousness of the leader. A conscious leader is an individual with a highly developed capacity for self reflection, a capacity we call *reflective awareness*.[22] Built on this underlying core capacity, we further suggest to group key competencies of responsible leaders along the roles identified for business. De Woot describes these roles as entrepreneurship, leadership and statesmanship, which serve as an excellent basis for linking the cornerstones of responsible and sustainable business to those of responsible leadership. These roles are further complemented with qualifying enablers and descriptions of perspectives as described below (also see Figure 3.2).

1. **Reflective Awareness** is expressed by the universal perspective of the leader, reflected in the way they relate to themselves, their environment and various aspects of the world. This dimension is defined by an evolved level of consciousness and personal awareness, clarity, focus and commitment on a personal and organizational level, deep values and ethics, humility and humanity, empathy and resonance with others, representing a fundamental, non-negotiable foundation of a globally responsible leader.

Source: Katrin Muff.

Figure 3.2   Four dimensions of globally responsible leaders

2. **Sustainable Entrepreneurship** is reflected in a visionary and long-term perspective. This dimension is defined by an advanced capacity for creative, critical, and divergent thinking, both street-smart and an evolved intellect, the ability to question the status quo and to dismantle complexity, a facility to handle general management challenges and to solve problems integrally, the ability to lead organizational change and sustainability transformations including implementation skills, and advanced mastery of all relevant subject knowledge to get any given job done. The sustainability aspect is reflected in the ability to think and act for the long term and the capability to integrate sustainability aspects into the organization.

3. **Holistic Leadership** is reflected in an ethical and inclusive perspective that integrates the demands of different stakeholders. This dimension is defined by strategic skills, extraordinary communication skills, an excellent adaptability and attitude towards learning, a talent as a motivator, enabler and team stakeholder, an awareness of patience versus impatience or doing versus being, the capacity to span boundaries and bear tension, an interest in uncovering unintended consequences of actions taken, respect for diversity, adhesion to ethics and human values.

4. **Enlightened Statesmanship** is demonstrated through a societal and political perspective. It includes the ability to formulate an inspiring

higher-order vision, a sensitivity and awareness for societal concerns, a capacity to talk to the general public in clear language, to serve a cause larger than oneself, a drive to serve the common good, the ability to create and function within broad stakeholder networks, fluency with all aspects of sustainability, and a profound desire to be of service.

Responsible leaders in this emerging new world will need to largely invent how they will lead. They will co-invent their leadership in the context of their everyday jobs, co-creating the road not yet traveled in relationship with partners, peers and stakeholders. Mirvis and de Jongh suggest four domains for developing competencies to lead a responsible company: self-leadership, shared leadership, enterprise leadership, and ecological leadership.[23] These domains suggest that beyond an effective self-management of a leader there is an element of shared leadership and enterprise leadership which moves the boundaries from hierarchical management systems to bottom-up, multi-level and cross-functional forms of collaboration that span countries and culture.

Learning how to operate in and exert authority in fluid, loosely structured teams and task groupings is a crucial part of a future leader's daily bread. The idea of someone being "in charge" contradicts models of shared leadership and responsibility where all the stakeholders share a vision and have an informed sense of what it takes to operate responsibly. We are experiencing spontaneous social networks and organic ways that people who share a common purpose self-organize according to systems that have so far been ignored. Socio-political movements such as Occupy Wall Street (United States) and Les Indignés (Europe) represent the first showcases of entirely new forms of organizing action.

Imagine if all leaders in charge of organizations of any type possessed such capacities and perspectives. Imagine how easily they might collaborate, not only within their organizations, but also beyond their immediate narrow set of stakeholders, embracing the existing and emerging regional and global challenges we all currently face.

We are concerned that Western thinking continues to dominate this discussion and that we are unable to embrace the true essence of what a great leader may be able to represent. In Eastern thought the concept of leadership is totally absent as they look at the act of creation from a different ontological perspective. Eastern societies have not, however, found ways to embody these thoughts into a current practice of leadership in their modern societies. The polarity of demands between being and doing seems to stretch the limits of human capabilities. Yet, we should not concede defeat. Bridging Eastern with Western thought may well provide one way forward in a journey. We will build the bridge.

NOTES

1. Nohria/Khurana (2010: 5).
2. Ernst/Chrobot-Mason (2011).
3. Graves (2005).
4. GRLI was founded by the UN Global Compact and the European Foundation for Management Education (EFMD). PRME has included the UN Global Compact AACSB International, EFMD; the Academy of Business and Society (EABIS), Aspen Institute's Business and Society Program, GMAC, Net Impact on its board with active support by the business school associations CEEMAN, CLADEA, AABS and AAPBS.
5. Jullien (2009).
6. Jung (2010).
7. GRLI (2005).
8. Ghemawat (2011).
9. GRLI (2008).
10. Pless/Maak (2011: 4).
11. Khurana (2007).
12. Carroll/Buchholtz (2011).
13. Mirvis/de Jongh (2010).
14. Wood (2010).
15. Colby et al. (2011).
16. Gentile (2010: 160).
17. McCall (2010: 682–686).
18. Gardner (2011).
19. John North is an associate at the Albert Luthuli Center for Responsible Leadership at the University of Pretoria, South Africa. He contributes to ongoing research and is in the process of completing his doctorate.
20. Mirvis/de Jongh (2010: 36).
21. Quinn (2004: 88).
22. Muff (2006).
23. Mirvis/de Jongh (2010: 37).

4. Imagine management educators as custodians of society

> For me, everything has to start from school. It is where we learn values. These are not emphasized in our lives as professionals.
> Carlos Ramos, youth representative, Peru

THE LANDSCAPE OF MANAGEMENT EDUCATION

The landscape of management education and research is both densely populated and diverse. While many of us immediately think of business schools as key representatives for management, we also find schools of business and management nestled within larger universities, leadership and executive development institutes, corporate universities, and professional training centers in both private and in public settings – such as in the military or in religious groups. Also, we tend to forget that informal on-the-job learning is more effective than most types of formal learning.

In terms of research, traditional academic research is conducted within management departments or in business schools. The decreasing relevancy of academic research has, however, opened a space for other research providers to satisfy the needs of business and the economy. Such providers include consultancies, think tanks and, increasingly, collaborative platforms currently emerging both virtually and in real life, such as groups of concerned citizens who wish to address a particular problem. When we examine how these needs are addressed in different regions of the world, we discover that there are significant differences in how education and research is conducted across different cultures and states of economic development.

Current studies suggest that more than 70 percent of professional education takes place in the form of job-related informal education, rather than through off-the-job classroom-based learning. Formal education provided by universities and business schools represents only about 10 percent of what people learn about their jobs.[1] On-the-job learning is often unstructured and takes place informally through discussions with co-workers, self study, mentoring by managers and similar methods. Interestingly, informal chats with colleagues are significantly more effective than instructions from managers.

Leadership is also a topic that is formally and informally addressed in a great diversity of books, films, and other media. We are also influenced by the culture we live in: our home enviroment, our communities and at work. Unsurprisingly, learning is particularly effective as a *response* to personal challenges (such as changing jobs), which is further supported by mentors, peers and self reflection. Rightly or wrongly, our reflective ability is a key factor in the informal learning process.

Corporate universities and in-house training offer development programs to improve skills and competences required on the job and to operate successfully within the given culture of an organization. Those emerging leaders earmarked as high-potential talent often benefit from a leadership training track that consists of a combination of job rotations, vertical and horizontal promotions, expatriate assignments and formal executive training courses, provided both internally and externally. In the U.S. alone, businesses spend 50 billion USD a year in training and development – a quarter of which is allocated to leadership development.

Some 40 percent of adults are engaged in continuous training at any given moment in their career.[2] Leadership and management training represent an important part of life-long learning. Continuous education serves to acquire knowledge, skills and competences in a life-long learning process, which often includes courses triggered by a personal sensitivity or interests that broaden the mind and enables the personal development of an individual. Such personal learning journeys tell a unique story; for many managers, entrepreneurs and emerging leaders, training resembles the colorful patchwork commonly seen on a quilt. Depending on the appetite to learn, learning individuals will weave courses of shorter and longer duration into their personal and professional lives, paid either out of their own pockets or by their companies.

Executive development is often narrowly defined as non-degree programs offered by top-level business schools. There is some debate about the nature of business school education as a form of professional development; not everybody agrees that such an education is part of the mission of a business school. Ideally, executive training should address developmental areas neglected during basic business and management education, allowing future leaders to understand their ambitions, limitations, vision and values in their journey. Such training also represents an important occasion to network with other leaders, to test one's journey in the context of others, to reflect on success and failure; and to step back from the daily burdens any given job entails. While business schools train a million MBAs each year (200 000 in the United States alone[3]), there are tens of millions people worldwide who participate in leadership, personal and professional training every year.

Girl Scouts and Generals

Research on leader development remains at the periphery of management research. So much of who we are and how we will act as leaders is related to the environment in which we grew up and the leaders around us. Leadership training happens in more places than we imagine, from girl scouts to military training. Practical business and management training is offered by private and state-owned institutions and ranges from training a few days or weekends, to certificate courses lasting several years and culminating in professional recognition. In many European countries (Finland, Austria, the Netherlands and Switzerland in particular) vocational training continues to be a very popular and highly valued form of education. In Switzerland, 75 percent of young adults choose an apprenticeship, nearly half of them in business. The three-year commercial apprenticeship entails a combination of on-the-job training and formal course work. A young adult thereby experiences a sense of freedom and personal responsibility by earning a salary relatively early in his life, compared with a small minority of his friends who complete a high school diploma before enrolling into a university.

Universities and business schools make by far the smallest contribution to management education (10 percent). These higher education institutions differentiate between undergraduate, graduate, postgraduate and doctoral degrees. Undergraduate education is for high school graduates with no formal work experience, most often a three- to four-year (predominantly full-time) degree that culminates in a Bachelor in Business, Management or similar qualification. Graduate education encompasses the so-called pre-experience degrees for Bachelor degree holders without work experience. The Bologna Reform in Europe resulted in the introduction of more than 1500 new master's degree programs in the past decade. In Europe, the MBA degree is considered a one-year postgraduate degree requiring at least three years of professional experience. In the United States, the MBA program is most frequently a pre-experience two-year master's program, with only some schools requiring work experience as a prerequisite. In the U.K., students jump from undergraduate directly into postgraduate education, adding to the general difficulties of comparing regions. As a result of the rising level of unemployment among the youth there is an increasing trend in Europe to complete a pre-experience Master's in Management instead of waiting for admission into an MBA program.

There is some internal debate whether a master's degree should enable graduates to enter the job market, or whether it serves as a first step towards an academic career and doctoral studies. Teaching-oriented schools tend to offer master's degrees with specializations that are tailored to ensure a smooth integration into the workforce. On the other hand, we see an increasing shortage of PhDs, which may be interpreted as a lack of perspective an academic career offers compared to a fast-moving and often highly paid career in business or management.

What is the difference between management education, business education and leadership education? We have witnessed many heated debates on this subject during the creation of the 50+20 vision. Given the confusion and contradictions related to the different interpretations of the terms, there is a need to provide clarity on our usage of these terms.

To us, business education focuses on transmitting skills, competences and knowledge required to succeed in business, including the broad functions in business, such as finance, accounting, HR, marketing, sales and other aspects.

Management education seeks to equip managers serving in any type of organization, including NGOs, governments and business with the skills, competences and general knowledge to successfully manage an organization – including leadership, managerial, strategic, collaborative, socio-political and of course entrepreneurial skills.

Finally, leadership education encompasses skills which ensure that a leader can lead and engage a group of people towards goals worthwhile pursuing. Such education should include ethics and value-based personal development.

Who is in charge of management education? As we have seen, the field contains many stakeholders, situations and markets. Prospective students can choose from degrees and non-degree programs, vocational and non-formal training. Besides teaching and training, there are the research and of service aspects to consider. Currently, no single formal entity represents management education, nor is there an overarching structure that helps ensure that all stakeholders develop the leaders our future needs.

WHAT VALUE DO BUSINESS SCHOOLS GENERATE?

Over the last quarter century, business schools have been the major success story in the world of higher education, at least when measured in terms of a growing demand. Compared to all other stakeholders in management education, business schools enjoy an unparalleled visibility, with the MBA recognized as the only truly global degree[4] in higher education.

However, over the past decade business schools have also been criticized with regard to their fundamental nature and value. Increasingly, they are also criticized for having become too customer and business focused at the expense of a professional orientation and their contribution to society. McIntosh[5] comments how "more learning is taking place on the streets than in institutions like universities".

Business schools claim that they create value for many various stakeholders; for themselves, for their customers (students and corporate clients), for the scientific community and society. Specifically, they create value for themselves by making money, by enhancing their own reputation and also by attracting and hiring highly regarded professors who amplify the school's status and image. Business schools further create value for their customers by enriching careers, salaries and by helping to improve the performance of their corporate clients. Next, they create value for the scientific community by contributing new research and building knowledge. Lastly, business schools claim to create value for society by educating people for a responsible engagement in society and politics, and by creating knowledge to solve societal problems.

But how good a job are business schools really doing in creating value for *society*?

The Rise of the Business Schools

The history of business schools is dominated by two highly influential reports: the Carnegie and Ford Foundation Reports, both published in 1959. Until then, business schools were criticized for being an overly vocational training ground where experienced managers recounted anecdotes to well-bred young people who were only after big profits. Many business educators felt that their field was frequently marginalized by other disciplines, particularly by economists. Based on the two reports, five doctoral programs were established at Harvard, Carnegie-Mellon, Columbia, Chicago and Stanford, with the objective to create rigorous and scholarly business programs. These programs were considered crucial to make business administration a more respectable academic discipline. As a consequence, management education was propelled into a rigorous, demanding, competitive arena of scholarly research and teaching. Fifty years later, the greatest cost driver within the traditional business model of a business school is *faculty salaries*. Increasing competition amongst schools, the market pressure of rankings and the decreasing pool of PhD candidates may well force traditional business schools to rethink their business model to remain competitive in an increasingly global economy.

In 1988 the Porter-McKibben Report, sponsored by AACSB, reminded business schools that the leadership skills of their graduates needed significant improvement. In that same year BusinessWeek published its first ranking of MBA programs, which proved to be far more influential than the Porter-McKibben Report. After analysing the historic development of business schools in the US, Khurana concludes that leading business schools moved from a "tyranny of the faculty" to a "tyranny of the markets".[6] Both forms of tyranny display a tendency to restrain or even cripple leadership in business schools.

Let us examine faculty dominance and market dominance in more detail:

Faculty dominance has many faces. A faculty has a defining role in designing courses, programs and pedagogy. However, most of a faculty has little or no training in pedagogy or andragogy. As a result, education is seen through the lens of teaching rather than learning. Teaching is most often one-sided and hierarchical: students are taught, examined and graded, and are not treated as partners or co-producers in a two-way learning process. If students have learned what they were taught, they pass the exams and receive good grades. In addition, research is seen as the prerogative of the individual faculty, not as a social obligation.

Faculty decides on research areas, approach and methodology, forms of cooperation, international orientation, theoretical or practical focus, as well as the forms and channels of publications. They are free to define these areas according to their own scholarly and methodological preferences and experiences, their reputation-building strategies, their economic interests and their political convictions. A business school's ability to have their faculty accept its research priorities and programs is generally limited. The higher the scholarly reputation of the faculty, the more likely it is that status and attractiveness will be employed to extract extra benefits and freedom demanded by the school. Engagement for institutional self-management and development (such as program management, leadership roles in committees and faculties) become the domain of the less reputable faculty. A faculty even has the ability to depose presidents and deans who propose a mandate to transform the institution, or who become too strong over the period of their tenure – as recent events in Europe have demonstrated.

Market dominance concerns a focus on the institution, not on the individual faculty, where business schools build and strengthen their brand name through institutional strategies. Financial well-being and success, revenues, costs and surplus play important roles. An institution uses marketing and communications to position the school and their particular strengths in an increasingly competitive and transparent landscape.

Accreditations and rankings are used to measure and demonstrate the comparative success of a business school, which are made widely known to different stakeholders and the public. Accreditation and rankings have become processes that are managed by dedicated faculty and administrators who will make their demands known internally, thereby challenging faculty dominance. Business schools develop and manage their alumni base to make their names known and to create additional sources of income, investing in attracting high-profile faculty members and carefully developing international networks of business school and corporate partners who are expected to reflect favorably on the school's own reputation.

As a result, collaborative dynamics between business schools and faculties are replaced by *competitive* dynamics. Openness and sharing give way to secrecy and conservatism. Students are selected from a pool of applicants; the bigger the pool and the lower the rate of acceptance, the higher the school's reputation. Further, the higher the reputation, the more the fees can be increased – thereby restricting their educational offers to wealthier students who are seen as customers who buy a service and whose demands have to be fulfilled. Success is measured in "customer satisfaction" surveys and course evaluations. Their results are used to improve teaching methods, but also to evaluate faculty performance. It should not come as a surprise that the fundamental educational purpose often gets lost in the process.

Faculty dominance and market dominance are both present in varying degrees in today's business schools. They force specific orientations on business school management, be it the research interests of a faculty or the market focus of the institution. Both approaches have clear limitations. Both create problems. Business schools teach a particularly biased content in business functions, ignoring the fact that these functions have negative impacts on the sustainability performance of companies. As part of their undeclared context, business schools ignore public interest in favor of private interests. They inculcate the value of money, personal enrichment and greed over communal values, and do not teach their students how to deal with water, food, habitat and shelter, transportation, energy, urbanization – the most common challenges we face today.

The current challenge for business schools is therefore one of re-legitimization – of regaining legitimacy that was lost in the wake of corporate scandals (Enron, Parmalat, UBS), during the recent financial and economic crises, or unresolved humanitarian, political and environmental crises.[7] If business schools want to attract and inspire talented students, secure political support and regain public trust, they must start looking beyond their own interests, those of their faculties and their direct markets.

To add to the challenge, business schools and management education is faced with a new problem that until recently seemed to be reserved for other fields of study. In light of the public debt crisis, the financing and affordability of education has moved up on the public agenda, as well as becoming a core political issue for business schools. Governments are reducing their financial support for public education. Increasingly high tuition levels and fast-rising student debt are exacerbated by an increasingly competitive job market, resulting in an explosive situation for students and graduates.

Management education faces multiple challenges. How will public universities and business schools address faculty salaries, PhD shortages, and funding limitations? Will the use of technology give rise to new program types? What risks and opportunities result from the changing financial equations for various existing program types? What do mergers between schools really contribute? Does it make sense for the government to continue to invest their funding directly into institutes of higher learning, or do alternative models such as life-long educational coupons for citizens make more sense? Finally, what would the consequences be of such alternatives, both for the life-long learners as well as public and private educational providers?

Clearly, it is time for business schools, and indeed all stakeholders in the field of management education, to seriously consider their contribution to society. What will it take to implement a research vision which will produce research that is useful and accessible in understanding and resolving the big societal issues? How will we develop an educational vision that generates the kind of managers and leaders society needs? How can they ensure that participants are equipped with the social awareness and leadership competencies required to secure the needed trust, or to handle the most pressing economic and social issues? In effect, management education institutions themselves will need strong leadership to steer their own organizations through a process of transformation in increasingly difficult times.

WHO SHOULD BENEFIT FROM MANAGEMENT EDUCATION?

In the middle of the twentieth century, business students were less well regarded than their colleagues in law schools or medicine. Since the 1970s however, the intellectual gap has been largely closed[8] and business schools are attracting highly talented students to a point where business studies have become the most popular study programs in most universities around the world. Yet, there is a strong sense that business students are different from students in arts and sciences. MBA students typically possess an engineering, business or natural science background, and only seldom a background in arts or humanities. More than others, business students are focused on the direct instrumental value of their studies. They study primarily to reach a clear goal, an attractive and well-paid future career and expect to get there as efficiently and effectively as possible. In contrast to this instrumental orientation, arts and sciences graduates are seen as being motivated by intellectual and cultural curiosity.

This motivational divide has consequences. The U.S. National Survey of Student Engagement, for example, finds that business majors are less likely than students in most other fields to discuss ideas from their courses outside of class, to read books on their own for personal enjoyment or academic enrichment, or to attend cultural events such as art exhibitions, plays, music or theater performances.[9] Although the more complex conditions of the twenty-first century (including business and life in general) demand greater flexibility of mind and a broader understanding, the dynamics in business schools are moving in a different direction. Management students are considered to display a lower capacity for caring about a world beyond themselves, and are less likely to contribute to the greater good of society.

The career ambitions of management students are often oriented toward a particular set of career paths. Consulting firms and investment banks – which offer considerably higher financial incentives and career flexibility than many other employers – are the preferred choice of students graduating from elite business schools in the Western world. Often, MBAs and other business graduates receive higher starting salaries than graduates of advanced degree programs in almost any other field. An MBA or a business degree from a leading business school has become a "golden passport" to financial well-being.[10] Such a mix of financial incentives has naturally become attractive to strongly career-minded students; their focus shifts "from learning to earning" while business schools respond with a corresponding emphasis on career development and a strong market orientation.[11]

Entry level requirements are another concern. Rating and accreditation agencies reward schools for selecting as few possible students from the largest pool of candidates. This means that the degree of improvement of a student at Yale is significantly lower than at Penn State,[12] where the performance level at the beginning of studies is significantly lower on average. At Yale, students can expect to progress slightly from very good to excellent, whereas at Penn State they leap from good to very good, a significantly larger improvement. Does Penn State not contribute as much (or possibly even more) value to society than Yale? Why should Penn State suffer in rankings for refusing fewer students than Yale? The fact is that the stereotype of the career-minded and income-driven business student runs the risk of creating a homogenous, self-centered system, scaring away students with different backgrounds and mindsets. Such a system reduces the diversity of students and available learning perspectives, while stifling much-needed debate and practical experience in the classroom.

"We Happy Few"

Let us look beyond business schools, which have been accused of providing undergraduate and graduate education mostly for the rich and successful. Is executive development any different? Many business schools have embarked on executive education – some of which have made it their core business.[13] While this has led to a broadening of their customer base by serving business organizations more directly, executive development has certainly not reduced elitism in business schools. How have other stakeholders in management education been doing? Is it not the task of corporate universities to train the few selected high potentials? Further, don't companies mostly select the high performers for leadership and executive training? Aren't only the highly motivated persons of a certain income group willing and able to invest personal time and money into continuous education of one form or another?

What of other emerging, existing or potential leaders around the world? What about the entrepreneurial potential in the emerging and developing countries – those economies that will determine much of the future fate of our planet, depending on how they deal with the unintended environmental and social impact of their economic decisions? Today, stakeholders in management education serve predominantly large corporations, the financial sector and consultancies, and educate students for these sectors. We believe that management education should reach more distantly placed groups, independently of wealth, education or their place in the world.

Current and future employees in publicly owned companies, governments, universities, hospitals and professional service organizations also need management education to run their operations more professionally. These sectors are particularly important, given that in countries like China public sector enterprises represent 80 percent of the economy, while the social economy makes up 50 percent of the remaining private and public sectors of the economy.

In India, the estimated market size of higher education is estimated at 10–15 billion USD, with a growth rate of 20 percent. The country launched more than 5000 new colleges in 2011 alone – but the reality is different in mature markets. Currently, Indian higher education is capable of supplying 0.6 million qualified professionals, compared to a current need of 89 million. By 2020, the labor pool will increase by 100 million young men and women. India must, somehow, find a way to build 1000 universities and 50 000 colleges in the coming decade. In management education alone, 1100 of the current 3000 institutions have been created in the past decade. These institutes can receive a total of 100 000 students a year, far below what the market for students demands.[14]

The degree of innovation in technologies that enables the creation, transmission, distribution, deployment, application and use of education is rapidly expanding. Today, textbooks are rented by chapters for limited periods of time online. Half of the bestselling management and leadership books sold on Amazon.com are sold for electronic or audio use. The future of management education is digital, leaving little room for printed works. We can imagine a future where students learn functional knowledge via their mobile reading and writing devices, including standard testing of basic disciplinary knowledge.

Given all these changes, management education can no longer afford to act as a vehicle to (greater) financial well-being for the already wealthy and privileged minorities. On the contrary, management education should focus its efforts on attracting and serving existing or would-be entrepreneurs, employees of family-owned and small to medium enterprises (the majority of companies in the world), the public sector, as well as the growing number of social entrepreneurs and leaders in the not-for-profit and charity sectors. Similarly, social enterprises, government and non-government organizations, whether operated for or not-for-profit, desperately need to be well managed. Management education should above all create a deeper context for itself by providing a public service.

HOW CAN MANAGEMENT EDUCATION HELP CREATE A BETTER WORLD?

Our vision does not focus on technological innovation, although we consider new technologies to function as an enabler that will help transform management education in important ways. For one, innovation will enable education to reach more parts of the world. We shall focus the vision on new approaches of how knowledge is transmitted, what competencies are developed and what services are provided and to whom – and how and where engagement in society and the world occurs.

Management education must play a critical role in addressing the global social and environmental challenges, as well as the dilemmas and issues they create for business. It needs to fundamentally rethink its purpose and how its customers should be served. Business schools should cease conforming to the current business and economic system; instead, they should start *transforming* the system. We believe that the mission of business and management educators in the twenty-first century is to become custodians on behalf of society, to enable and create the business system needed for a world worth living in.

Unlike other fields in the social sciences, economics and finance are domains where the prevailing "mainstream" has regressed to dogma – a domain where alternatives have little chance of being discussed, much less properly researched. Our economic system is in shambles, yet the few places where alternative systems are discussed are amongst independent think tanks, often financed by donors and foundations. Business schools only rarely address societal issues or discuss important public policy questions. It seems as if the many thousands of economics and finance researchers around the world are led by an invisible hand to follow the self-restrictive mainstream, releasing endless publications containing ever narrower refinements to the same business problems.

Since the mid-1980s we have known that ongoing growth is neither a realistic scenario for the developed world due to demographic shifts, nor is it an option when considering planetary boundaries. Yet, business schools have generally ignored the question of how business could operate within a different paradigm than the current growth scenario. Who would be better placed than business and management scholars to conduct research on alternative models and strategies, and follow up on attempts to conduct business differently? Who better than players in management education to organize debates and discussions around alternative business and economic models?

But what does it mean to be a custodian on behalf of society? We imagine a center of learning, placed in the *midst* of society, where new ideas are born, where participants and contributors may exceed their assumed potential. Imagine a place where all stakeholders of society meet to explore their potential and together advance their knowledge, their skills and competences, co-creating a learning experience in service of society and the world. We imagine education and research as contributing factors that positively influence the development of society, perhaps in the form of a future-able university organized around issues rather than disciplines. We imagine a funding system that does not fund schools and universities directly but rather provides each citizen with an annual learning voucher that can be invested at the institution of choice, thereby allowing the market to decide which educational propositions are appreciated and which are not.

Management education needs to train those without the means to do so themselves, and develop ideas, products and services that benefit the bottom of the wealth pyramid.[15] This requires rethinking how management education can be delivered to those with the ambition, entrepreneurial energy and dedication in regions and social classes that have been either overlooked or ignored. It goes without saying that such education should ideally be provided for free.

Another important aspect concerns the age of learners. The majority of business schools cater for people in their 20s to 50s. Management education, however, needs to embrace the learning needs of those less than 20 years of age, potentially in cooperation with or in addition to elementary schools. At the other end of the spectrum we need to serve those in their 50s and beyond, people looking to re-orient themselves in their lives as they shape their "second adulthood", while addressing related opportunities to learn and help older generations to realize their potential contribution to society.[16]

Above all, we imagine an open space for people all along their life-long journey of learning, with the possibility to shift back and forth between residing in a place of learning for educational, reflective or research purposes, and more hands-on functions in society – be it as an entrepreneur starting up a new business in an emerging country, in government, or in organizations that provide products and services that help transform society. The space should be open in the sense that anybody is welcome, no matter their origin or their academic qualifications. Citizens should be able to pass through the open space, and not be limited to their own national borders. We imagine a sense of timelessness in this space, with places to think, walk, reflect and simply be. Imagine a personal place that seeks to fully develop the potential of those with a wish to grow and participate in developing a better world, a place that encourages new forms of ethics celebrating the ability to be fascinated, as well as the capability to persevere, far away from the consumerism present in so many places of education.

Consider a place of diversity in every sense of the word, including diversity in the type of education and research, embracing both highly academic discourses as well as applied and concrete discussions. Next, we may add diversity in the ways various projects are financed, and where fees are adapted to prevailing circumstances. We further envision diversity in terms of methodology and pedagogy, including collaborative work, online learning, field and practice work – or a blended combination as required. We also urge diversity in terms of co-creating one's own learning program, with the ability to shift between different disciplines, and benefiting from the modular approach adopted by higher education. Finally, we encourage diversity in the sense that there will be many such places available, from collaborative workspaces to pop-up business schools and, of course, more traditional centers of management education.

Imagine a place where risk-taking is encouraged, a place that is alive with unconventional thought, insightful questions and laughter, where creativity blooms across all generations, and where qualifications are quite irrelevant. We imagine a place that enables a new lifestyle that offers different levels of immersion between work and learning within a new, open society.

NOTES

1. OECD (2012) and Jennings (2012: 2).
2. OECD (2012).
3. GMAT report (2007).
4. Mintzberg (2004).
5. Malcolm McIntosh works at the Asia Pacific Centre for Sustainable Enterprise, Griffith University in Australia. He is general editor of the *Journal of Corporate Citizenship*.
6. Khurana (2007: 363).
7. Starkey et al. (2004: 1527); Podolny (2009).
8. Khurana (2007: 326–327).
9. Colby et al. (2011: 40).
10. Khurana (2007: 329).
11. Datar et al. (2010: 81–83).
12. Gladwell (2011).
13. IMD, Lausanne, Switzerland, is an excellent example with approximately 90% of their revenue generated through executive training and the remainder accounting for their MBA and Executive MBA programs.
14. Popli (2012).
15. Prahalad (2005); Hart (2005).
16. See work by Richard Boyatzis for information on learning needs at different ages in the life cycle.

PART II

The vision

5. A vision of management education for the world

If we want another state of the world, we should find another lowest common denominator, one based on a human being's best attribute: love.
Sofia Borodulina, GRLI Young Ambassador, Germany

DESIGNING THE VISION OF MANAGEMENT EDUCATION

The 50+20 vision is primarily aimed at those who sense that something is fundamentally amiss with the world, and who realize the need for deep changes in the way we live. Our primary goal is to describe a vision for the transformation of management education, in which the common tenet of being the best in the world is revised in favor of creating businesses that are designed and led to achieve the best *for* the world. Given that the very foundations of business and management education are critically examined, the vision concerns business, management and leadership education in general. Stakeholders in this landscape include not only business schools, leadership and executive development programs or corporate universities, but also think tanks, business consultancies and vocational training centers.

Business schools are – at least in the public eye – key representatives of management education. Substantial material exists which describes how business schools are performing, including increasingly critical voices concerning their performance over the past decade. Interestingly, we find very little available material concerning the wider landscape of management education, in contrast to the wealth of information and critical analyses on business schools. Despite this lack of information, the vision is not limited to business schools but rather addresses the whole management education landscape, defining and developing key roles its various players can fulfill.

The 50+20 vision seeks to define areas of responsibility and opportunity, identifying clear roles which management education can play in order to assume responsibility in contributing to the creation of a society and

EMERGING BENCHMARKS

Participants of the 50+20 project recognized the need to chart an entirely new course for management education by proposing something revolutionary, daring and altogether new and different. We require different standards and examples against which we can measure a collaborative rather than competitive approach. We call these examples *Emerging Benchmarks*.

Throughout the 50+20 Agenda we include a small selection of initiatives across the globe as a sample of what we have uncovered to date. A growing list of Emerging Benchmarks can be viewed and discussed at 50plus20.org/benchmarks. *Emerging Benchmarks* was also the title of a mobile exhibit and prototyping platform where management education for the world was demonstrated and shared during the RIO+20 Summit. The exhibit consisted of artistically designed and decorated two-seater benches, commissioned from artists around the globe and constructed from reclaimed materials. When arranged in a learning circle the benches are symbolic of a commitment to reclaim management education for the world, and provide a physical metaphor for the collaboratory: a concept central to the 50+20 vision. The benches were used to host collaboratory prototype sessions during RIO+20.

EMERGING
BENCHMARKS

world worth living in. These roles can be embraced by any player involved in management education, including corporate universities, consultancies, executive training centers, vocational training, think tanks or research centers – as well as business schools and management departments within the larger universities.

Thus far we have examined what is needed in society and the world, and what different players in the field of management education can contribute to make the world a better place. But what about our own stakeholders? We engaged with key representatives of our broader community to better understand how various stakeholders interrelate and influence each other in the complex system of management education. During our retreats we shared and developed points of view with members of this community as equal partners. The global survey, the resultant discussions and the integration of new contributors into our visioning process stirred a very different felt sense towards these people. Our shared experience led us to identify a potential paradigm shift from a more mechanical "stakeholder involvement" to a "community engagement" approach: an emotive, whole-person collaboration similar to an animated family discussion.

The perspectives and expectations of our community point toward a very different model of management education. These views further shaped our thinking as we continued to study the challenges of the world, the economic system, business, leadership and management education. In the process we developed a sense of tapping into the higher consciousness of the broader global community concerned with the future of management education. From this larger field, a new vision slowly emerged, outlining a new type of management education.

A NEW VISION FOR MANAGEMENT EDUCATION

Rather than train managers for organizations that operate within twentieth century logic, management educators need to answer the call of service to become custodians which provide a service to society. The 50+20 project is searching for ways to tackle the challenge.

The management school of the future understands that transforming business, the economy and society begins with its own internal transformation. A school that embraces the vision will make the leap in a transparent and inclusive manner, leading by example by *being the change* it wishes to progress. More concretely, we envision three fundamental roles in management education which refine and enlarge the current purpose of education and research:

- *Educating* and developing globally responsible leaders;
- *Enabling* business organizations to serve the common good; and
- *Engaging* in the transformation of business and the economy.

We also refer to the vision as the *Triple E vision:* Educating, Enabling and Engaging.

Each of these roles holds significant implementation challenges and is supported with enablers that aim to facilitate the transformation of any management educator interested in embracing the vision.

The 50+20 vision is founded on the insight that providing responsible leadership for a sustainable world is first and foremost about creating and holding a *space* for the incarnation of these three roles. The various visioning exercises conducted in the creation process of the vision revealed a

Educating
• Transformative learning
• Issue-centered learning
• Reflective practice and
  Fieldwork

Enabling
• Research in service of society
• Supporting companies towards
  stewardship
• Accompanying leaders in their
  transformation

Engaging
• Open access between
  academia and practice
• Faculty as public
  intellectuals
• Institutions as role models

Collaboratory
• The preferred place for
  stakeholders to meet
• Collaborative action learning and
  research platforms

Figure 5.1   The vision for management education for the world

profound and multi-dimensional connectedness with a larger field – from the single individual human being to organizations, societies, animals, plants and the natural world in general. This larger field is directly related to the philosophy of creating a space.

The central feature of our vision is expressed in the *collaboratory* (the inner circle in Figure 5.1) – a powerful space of co-creation in service of resolving issues relevant to local, regional and global societies. The collaboratory represents the core mission of management educators adopting the role of transient gatekeepers who hold a space for responsible leadership for a sustainable world. Holding such a space enables an individual to connect to their full potential, while also reconnecting with all parts of society and the world. We found the circle of the collaboratory to be an appropriate symbol, representing a universal meeting place for discussing communal matters.

Educating, Enabling and Engaging

Implementing each of these new roles represents a challenge in its own right. While not every player in the landscape needs to embrace all the roles, management educators may want to use this vision to reflect on their strategic choices for the coming decades.

The realization of this vision requires individuals with a certain mindset, typified by a deep awareness and understanding of the global challenges we face, a sense of urgency to bring about change, and an unwavering belief that all of us "own" the responsibility to create change and contribute to making the world a better place.

Our vision consists of the three roles for management education (Educating, Enabling and Engaging), each of which is supported by three underlying enablers. These elements represent not only the essential roles of management education for the world but also point to three different levels of engagement:

- **The Individual Level**: educating and developing globally responsible leaders.
- **The Organizational Level**: enabling business organizations to serve the common good.
- **The Societal Level**: engaging in the transformation of business and society.

Let us consider each of these roles in more detail to gain an understanding of the underlying enabling forces.

Role 1: educating and developing globally responsible leaders
Educating globally responsible leaders is fundamentally different from what management education has achieved to date. Rather than acquiring desirable traits or isolated knowledge, leadership development is about developing the potential to act consistently on behalf of society. It requires the development of capacities that may lie dormant within a leader or an organization, including the ability to embrace complex transdisciplinary issues and hands-on collaboration with other members of the larger community. A systems-based approach is important to develop the key dimensions of globally responsible leaders. Holistic development approaches provide a healthy foundation to treat the human being, the organization

and society as an open, emergent and dynamic system that progresses (and can regress) without ever acquiring a perfect state.

Our interaction with various societal groups also identified the challenge for management education to assume a very different attitude towards educating potential leaders in developing countries. A key issue is that the poorest are denied access to management education, together with many more from the developed world. No comprehensive vision of the future of management education can leave this situation unaddressed.

Different cultures (simplistically defined as Eastern and Western) hold different views on what it takes to develop a leader and what roles they play in society. Insights from all approaches enable marrying the art of *being* and *doing*, bridging the interdependence with the world and the leader's inner values into an ethical and globally responsible approach. Prolonging the dimension from *me* to *we* and to *all of us*, and developing a reflective awareness and a felt sense of being truly connected with other sentient beings opens up new perspectives of collaboration, purpose and direction.

We need to adopt whole person learning in order to educate our leaders. This requires pedagogies which are very different to the dominant paradigm of management education today, which is built on the "sage on the stage" and the case study method, reflecting a cognitive intellectual approach which assumes a defined set of pre-established knowledge which can be captured, packaged and shared. Traditional techniques largely focus on what others have done in the *past*, which might conceivably make sense in a stable system – but not in todays world, where the challenge is to forge an entire future that is different in almost every respect from the present. The pedagogical framework for developing a whole-person human leader equipped with the required skills, competences and knowledge to "walk on the bridge as it is being built" has only started emerging recently.

Currently, we consider the three key enablers for educating and transforming globally responsible leaders to be:

- **Transformative learning:** Leadership development is first and foremost personal development, meaning that we need to go about developing the *whole person*: mind, heart, body and soul. At its core, transformative learning transforms problematic frames of reference into perspectives that provoke exploration into previously unknown solutions. The ability to consider different and new perspectives occurs through the development of consciousness, leading to a new way of relating to oneself and the world. The entry ticket for transformative learning is a powerful and safe learning environment. Such a transformation may be achieved by multiple avenues. A common denominator for any of the applied methods is that they trigger personal responsibility in co-creating a world within an evolving, inter-dependent movement. One of the goals of transformative learning is for future leaders to develop and expand their *reflective awareness*, which is considered the basis of globally responsible leadership.

- **Issue-centered learning:** Future-relevant learning needs to be organized around societal, environmental and economic issues both globally and locally – rather than around disciplines. A key element of issue-centered learning is a transdisciplinary, systemic approach to problems and dilemmas, potentially enabling complex decision-making processes. Another element is the active involvement and participation of societal stakeholders. Subject knowledge (such as finance, marketing, human resources and strategies) is acquired alongside issue-centered learning. When learning is conducted around issues, subject experts and teachers act as curators of knowledge and contribute relevant expertise when appropriate, favoring the integration of theory within a practical context. The collaboratory is a good example of issue-centered learning and represents a significant evolution from the traditional case study method, providing a new methodological approach to develop functional knowledge, transdisciplinary breadth and critical thinking.
- **Reflective practice and fieldwork:** Most learning occurs on the job, while common wisdom dictates that leaders cannot be developed without work experience. At the same time, adding fieldwork and practice to a curriculum is not enough. The path towards skilled performance in a new domain needs to be accompanied by guided reflection. The ability to self-reflect cannot be learned in one day but resembles the daily practice of personal hygiene. Fieldwork as part of a course should include exposure to different social domains, particularly in emerging and developing countries.

Role 2: enabling business organizations to serve the common good
Business organizations require a shift in philosophy in order to transform from the current paradigm of short-term profit maximization in the interest of shareholders to a paradigm of creating sustainable value for society and the world. Such a shift implies *moving beyond* the conventional triple bottom line approach of balancing issues of people, profit and planet to simultaneously create positive environmental value, positive social value and positive economic value in every aspect of a business and its related

supply chains. This may require not only practical tools and methods to change practice inside organizations, but potentially includes the fundamental re-design of the modern corporations as well as the legal and other frameworks in which they operate.

Such a shift will favor the common good. We define the common good as the greatest possible good for the greatest number of individuals: a world where all citizens live well and within the limits of the planet. The common good requires that business organizations direct their economic and technical creativity towards societal progress. In the context of management education, this presents opportunities for the creation of new hybrid models between consultancy and academic research, between business schools and corporate universities, and between personal and professional development.

The three enablers for business organizations to serve the common good are:

- **Research in service of society:** Future management education should adjust its research orientation to serve society by encouraging the creation of businesses, business methods and solutions which address global and local challenges around environmental, societal and economic issues. Such an agenda includes a critical reflection of dominant theories in management, finance and economics. In future, researchers should redefine their role primarily as developing, testing and adapting alternative research methodologies that allow future-oriented problem solving. They should further engage in an ongoing dialogue with stakeholders in order to jointly identify research topics and add value by ensuring academic rigor and a critical academic perspective (see the collaboratory). As a result, management education institutions would develop solutions for societal stakeholders rather than their peers.

- **Supporting companies towards stewardship:** Creating long-term societal value requires organizations to view their business in the context of environmental, societal, economic, political, cultural and systemic dynamics. Understanding and evaluating the potential impact of strategic choices requires a new framework to evaluate if and how companies can embrace stewardship and how they can take steps to implement the related transformational changes. Such a framework includes the development of useable and comparable measures between and within industries. We suggest adopting a hybrid model, situated between current consulting and traditional academic research, helping organizations with simulations, crowdsourcing, research action labs, reporting and analysis beyond the existing limits and the framework of day-to-day perspectives within an organization.

- **Accompanying leaders in their transformation:** Leadership development is a life-long learning adventure that progresses along different stages of mastery. Retraining *existing* leaders in positions of responsibility is a different challenge. Businesses adopt stronger leadership by enabling their managers and leaders to think "outside the box", to determine how to make their business truly sustainable. We envision combined corporate university, business school and leadership centers to facilitate the learning process of an executive, both on the job and away in guided reflection – a concept further discussed in our framework of the "leadership sanctuary".

Role 3: engaging in the transformation of business and the economy
Leadership is needed to manage the debate concerning the necessary transformation of the economic system towards a system that serves societal progress. The scale of the task across the world requires multiple simultaneous approaches across the globe. As sustainability and scenarios beyond growth gain momentum, management education providers will need to support business and other stakeholders in achieving the challenges ahead. Business and management scholars can lead the public debate concerning new economic and business models, enabling the general public to understand the stakes and direct relevant community action to drive these changes. This will require new and wider forms of collaboration between academia and the professional world. Management educators themselves must become role models supporting the concept of the common good.

The three enablers for engaging in the transformation of business and society are:

- **Open access between academia and practice:** The management school of the future has no walls that prevent a free and liberal exchange between various contributors to learning and research. Titles and tenure are no longer venerated. Both professors and practitioners will shuttle back and forth between management schools and applied work in organizations, be it in business, public office or NGOs. Likewise, the management schools' doors are open to experienced practitioners from business and any other field of activity, to reflect on and contribute their insights, experience and knowledge to the learning and research environment. These forms of interaction serve as a key ingredient when creating an effective platform for action-learning and research (the collaboratory).

- **Faculty as public intellectuals:** The far-reaching changes in our economies and societies require that scholars accept the role of public intellectuals, addressing critical developments and providing knowledge and expertise to public debates. Business and management scholars need to move away from highly ambitious scholarly work chiefly aimed at other scholars or the scientific community. The regular tasks of all business and management faculties should be to serve as public intellectuals who are pro-actively engaged through their research, teaching and public services. Further, management schools need to find ways to reward these tasks through performance appraisals and promotions.
- **Institutions as role models:** Management educators need to fundamentally rethink their own organizational models in order to become role models for a world seeking socially, environmentally and economically just organizations that contribute to the well-being of society. Such a change will involve new models in funding, decision making, governance, compensation and value creation. Faculty and administration are challenged to display the same levels of globally responsible leadership they would wish to see in their fellow learners and participants. As such, the organization serves as a showcase of transformation, thereby shaping the revised definitions of for-profit and not-for-profit organizations under the new paradigm of *shared value creation*. Ideally, management educators become role models in a learning journey that reveals new methods of leading and managing an organization.

THE COLLABORATORY – THE ESSENCE OF THE VISION

The philosophy of the collaboratory involves a circular space that is open to concerned stakeholders for any given issue. Action learning and research join forces in collaboratory – where students, educators and researchers work with members of all facets of society to address current dilemmas. The collaboratory is a key feature of the 50+20 vision, a new philosophy in promoting management education for the world – as seen in the context of the three roles and corresponding enablers discussed previously.

The collaboratory represents an open-source metaspace: a facilitated platform based on open space and consciousness building technologies. Once understood, a collaboratory can be established anywhere, virtual or real, within companies, communities – or within a management school.

Its primary strengths lie in enabling issue-centered learning, conducting research for a sustainable world, and providing open access between academia and practice. The collaboratory also offers a powerful alternative for public debate and problem solving, inclusive of views from business and management faculty, citizens, politicians, entrepreneurs, people from various cultures and religions, the young and the old. Everybody must have a voice, hence the need for a transdisciplinary approach.

A collaboratory is conducted without formal separation between knowledge production and knowledge transfer, while focusing on visceral real-life issues and providing solutions that are driven by issues, *not* theory. Participants in a collaboratory employ problem-solving tools and processes that are iterative and emergent. Proposed solutions are directly tested, contested and modified while supporting both knowledge production and diffusion, which occur in parallel.

If management education today is characterized by the lines of chairs facing a combination of screen, lectern, stage and whiteboards, the collaboratory symbolizes management education for the future. In this approach the knowledge that traditionally was supposed to reside at the front of the room is replaced by knowledge drawn from the community of the circle, the extended and globally connected community surrounding the circle and the co-creative wisdom of the collaboratory process itself.

The Co-creation of Meaning

Of course, the idea of open and equal collaboration is nothing new. Sometimes it works, sometimes not. One may easily mistake the philosophy of the collaboratory as a free-for-all gathering of affable individuals who automatically become friends and miraculously agree on credible resolutions without encountering any significant obstacles. We know all too well that without the proper systemic approach a gathering of this kind may disintegrate following (for example) a prolonged argument over the minutiae of an issue under discussion. Skilled facilitation and a robust methodology are therefore required to address the complexities of vested interests, group dynamics, and problem resolution. To us, the collaboratory is a living experiment whereby we co-create its meaning, its power and strength during each session held around the world.

Paradigm-shifting innovations do not usually occur in well-established institutions, but tend to emerge amongst the outliers: the smaller, hidden and often ignored pockets of creativity that are also part of the colorful landscape of management education. We refer to these innovative initiatives as *emerging benchmarks*: an initial set of examples related to the three proposed roles for management education. Collecting

Figure 5.2　Benches define the circular space of our collaboratory

emerging benchmarks runs parallel to the 50+20 vision development, and will continue as the initiative grows.

We consider benches a useful visualization for a new paradigm of joint learning and research. The term 'benchmark' was derived from cobblers who measured their customers' shoe sizes by placing their feet on a bench and marking an outline, or rather a *measure*. The outline formed by such a measure resembles a footprint which symbolically reminds us of the social and environmental impact of our actions and urges us to tread lightly and with care. We may progress the metaphor further: sitting on a bench involves sharing one's own space with another individual in a public space. The proximity of an adjacent stranger sharing the same view provides a different kind of exchange when compared to individuals sitting oppositely in single chairs. A series of benches can further be used to create a circle of learning (see Figure 5.2).

Finally, benches are often perceived as a temporary place for rest, reflection and brief reunions – reminding us of the transient nature of our activities and existence while stressing both the common origin and purpose we share as global citizens.

The Evolution of the Collaboratory

The term *collaboratory* was first introduced in the late 1980s[1] to address problems of geographic separation in large research projects related to

TOWARDS AN ECONOMY THAT SERVES EACH INDIVIDUAL

A public interest organization in Switzerland believes that globalization can and should serve and enhance the common good. At an international summit hosted annually they bring together over 200 entrepreneurs, economists, politicians and NGO representatives for the purpose of bringing more humanity into the process of globalization and making practical recommendations to leaders for an economy serving the human person and the common good. They aim to inspire and equip an emerging generation of leaders who may implement key recommendations from these Summit meetings through a number of selected projects.

 EMERGING BENCHMARKS

travel time and cost, difficulties in keeping contact with other scientists, control of experimental apparatus, distribution of information, and the large number of participants. In their first decade of use, collaboratories were seen as complex and expensive information and communication technology (ICT) solutions supporting 15 to 200 users per project, with budgets ranging from 0.5 to 10 million USD.[2] At that time, collaboratories were designed from an ICT perspective to serve the interests of the scientific community with tool-oriented computing requirements, creating an environment that enabled systems design and participation in collaborative science and experiments.

The introduction of a user-centered approach provided a first evolutionary step in the design philosophy of the collaboratory, allowing rapid prototyping and development circles. Over the past decade the concept of the collaboratory expanded beyond that of an elaborate ICT solution, evolving into a "new networked organizational form that also includes social processes, collaboration techniques, formal and informal communication, and agreement on norms, principles, values, and rules".[3] The collaboratory shifted from being a *tool*-centric to a *data*-centric approach, enabling data sharing beyond a common repository for storing and retrieving shared data sets.[4] These developments have led to the evolution of the collaboratory towards a globally distributed knowledge work that produces intangible goods and services capable of being both developed and distributed around the world using traditional ICT networks.

Initially, the collaboratory was used in scientific research projects with variable degrees of success. In recent years, collaboratory models have been applied to areas beyond scientific research and the national context. The wide acceptance of collaborative technologies in many parts of the world opens promising opportunities for international cooperation in critical areas where societal stakeholders are unable to work out solutions in isolation, providing a platform for large multidisciplinary teams to work on complex global challenges.

The emergence of open-source technology transformed the collaboratory into its next evolution. The term *open-source* was adopted by a group of people in the free software movement in Palo Alto in 1998 in reaction to the source code release of the Netscape Navigator browser. Beyond providing a pragmatic methodology for free distribution and access to an end product's design and implementation details, open-source represents a paradigm shift in the philosophy of collaboration. The collaboratory has proven to be a viable solution for the creation of a virtual organization. Increasingly, however, there is a need to expand this virtual space into the real world. We propose another paradigm shift, moving the collaboratory beyond its existing ICT framework to a methodology of collaboration beyond the *tool-* and *data-centric* approaches, and towards an *issue-centered* approach that is transdisciplinary in nature.

Hold that Space

Translating the concept of the collaboratory from the virtual space into a real environment demands a number of significant adjustments, leading us to yet another evolution. While the virtual collaboratory could count

---

BUILDING HOPE ON THE AFRICAN CONTINENT

A South African University has restated its mission to be a true builder of hope on the African continent, and to blaze new trails with a "science for society" strategy that puts its strengths and expertise at the service of human need. The project, which has received considerable funding from internal and external sources, enables research on local, regional and African challenges and provides opportunities for learning and growing new generations of thought leaders.

EMERGING
BENCHMARKS

on ICT solutions to create and maintain an environment of collaboration, real-life interactions require facilitation experts to create and hold a space for members of the community, jointly developing transdisciplinary solutions around issues of concern. The ability to hold a space is central to the vision of management education.

The technology involved with holding a space implies the ability to create and maintain a powerful and safe learning platform. Such a space invites the whole person (mind, heart, soul and hands) into a place where the potential of a situation is fully realized. Holding a space is deeply grounded in our human heritage, and is still considered an important duty of the elders amongst many indigenous peoples. In Western society, good coaches fulfill a similar role, including the ability to be present in the moment, listening with all senses, being attuned to the invisible *potential* about to be expressed. As a result, what needs to happen, *will* happen. Facilitation and coaching experts understand the specific challenges involved in setting up an environment in which a great number of people can meet to discuss solutions that none of them could develop individually. Coaching and facilitation solutions already exist to create and hold such spaces, but are nevertheless distinctly different in a felt sense from the ICT-driven virtual collaboratories we have seen over the past two decades.

The evolution from the virtual collaboratory bears its own challenges and opportunities. In the co-creative process of the 50+20 vision, we learned to appreciate the power of the collaboratory both in real-life retreats as well as interactions between our gatherings. We propose that the next evolutionary step of the collaboratory will include both the broader community of researchers engaged in collaboratories around the world, as well as stakeholders in management education who seek to transform themselves by providing responsible leadership.

In our new definition, *a collaboratory is an inclusive learning environment where action learning and action research meet*. It involves the active collaboration of a diversified group of participants that bring in different perspectives on a given issue or topic. In such a space, learning and research is organized around issues rather than disciplines or theory. Such issues include: hunger, energy, water, climate change, migration, democracy, capitalism, terrorism, disease, the financial crisis, new economic models, management education that serves the world and similarly pressing matters. These issues are usually complex, messy and hard to resolve, demanding creative, systemic and divergent approaches. The collaboratory's primary aim is to foster collective creativity.

The collaboratory is a place where people can think, work, learn together, and invent their respective futures. Its facilitators are highly experienced coaches who act as lead learners and guardians of the collaboratory space. They see themselves as transient gatekeepers of a world in need of new solutions. Subject experts are responsible for providing relevant knowledge and contributing it to the discussion in a relevant and pertinent matter. Students will continue to acquire subject knowledge outside the collaboratories – both through traditional and developing channels (such as online or blended learning).

As such, the faculty is challenged to develop their capacities as facilitators and coaches in order to effectively guide these collaborative learning and research processes. To do this, they must step back from their role as experts and rather serve as *facilitators* in an open, participative and creative process (see Figure 5.3). Faculty training and development needs to include not only a broad understanding of global issues, but also the development of facilitation and coaching skills.

The circular space of the collaboratory can become the preferred meeting place for citizens to jointly question, discuss and construct new ideas and approaches to resolve environmental, societal and economic

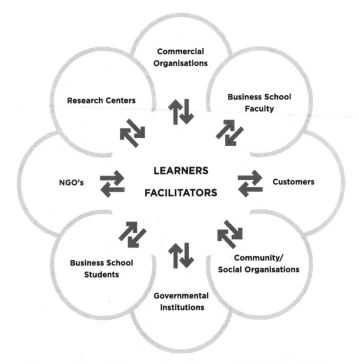

Source: Fernando D'Alessio, Director General founder of CENTRUM Católica.

Figure 5.3   Participants in a collaboratory

BIOSPHERE RESERVES AS A GLOBAL BUSINESS SCHOOL PROTOTYPE

UNESCO's World Network of Biosphere Reserves is, in effect, an example of the new style of business school. Its aim is to encourage sustainable development, and to do this it practices action-oriented learning. This shared vision of sustainable development practices is creating an ever-evolving global campus for learning about how to develop human social and economic practices in order to increase levels of sustainability.

 EMERGING BENCHMARKS

---

challenges on both a regional and global level. Collaboratories should always reflect a rich combination of stakeholders: coaches, business and management faculty, citizens, politicians, entrepreneurs, people from different regions and cultures, youth and elders. Together they assemble differences in perspective, expertise and personal backgrounds, thereby adding a vital creative edge to every encounter, negotiation or problem-solving session.

We envision that the collaboratory of the future will contain a number of attributes and approaches. Most importantly, the collaboratory will be centered on real-life challenges, providing solutions that are problem driven, not theory driven. Problem definitions will be systematically created and assessed by professors, experts, students, researchers and practitioners, taking into account environmental dynamics, social dynamics, political dynamics, anthropology and systems dynamics. Addressing complex global problems requires a transdisciplinary and systemic approach, employing individuals with variable perspectives in order to understand and resolve an issue. Members of a collaboratory will employ problem-solving processes that are iterative and emergent, without formal separation between the production and transfer of knowledge. Finally, proposed solutions must be directly tested, contested and modified while supporting both knowledge production and diffusion, which occur parallel to one another.

As such, a collaboratory becomes a powerful tool to hold a space for future-relevant learning and research. Research will support the resolution of global issues by embracing action research as a standard approach, as well as employing various future-oriented methodologies. Subject experts,

including professors from various disciplines serve as knowledge curators, selecting which types of information and input are appropriate to
help uncover new solutions. Educators meanwhile ensure that students
are able to integrate the experience in the collaboratory through effective
facilitation and coaching methodologies, including self reflection, creativity, systemic and critical thinking. As a result, a collaboratory is a place
where action learning and action research join forces, where students and
researchers work with all facets of society related to the issue under exami-
nation. The collaboratory is the key feature of our vision, a distinguishing
factor in promoting management education for the world.

CLARIFYING COMMUNITY EXPECTATIONS

In collaboration with the youth organization Challenge:Future,[5] we asked
1091 students from the age of 18 to 32 years from 79 countries: "Which
group of people is most responsible for not acting on time, even though
humanity is approaching an ecological catastrophe?" On a scale from 1
(not responsible) to 6 (responsible) the students were asked to rate the
different groups.

Today's youth considers "us as human beings" and "political leaders"
as by far the most responsible (51 percent and 43 percent respectively),
followed by "international organizations" (31 percent), "business" and
"the educational system in general" are considered somewhat responsible
(24 and 22 percent). It was noteworthy to find to what degree our current
youth considers *itself* co-responsible ("we as human beings"), while
they attribute only a small responsibility to "business schools" and "the
financial markets" (15 percent and 16 percent respectively).

To understand what other members of the community have to say
about the future of management education, we conducted a global survey
and collected 145 responses from 37 countries (see Appendix 1).

The responses gathered from our community suggest a fundamental
shift in priorities, a swiftly growing awareness of the broader issues that
affect us globally. In our visioning work we incorporated these responses
into the larger societal context and derived a vision that suggests three
revised roles for management education. We embrace the example set by
the youth and suggest that management education should assume a sense
of *co-responsibility* in shaping tomorrow's world. Management education is very well positioned to play a vital role in addressing the concerns
outlined above.

In order to understand how management education can play this three-
fold role as a custodian for transforming business and the economy, we

EXCERPT FROM THE 50+20 GLOBAL SURVEY (SEE APPENDIX 1)

Insights are grouped into three areas:

a) *Understanding priorities, measures of success and future focus of business schools*

The majority of respondents want business schools to focus on developing future leaders who drive global problem solving with all stakeholders, rather than simply training skilled professionals for business. A surprisingly high number of respondents urge business schools to focus on the bottom 4 billion of the pyramid (developing and emerging countries), a perspective that is largely ignored today. Entrepreneurs, SMEs (small and medium-sized enterprises), organizations of all types (NGOs, start-ups, MNCs, not-for-profit, government organizations) and individual students are listed as other top stakeholder groups requiring the attention of business schools.

When asked how the success of business schools should be measured, we noted that a graduate salary increase and school rankings are considered largely irrelevant, whilst research is not selected as a measure at all. By contrast, respondents measure the success of a business school solely by the competencies, abilities and skills of graduates, namely: the ability to adopt different perspectives and understand the larger picture, holistic decision-making skills, including societal and environmental factors, entrepreneurial skills and leadership skills. While the challenge remains to effectively measure these competencies, we may still wonder why these factors are mostly absent from current business school ratings and rankings.

b) *Understanding educational priorities of the future*

Developing leadership skills ranks as the clear priority when considering future educational priorities. For young students, leadership skills are defined as ethics, values and developing the person, while professionals and executives prefer responsible, sustainable and ethical behavior. Executives are further expected to understand the larger context of business, societal and environmental issues. Leadership competences that are perceived to require most attention include deeply engrained ethics and responsible behavior, critical reasoning and holistic decision-making, as well as possessing reflective skills.

When asked how such leaders can be developed, respondents favored state-of-the-art pedagogical approaches, including experimental learning situations for personal leadership skills, hands-on learning situations, embodied and experimental learning, values-based learning and co-creating the curricula with students.

c) *Understanding research priorities of the future*

Respondents' answers also indicate new priorities for management research, such as resolving societal and global issues, inter-disciplinary issues in business and transdisciplinary issues of business and other sectors. Our respondents placed particular emphasis on how business should be responsible and sustainable, how to develop globally responsible leaders, the role of business and its responsibility towards consumers, society and the planet, as well as new measures for economic, social and environmental effectiveness of business.

We further found a clear consensus that future research should be conducted in an interdisciplinary way, as action research and in a transdisciplinary manner, addressing larger issues with input from non-business fields. Stakeholder respondents overwhelmingly expressed that research objectives should address emerging future issues rather than studying current and past phenomena. Respondents further believe that management research should be conducted for business practitioners and various societal stakeholders rather than for an academic peer audience.

first need to examine these roles in more detail. In the following three chapters we discuss the three roles of management education and their primary enablers in detail, beginning with how management education can forge globally responsible leaders (Chapter 6), how to enable business organizations to serve the common good (Chapter 7), and how to enable business and the economy to work towards a sustainable society (Chapter 8).

NOTES

1. Wulf (1993).
2. Sonnenwald et al. (2003).
3. Cogburn (2003: 86).
4. Chin and Lansing (2004).
5. Challenge: Future is a global youth organization, see www.challengefuture.org.

6. Educating and developing globally responsible leaders

It is incumbent on education to prepare us emotionally and holistically, not just intellectually. Logic is no longer sufficient to thrive in today's and tomorrow's world.

An academic within GRLI

CHALLENGES IN EDUCATING MANAGERS AND LEADERS

The effectiveness and relevance of management education in general (with an emphasis on MBA programs) have been fundamentally questioned in recent years. Serious doubts linger around the ability of management education in general and business schools in particular to provide students with the skills needed to function at an executive level in modern organizations, or prepare them for the professional demands and challenges of global business in a pluralistic world.[1] There are several reasons for this:

Functional and Disciplinary Knowledge Acquisition

The dominance of business functions comes at the expense of an integrated management perspective which would address the external context, in particular culture, society, nature and history.[2] Few training options are available with regard to integrative thinking or the development of an interdisciplinary and integrated perspective. Although teaching methods have evolved to include case studies – thereby simulating the complexity of real-life business situations – business education remains fundamentally discipline based and entrenched in an isolated setting, with little opportunity to deal with messy real-world problems that cross boundaries.[3]

A Strong Focus on Analytical Skills instead of Soft Skills

Management functions have been reduced to analysis, or in some cases even to technique, whereby integration, synthesis and in particular soft skills are entirely neglected. Such skills are exactly what managers need most to succeed in their day-to-day tasks. Students tend to become knowledgeable about business but remain largely uneducated in the art and craft of management.[4] Business graduates are often surprisingly naïve about organizations and management due to an inability to ask critical questions or employ multiple perspectives to understand difficult situations. They similarly fail to understand that organizations are fundamentally political, why logical arguments are not necessarily accepted, or why people say "yes" but don't follow through, be it for cultural or personal reasons. Either way, graduates must become intimately familiar with the politics of human nature if they are to succeed.[5]

A Selective Focus Within a Narrow Market Paradigm

Current education favors the few big companies over the majority of small companies, as well as Western perspectives over other approaches. Education focuses on efficiency rather than effectiveness. Idealized markets have become the primary analytical framework for discussing business and society related issues. Business schools have proved to be very weak in providing alternative perspectives on society and the world.

A Distorted View on Ethics and a Lack of Attention to Self Knowledge

The dominance of amoral theories being taught effectively strips managers of their personal responsibility.[6] Graduates are unprepared to cope with current challenges in the roles, responsibilities and purpose of business in society.[7] Good judgment and practical reasoning are the result of critical reflection on one's own perceptions and values. Rarely are reflective spaces offered and used to develop a dialogue with oneself about how one intends to act as a manager and leader, or how insights may be employed for personal development and problem resolution. It is not sufficient to address values and ethics if the challenges are not connected with the students' efforts to make personal sense of them.[8]

Professional judgment is guided by knowledge, skills, ethics and values. Ethical sensitivity in action goes well beyond generating ethical awareness of issues; students need the chance to *practice* values-driven action in the context of practical management decisions. Only when students learn to move between the distanced, external stance of analytical thinking – the third person view – as well as the first and second person points of view from which they have to act when solving real problems, will they develop the required levels of empathy, character and integrity.[9]

In order to overcome the lack of integration between theory and practice, some business schools have supplemented their learning approaches with forms of applied learning, by placing the learning experience directly in the field. In order to better balance the different demands of knowing, doing, and being, business schools need to develop and use pedagogies of enactment (or engagement) to a much larger extent, requiring students to enact their understanding and skills in extended, supervised practice.[10] Such an approach will further require changes to the teaching faculty and their training methods.

The gap between the vision and the current situation in business schools is striking. The criticisms listed in this report chiefly concern business schools, but can be extended to many other forms of formal learning.

A Lack of Attention to Learning

Self-directed learning has decreased in parallel to the increasing demand for "edutainment" which renders students dependent on learning providers. The faculty mostly consists of subject experts with little to no pedagogical training to help assure and measure whether any learning has actually occurred. More often, acquired (memorized) knowledge is given precedence. The case method, meanwhile, does encourage strategic scenario thinking but creates the illusion that students can effectively handle a situation they have only encountered in theory.

Not only the contents of learning are viewed as reductionist: the fundamental process of learning and pedagogy do not adequately prepare students for their tasks and challenges as globally responsible leaders. Ever since the Carnegie and Ford foundation reports, business curricula

---

THE DREAM FACTORY: WORKING FOR THE COMMON GOOD

A not-for-profit initiative working in India empowers participants to create and lead their own social projects through issue-centered training in subjects ranging from leadership, organization building, project management, financial planning and fund raising. The institute offers a one-year program that uses a hands-on fieldwork approach, with a heavy emphasis on real world case studies. The curriculum is designed to support the "dream factory", where participants learn how to convert their dreams of social change into reality.

EMERGING
BENCHMARKS

have emphasized *knowing* at the expense of *doing* and *being*, with the latter focusing on values, attitudes and beliefs. In part, such measures were necessary to overcome concerns about the lack of academic rigor. As a result, however, we find not only a persistent knowing-doing gap among business graduates, but also a doing-being gap.[11]

For the most part students concentrate on acquiring knowledge, leaving little opportunity for them to practice what they have learned. Yet, in order to grow into effective managers and leaders they must first gain access to practicing skills. Teachers ask students to practice distant substitutes of what they think students should know, based on academic tradition and the teacher's limited understanding of real needs, pedagogy and didactics.[12]

CLARIFYING COMMUNITY EXPECTATIONS

EXCERPT FROM THE 50+20 GLOBAL SURVEY (SEE APPENDIX 1)

Currently, business schools train skilled professionals for business and to ensure literacy in management skills. What educational aspects do business schools focus on today compared to what our community thinks they *should* focus on in future?

Our respondents strongly believe that business schools should concentrate on developing leaders who drive global problem solving. Other areas that deserve attention include developing managers and leaders for all types of organizations, training skilled professionals for business, and ensuring literacy in comprehensive management skills.

The gap between expectations and current practice widens further when we asked stakeholder groups what business schools should focus on *most* in future. A majority of respondents indicate that creating entrepreneurs should be the primary focus of business schools. Other responses showed a preference for developing and emerging countries, small and medium-sized businesses, and organizations of all types.

Currently, business schools focus almost exclusively on educating leaders for the business sector, mostly for MNCs (multinational corporations), consulting companies, financial institutions and to a lesser degree SMEs (small to medium enterprises).

Our community, however, expects business schools to shift their focus quite dramatically, expressing a need for very different types of knowledge, skills and competences following graduation from a business school. Respondents favored developing leadership skills, awareness of future emerging business, societal and environmental issues, real-life exposure to the world, to business and work, as well as contextual insight into the role of business in the world (society, planet, history). These competencies are significantly different from what undergraduate and graduate students in business and management *currently* possess upon graduation. Rebuilding business schools to provide graduates with these abilities would therefore require a fundamental transformation.

What knowledge or skills should *executives* possess after completing their business education? Representatives of our community strongly favor leadership skills (responsible, sustainable and ethical behavior), and understanding the context of business, societal and world issues. Two other preferred responses included hands-on exposure to global issues (project work), along with testing business models serving society, the planet – and making money. It may come as a surprise to some executive training providers that the very essence of what was believed to be good executive education – namely providing a general management education (applying theories to business) – scored *lowest* with our respondents.

We believe that this shift has much to do with the change in expectations of what qualities a leader should possess. Respondents expect our business leaders to be innovators who are able to create long-term sustainable value, as well as individuals who work with stakeholders for a better society and world. Respondents also favored business leaders as people who connect deeper values to the organizational context.

What leadership competencies should be developed most? In order of preference, respondents in our community believe that leaders should learn deeply ingrained ethics and responsible behavior, critical reasoning and holistic decision making, reflective skills (personal development and self-knowledge), followed by collaborative skills and strategic thinking.

Some critics argue that management education has failed to provide students with the right competencies, citing a variety of reasons that largely concern a disregard for integrated thinking, external contexts (e.g. social, cultural), a strong ethical framework, self knowledge, and soft skills. These critical failures include a lack of integration between business theory and practice, but also between the task and the individual. When educating, we need to move beyond knowing by including the states of doing and being.

Such skills and competences require a very different approach to teaching and learning compared to what business schools with their dominant lecturing and case study methods have used thus far. When asked to rank different leadership development methods, our respondents' more popular choices include creating experimental learning situations for personal leadership skills, hands-on learning situations and projects, and values-based learning. Respondents also expressed a strong interest in cross-creating the curriculum (sharing the responsibility of learning), and facilitated issue-centered learning (joint learning). Teaching functional skills takes a distant last rank.

Given where we are, we consider three critical enablers to support the development of globally responsible leaders, namely:

● Transformative learning;
● Issue-centered learning; and
● Reflective practice and fieldwork.

Let's examine each of these three enablers in more detail.

TRANSFORMATIVE LEARNING

Most of us are never taught how to consider the viewpoints of others. We are largely unaware of how self-limiting beliefs are formed and transformed, or how we waste our mental and physical resources with thoughts and emotions that are disconnected from a particular context. By knowing ourselves and others we will better cope with uncertainty while maintaining a commitment to our own values, beliefs and ethics. Achieving such awareness requires a fundamentally different approach to teaching and learning.

Transformative learning involves *un*covering and *un*learning. Knowledge and intellect – whilst critically important – are by themselves not enough to produce a rounded leader. Responsible leadership requires a deeper empathy and values-based ethic: an innate understanding of oneself, as well as of colleagues, organizations, communities, the environment, and how all these factors relate to one other.

The key concept in transformative learning lies in the process of *perspective transformation*, enabling individuals to revise their beliefs and modify their behavior. We understand transformative learning not only as a rational or intellectual exercise but consider personal experience as a critical enabler to trigger a transformation in the participant. Such learning is embedded in a philosophy of whole person learning: respecting a person in their mental, emotional, physical and spiritual dimensions, and recognizing the need to develop all these aspects of the individual in order to progress towards an increasingly integrated and therefore "whole" person.

The understanding that no ideal state of leadership can be achieved corresponds to the parallel understanding that learning is life-long and continuous. The systemic and holistic approach to human, organizational and societal development highlights the dynamic, open and emergent nature of the system we call *leadership*.

Eastern philosophies offer an important alternate perspective to the dilemmas embroiling Western leadership concepts. In ancient Chinese and Indian philosophy the constant interaction between *being* and *doing*, the awareness of a continuous flow of life that includes a person and organization in a larger system is diametrically opposed to the Western hero who conquers the world through sheer willpower. Holistic developmental models point to a framework of consecutive levels of values within which human beings, organizations and societies navigate, progressing and regressing depending on the issue at hand and the state of evolution in that specific domain at a given time. Such alternate approaches encourage us to discard the so-called desirable leadership traits of the "perfect leader", in favor of *external* values and definitions.

Educere, the Latin root word of education, signifies to "lead out", implying that the source of learning is both inside and inherently present. Transformative learning is to a significant degree based on the fact that there is more to *un*cover and *un*learn than there is to *add on*. This concept is based on an understanding that the issues and challenges of the modern world require not only knowledge and intellect but also a deeper understanding of our own selves, of others, and of how we relate to each other. By knowing ourselves and others we can better cope with uncertainty and respond to unexpected challenges, while maintaining a commitment to our own values, beliefs and ethics.

Personal Journeys

Leadership development is first and foremost personal development. Enabling future leaders to feel authorized and to self-authorize themselves to be both fully human and professional requires a fundamental re-think of how management and leadership have been taught to date. The journey of developing the full potential of a human being is a personal as well as a collective effort. It begins with a personal choice, a desire to look inside, to connect to what drives and motivates us. We are required to dig deep down to render *sub*conscious reactions conscious, to reflect to what extent the things we feel, think and do are aspects of deeply instilled and almost automatic fear-based mechanisms. The path of personal development requires courage, patience, persistence, humility and compassion.

Increasingly, the path of personal development will lead us to become more reflected, conscious and truly *human* beings. Once we understand that all living organisms on Earth are part of a single community we gain the potential to become truly enlightened leaders. Such a journey is what leadership training needs to put in motion – and while no training can guarantee such an outcome, the end goal represents the core of a truly relevant management education for the future.

The starting base for transformative learning is the creation of a safe and powerful learning environment. Such an environment is defined by the degree of trust participants feel, their willingness to acknowledge their faults and to uncover unconscious blind spots. Transformative learning requires teachers with advanced coaching skills, who are able to hold both a safe space and the capacity for a powerful personal intervention when a participant is stuck or unable to see what is holding them back.

There are no easy ways to create such an environment, which requires the teacher's ability to expose their own personal inauthenticity immediately after they have been inauthentic, thereby establishing the depth of interaction through personal example. This competence requires a teacher who is comfortable with an appropriate degree of self-disclosure, paving the way for disclosure by the students themselves, who will likely show more willingness to candidly discuss the challenges they face and integrate feedback they receive in return. Such an ability requires a degree of humility and self-reflection – both of which are uncommon traits in the current landscape of management education, given how we prefer to view leaders from a third person perspective rather than expose ourselves as the potential leaders we are and could be. The third person perspective implies assessing leadership from a distance, usually by discussing how *other* leaders have performed rather than actually experiencing the leadership role personally.

To us, these concepts form the basis for developing future leaders: first and foremost, we must enable them to become whole persons equipped with the comprehensive skills, attitudes and competences to lead both themselves and others on a journey into uncharted territory. This includes engaging mind, heart, hands and soul. Once a powerful and safe learning environment is created (the teacher's responsibility) there are countless methods to create and provoke learning experiences that initiate a transformational effect. The common basis of all of these methods is a whole person philosophy, an approach that seeks to embrace and develop all aspects of an individual, including intellectual, emotional, physical and spiritual dimensions. Rather than listing or recommending specific methods,[13] we will briefly discuss the underlying themes of many existing and emerging methods.

Whole Person Learning (WPL)

The learning experience is both lived and reflected, bridging two fundamental concepts in adult education, including experiential and experimental learning. *Experiential* learning[14] involves a pragmatic, intellectual approach to learning, focusing on the analytical interpretation of an experience. Current practices such as internships, field trips and business simulations are examples for experiential learning. Experimental learning takes a phenomenological perspective and leaves experiences as they are without seeking to advance them to an intellectual interpretation.[15] *Experimental* learning differentiates between affective, imaginative, conceptual, and practical modes of psyche and focuses on what occurs *within* the learner. Experimental learning offers more ways of understanding and integrating an experience than experiential learning, thereby enriching the learning experience. Whole Person Learning (WPL) embraces all aspects of what it means to be human: feelings, senses, intuition, connection to others and the broader cosmic environment, as well as the mind and intellect, combining both experiential and experimental learning into a learning approach based on a philosophy that opens new avenues in pedagogy and andragogy.[16]

Person-centered Learning

The learning experience is built around the learner,[17] starting with where they are positioned in their development and in the world at the moment the learning occurs. This approach encourages the learner to identify what issues need to be developed and integrated next in their learning journey. The focus rests on *sharing* the journey of learning, rather than

---

EMBRACING THE ARTIST MINDSET TO CREATE A NEW ECONOMIC MINDSET

A U.K. University working with a Canadian leadership center employs dramatic arts as a way of developing practical leadership and management expertise. By tapping into the artist's mindset and specifically through the kinaesthetic approach, where you learn not through watching but doing, students and participants harness their creative capabilities in order to recreate their economic mindset.

EMERGING BENCHMARKS

---

on imparting knowledge that has been pre-determined by the teacher. Learning facilitation involves creating a process that places participants in the position of deciding what the information means to them and how to best integrate it into their learning and development.

First-person Learning

The learning experience is constructed in such a manner that the learner experiences what is being taught firsthand. Participants experience themselves as leaders from a first-person perspective, rather than discussing leadership from a third-person perspective. This approach is based on an ontological / phenomenological model[18] that seeks to develop leaders by assigning and exercising leadership as their natural self-expression. The process reveals both the actual nature of being a leader and opens up the source of one's actions when exercising leadership. Combining these two aspects provides a spontaneous, intuitive and effective response from the learner. The transformation is sought and achieved by uncovering and releasing the potential within the learner.

ISSUE-CENTERED LEARNING

Future-relevant learning needs to be organized around societal, environmental and economic issues both globally and locally – rather than around isolated business disciplines. A key element of issue-centered learning is a transdisciplinary, systemic approach to problems, potentially enabling complex decision-making processes. Problems are by nature

multifaceted and transdisciplinary. Anticipating side effects and consequences across multiple intricate systems requires considerable fluency in
systemic thinking, as well as a talent for distilling complexity.

Issue-centered learning is based on the idea that competences such as
holistic and divergent thinking, systemic understanding, consideration of
multiple perspectives and integral decision making are critical for future
leaders, who need to be trained and developed above and beyond merely
transmitting expertise. More explicitly, we believe that teaching disciplinary expertise in isolation may well have been the cause for numerous
problems the economic system is currently facing. Developing an understanding for unintended side-effects and consequences within a system
requires a degree of fluency in systemic thinking, including the ability to
dismantle complexity.

The world doesn't function within neatly separated disciplines. Problems
are by nature multifaceted and transdisciplinary. We cannot resolve existing and emerging challenges by dissecting them into sub-problems for
various disciplines to study. This is not to say that functional knowledge is
irrelevant or useless. On the contrary, disciplinary and functional knowledge are critical when professionally addressing issues across multiple
disciplines. It is a great mistake, however, to assume that we should *first*
teach functional knowledge – much as we have in business schools to date
– and simply add on a transdisciplinary issue-centered learning element at
the *end* of business studies.

Cart and Horse: a Non-optimal Sequence

Let us examine the problem in more detail. The conceptual framework
of underlying assumptions within which subject knowledge is currently
taught significantly influences the way students learn and integrate these
subjects. For example:

- When teaching discounted cash flow methodology in corporate
  finance we assume we wish to maximize shareholder profits.
- When teaching market segmentation strategies in marketing we
  assume a further advance in consumption levels.
- When teaching post-merger integration challenges in business strategy, we assume that the corporate culture of the buyer should
  dominate.

By the time students complete these courses they have already integrated
the underlying assumptions without ever consciously questioning them or
even being aware of them – a practice that has proven very detrimental to

business and economy. The only means of changing the flawed framework is to fundamentally re-think how functional knowledge should be taught. Critical and systemic thinking[19] may well become the most sought-after business competencies of the future.

Business and management education needs to be rebuilt by replacing the teaching of subject knowledge with issue-centered teaching, which enables critical and systemic thinking. Issue-centered learning is organized around societal, environmental and economic issues both globally and locally. These include issues such as water scarcity, pandemics and chronic health issues, poverty, climate change, pollution, migration, energy, renewable resources, unemployment, assisted death, management education, ocean depletion, fragile states, social inequalities and other pressing concerns.

Rising to the challenge of addressing and resolving global and societal challenges requires an understanding of human and societal developmental stages (the perspective from which stakeholders look at a problem) and the capability to navigate between the diverse fields of expertise (including technology, sociology, gen-tech, philosophy, psychology, neuroscience, medicine, architecture, engineering, bio-tech). Leaders for a sustainable future will learn to work with experts in these fields, and possess the ability to build bridges and lead a group of subject experts towards sustainable solutions.

An important element of issue-centered learning is the active inclusion of stakeholders in the process. Their presence in class discussion and practical fieldwork on global problems ensures that such issues can no longer be resolved by applying a single-disciplinary perspective. Such a collaborative approach will help ensure the emergence of a critical leadership skill, namely a fluency and ease in considering and shifting between multiple perspectives. A key outcome of this approach is the profound experience of participants becoming an integral part of something larger than themselves. This understanding empowers leaders to embrace their responsibility towards the greater whole, by which we mean their society and the world. An issue-centered education integrates multiple sets of disciplinary knowledge (such as finance, marketing, strategy, HR) when addressing a specific issue. The professor and subject expert assumes the role of the curator of knowledge, selecting what material is of benefit at what time, and which points of view are important to advance the debate. With this process, conventional wisdom is challenged by uncovering underlying assumptions of the dominant discourse – in any domain. As a consequence, subject knowledge is acquired predominantly in the context of a given problem, enabling students to anchor it within the tangible context of real stories.

Further, the concept of sustainability is systematically incorporated into classic business disciplines by linking their work to sustainable outcomes (including work from other parts of organizations and that of stakeholders). This approach broadens available content and puts sustainability to the fore. Table 6.1 provides a number of concrete examples for incorporating sustainability across disciplines.

New thinking, such as issue-centered education, is usually met with initial resistance no matter where the new ideas come from or how valuable they may be. Risk taking is a critically important competence for innovators, change agents, or indeed anyone who chooses to act responsibly in a time of crisis, complexity and competing values. Management educators of the future should deliberately invest in the study of risk and risk taking. The study of risk is a matter of astute scholarship and skill, while risk taking tends to be a blend of character, courage and wisdom. Both aspects require the sober eye of critical thinking.

We do not suggest that traditional disciplinary and functional knowledge are unimportant. Instead, we want to emphasize that most business education institutions mistakenly base their curricula on functional knowledge, occasionally supplemented by a bolt-on issue-centered learning module towards the end of a student's business studies. A stronger issue-centered learning approach would better enable future leaders to adopt "deep" sustainability solutions based on the triple bottom line of environmental, social and economic problems.

REFLECTIVE PRACTICE AND FIELDWORK

Reflective practice and fieldwork involves providing students with hands-on experience: an active fusion of traditional functional disciplines, question-based techniques and integrated skills. No textbook can serve as a substitute for true experiential learning. A related aspect of leadership creation concerns guided reflection: a critical but often ignored technique that instills a practice of both life-long (internal) and shared (external) learning, helping teachers understand their students' core issues and challenges. Such a process is a first step towards creating a shared learning journey, involving participants in co-creating a course syllabus and thereby encouraging them to assume responsibility for their learning.

The dominant part of management education takes place on and around the job. We believe reflective practice and fieldwork (internships and project work) need to be incorporated in all educational endeavors of significant duration, most particularly in undergraduate and graduate studies where students have virtually no working experience. One

Table 6.1   Incorporating sustainability across disciplines

Subject	Topics to incorporate	Sources
Economics	– New measures of economic performance: Beyond GDP, quality of life measurement – Green growth, green economy – Zero growth, prosperity without growth – Ecological economics – Steady state economics	– New Economic Foundation – New Economics Institute – Institute for New Economic Thinking – Club of Rome – Green Economy Coalition – Post Growth Institute – Steady state economics
Strategy	– Impact of sustainability issues and regulations on markets, industry, and stakeholders – Sustainable value creation – Sustainability strategies (sustainable products, brand reputation, cost of capital, risk reduction, license to operate) – Sustainability as a driver for business innovation – Sustainability and profitability – Sustainability management systems	– Sustainability Consortium – WBCSD: Vision 2050 – CERES Roadmap for Sustainability – UN Global Compact – Natural Step – Network for Business Sustainability – Conscious Capitalism Institute – ISO Standards on Environmental Management Systems (14001) and Social Responsibility (26000)
Corporate Governance	– Demands from external standards and codes of conduct: From the governance of ethics to the ethics of governance – Board responsibilities and structure and effective corporate stewardship – Corporate sustainability policies and internal processes	– UK Corporate Governance Code – Sarbanes Oxley Act (USA) – King III report on Corporate Governance (ZA) – Transparency International – AccountAbility
Human Resources	– Green jobs and decent work – Social protection and human rights	– International Labour Organization (ILO) – International Organisation of Employers (IOE)

Table 6.1 (cont.)

Subject	Topics to incorporate	Sources
	– Employer branding and war for talent – Sustainability as a source for motivation and loyalty – Training and development for sustainability – From human resources to "employee equity" and from human resources management to "people management"	– International Trade Union Confederation (ITUC) – Emotional Intelligence Consortium – The Loyalty Effect
Information Technology	– Green IT: energy and resource use in product design, life cycle, product use, recycling – Ensuring what matters is tractable and measured: enable traceability, transparent supply chains	– U.S. Environmental Protection Agency: Green IT – Greenpeace: Guide to greener electronics
Finance & Accounting	– Responsible investments – Sustainable finance – Microfinance, microinsurance – Sustainable corporate finance – Sustainability costs, eco-efficiency (waste, energy, water, hazardous waste treatment) – True / full cost accounting – Sustainability reporting and integrated reporting – Sustainability auditing and assurance	– UN Principles of Responsible Investment (PRI) – UNEP Finance Initiative – The Finance Lab – International Labour Organization (ILO) – International Financial Reporting Standards – International Federation of Accountants (IFAC) – Global Reporting Initiative (GRI) – International Integrated Reporting Committee (IIRC) – Corporate Register – Sustainability Assurance Standards: AA 1000 and ISAE 3000
Marketing	– Sustainable consumption: green consumer behavior, ethical consumption	– World Economic Forum: Sustainable Consumption

Table 6.1   (cont.)

Subject	Topics to incorporate	Sources
Marketing (cont.)	– Sustainable lifestyles: Lifestyle of Health and Sustainability (LOHAS), sufficiency – Personal sustainability – Sustainability marketing: sustainable products, sustainability communication, greenwashing – Life cycle analysis, carbon footprint analysis, water footprint analysis, ecolabelling – Marketing to the bottom of the pyramid	– Sierra Club: Sustainable Consumption – National Geographic: Greendex – Manchester University: Sustainable Consumption Institute – EU Ecolabel – Global Ecolabelling Network (GEN) – Ecolabel Index – ISO Standards on Ecolabelling (ISO 14020 series)

inspiration for this approach is the German "Wanderjahr" ("wandering year" by a guild-trained journeyman).[20]

The 2011 Carnegie Foundation report on undergraduate business education in the U.S. urges business education to integrate liberal learning practices in order for students to:

- Make sense of the world and their place in it.
- Use knowledge and skills as a means to responsibly engage with the world.
- Instill in students a sense of responsibility for the common good, guided by commitment and values.

Work in practice or in the field involves cultural exposure, team work, personal development, exposure to and working with complex global dilemmas. Learning by doing is an important part of a learning process. In fieldwork and practice, students engage with real problems affecting organizations, communities, or the world. Such hands-on experiences are essential in the learning process since many of the issues facing business, government, society and the world today are beyond the boundaries and scope of authority of any single sector, just as they are beyond the capabilities of any single institution. Government, business, the judiciary, not-for-profit organizations, unions, religious groups, and the media must work together to address existing and emerging issues.

Given that big global issues are invariably multi-dimensional, fieldwork requires the student to integrate across traditional functional disciplines, as well as integrate knowledge with skills. Functional subject knowledge can not only be comprehended but also "owned" by the student through applied systemic thinking, holistic decision making, and the practice of leadership skills in the context of a living laboratory. Experiential learning results in a deep integration of knowledge, enabling the prepared student to apply this knowledge in the pursuit of innovative solutions to real problems.

An eagerness to start a small business and the ability to set up new ventures is an important outcome of experiential learning. Incubators form an integral part of educating globally responsible leaders, providing emphasis on entrepreneurship and microenterprise / small business development.

The consensus among stakeholders of management education is that leaders cannot be developed without a solid foundation of work experience. Reflective practice and fieldwork (such as internships and project work) need to be incorporated in all educational endeavors of significant duration, particularly in undergraduate and graduate studies, where students have virtually no working experience. At the same time, there is little value in having participants take part in hands-on fieldwork if their experience is not thoroughly and professionally reflected upon. A key enabler to ensure integration of knowledge is the support of practice and fieldwork through guided reflection – an aspect long ignored and undervalued in the informal learning process. Reflection includes the following considerations:

- What have I learned in terms of knowledge, insights, skills and competencies?
- What did I *not* expect to learn? What took me by surprise?
- What did I learn in my interaction with others?
- What did I learn about myself? What situations did I find particularly challenging or rewarding?
- What else would I like to investigate further, learn more about, and / or explore?

The *art of asking questions* is a preferred Zen method of teaching and the Socratic approach to study. Similarly, enabling learners to ask good questions is a higher purpose of education, helping them uncover solutions that leap-frog above and beyond current practices. Question-based learning has been shown to develop problem-solving skills and logical reasoning as well as reflective thinking.[21] It represents an essential factor in educating leaders to embrace problems we don't yet know, or in reaching solutions

DEVELOPING REFLECTIVE AWARENESS AMONGST THE YOUTH

A global leadership education initiative is collaborating with graduate and MBA programs, colleges and high school students to unlock human potential by providing leadership training to a broad group of youthful participants, helping identify and train our future leaders. The initiative fosters a greater understanding of leadership and personal development through a transformative learning process that enhances self-awareness, self confidence, interpersonal skills and greater clarity of future challenges and goals.

 EMERGING BENCHMARKS

that don't yet exist and are often based on technologies and techniques that have not yet been developed. A key benefit of question-based learning is therefore the development of a broader understanding.

Guided reflection is a critical enabler for a learner to advance in their personal journey to mastery in the field of their choice. It enables the understanding of where a learner is and what challenges need to be embraced. Guided reflection further installs a practice of life-long learning, as well as opening the pathway to *shared* learning, helping a teacher understand their students' core issues and challenges. Such a process is a first step towards creating a shared learning journey, involving participants in co-creating a course syllabus and thereby encouraging them to assume responsibility for their learning.

NOTES

1. Colby et al. (2011); Pfeffer/Fong (2004).
2. Martin (2007).
3. Khurana (2007: 305).
4. Mintzberg (2004).
5. Datar et al. (2010: 92).
6. Ghoshal (2005); Khurana (2007).
7. Gentile (2010); Swaen et al. (2011); Bieger (2011).
8. Colby et al. (2011: 65–69).
9. Colby et al. (2011: 68, 82); Gentile (2010).
10. Colby et al. (2011: 89–110).
11. Datar et al. (2010: 104).

12. Colby et al. (2011: 89).
13. There are many methods including Appreciative Inquiry by David Cooperrider, Spiral Dynamics by Clare Graves and Don Beck, Community Building by Scott Peck. For a helpful overview see also Van Velsor et al. (2010).
14. Experiential learning as defined here is an intellectual account based on the paradigm of scientific inquiry, in the tradition of Dewey, Lewin, Piaget and Kelly. Also further developed by Jack Mezirow, David Kolb, etc.
15. John Heron, Lyle Yorks and others.
16. GRLI and Oasis School of Human Relations are actively developing Whole Person Learning in Europe.
17. Rogers/Freiberg (1994) translate insights from therapy to the classroom.
18. Erhard et al. (2012).
19. Systemic thinking views problems as part of an overall, interconnected system (see Bertalanffy, Checkland, Capra, Weinberg, Senge and many others).
20. The journeyman years of many guilds flourished in the medieval years until the early twentieth century. Today, there are approx. 10 000 journeymen on the road world-wide. The purpose of these years abroad and away from home was to acquire latest practices from other regions, to gain life experience and to test the application of one's knowledge in various new circumstances.
21. De Jesus et al. (2005).

7. Enabling business organizations to serve the common good

Globalization rules our lives, rules over wealth or poverty, creates winners or losers. Why have we been told that it isn't possible to let everyone benefit in some way? Why do we consider the idea of a selfish human being more true to reality than a sharing human being?
Sofia Borodulina, GRLI Young Ambassador, Germany

CHALLENGES IN SUPPORTING BUSINESS MANAGEMENT

As with the current economic model, most management education organizations inhabit a realm that is desynchronized with the increasingly distressing realities of our world. Management education needs to evolve in order to make itself useful again by becoming a service to society that works towards the common good.

Academia is increasingly criticized for being out of touch with the business world. Scholars often retreat into their own secluded academic domains, sustaining a never-ending carousel of refinements to economic problems that are as incomprehensible as they are meaningless to businesses operating in the real world. Many management scholars are more concerned about a rigorous research process leading to defensible theoretical generalizations, rather than addressing tangible economic problems. The fact that the value of scholarly work is defined chiefly by the frequency of citations by other business scholars suggests that the current approach is not practically useful – except perhaps to academia itself.

We consider three key enablers to be of particular relevance in supporting business organizations to serve the common good:

- Research in service of society;
- Supporting companies towards stewardship; and
- Accompanying leaders in their transformation.

The competences and skills needed to excel in all three areas vary. Clearly, no single management educator is required to offer all these dimensions with equal expertise or priority. This chapter provides an insight into the current dynamics and challenges in the three domains, allowing management educators to determine where and how they wish to play their role in enabling business organizations to serve the common good.

While there are many players in management education active in supporting companies, providing research and leadership development, three classical types come to mind: consulting companies, business schools and executive training centers. We will investigate research and consulting dynamics in the field of business and management – but first, we need to study management consulting companies and providers of business and management research, such as business schools and management departments of universities.

The Scramble for Acceptance

In 1962 Marvin Bower (then Managing Director of McKinsey & Company) addressed MBAs at Harvard, where he described management consulting as "one of the new professions". For the past half century, management consulting firms fought widespread public apprehension that advice proffered by consultants constitutes little more than corporate pandering. As long as both insiders and outsiders considered management consulting as a young profession, consultants could continue to dismiss any perceived ethical failings as symptomatic of a field in adolescent development. Management consulting firms therefore invested heavily in professionalizing consulting work in a quest for increased autonomy and respect, a goal they didn't quite achieve by the end of the twentieth century.[1]

Business schools were in a comparable situation just half a century ago. Business scholars felt they were the underdogs to the powerful scientific community of economists, whose adherents didn't take business studies quite as seriously as they should. Business scholars embarked on a drive to professionalize business and management studies, resulting in research efforts that have drifted far from the real world of business and management, laying a theoretical foundation of the field by means of increased specialization and segmentation. Today, business and management scholars are well respected by their colleagues in other fields – including economics. However, these scholars are no longer in touch with business and management, at least not in the forms that are applied and exercised in a realistic setting.

Meanwhile the management consultancies stepped in, filling the gap left open by business and management research while they pursued their goal for autonomy and respect. The market for consultants expanded at a double digit pace during the 1990s, reaching the point where the

Managing Director of McKinsey no longer needed to charm MBAs into joining his firm, a position which in 1997 was considered a dream job both in Europe and the U.S. At the end of the twentieth century, an entry-level position in a management consulting firm had become the preferred path for promotion to the very highest executive positions throughout the world. Today, McKinsey can boast that they have produced more CEOs than any other institution. At the same time the firm still seeks the respect of management scholars. McKinsey sees itself much as academic organization and consider their senior partners like tenured faculty: leaders in their own right.[2]

Management consultancies are criticized both by clients and management scholars. Apart from their overuse of buzzwords and predilection for management fads, one important criticism centers on their failure to develop strategies and plans that can be realistically executed by their clients. Some argue that the mismatch between advice provided and the ability of business leaders to implement a proposed change results in substantial damage to organizations.[3] Alternately, advice provided by management consultancies contains gaps and inconsistencies that may prevent a positive outcome.[4] Others claim that management consultancies do little more than state the obvious while lacking real experience upon which to base their advice, offering generic strategies and plans of no relevance to a client's particular problem. Another concern is the promise to deliver sustainable results which are difficult to measure and implement, given the disconnect between the client and firm once a project is finalized.

On the other hand, management consultancies *do* hold the ability to translate abstract theoretical knowledge developed by management scholars into the straightforward language that business executives understand. Critical voices in academia admit to a certain envy concerning this rare ability, wishing instead that business and management scholars in business schools conducted research with higher practical relevance.

Scaling the Ivory Tower

Criticism of research conducted by business and management scholars is well documented. While there have been notable scholarly contributions to management practice (especially in the fields of strategy and finance), management research is primarily oriented towards developing theory and thereby enhancing scholarly reputations within academic circles,[5] resulting in a profession displaying a wide gap between researchers and practitioners.[6] While medical, engineering and law schools engage in their respective professions, business schools do not command the same attention from managers. Critics bemoan the retreat of management academia into their own secluded domain, which in effect has led to the creation of an "incestuous loop".[7] The result of this withdrawal leaves scholars writing ever more sophisticated papers to each other, discussing problems defined only between themselves, while the value of the work is defined chiefly by the *frequency of citations by other business scholars*. Research impact as defined by citations has become a yardstick for recruiting and promoting such scholars, as well as measuring their scientific performance and reputation. Ultimately, business schools are increasingly decoupled from the world of practice, having lost the balance between scientific rigor and practical relevance.

Overall, the extent of damage is far greater to business schools than management consultancies. Business school research is increasingly referred to publications in discipline-based academic journals published in English and included in the Social Science Citation Index, or a list of publications used by the *Financial Times* for their business school rankings. Most management research comes from Europe and North America, having failed to embrace the new global context by ignoring emerging and developing countries. More fundamentally, management scholars are criticized for concentrating on "reporting research", re-creating and explaining past developments instead of creating *new* knowledge to build a different future.

Research insights developed at business schools may have increased their academic legitimacy, but only very rarely touch the world of practice. Practitioners, who include managers, public officials or students, don't read the scientific journals, and if they do read them they don't find them useful.[8] There are three different explanations for this gap – framed as a *knowledge transfer problem* – that may be solved by better *translating* the results of management research into languages, publications, frameworks and tools that managers can and do use in their work. In this way, research results could be made useful in practice.[9] However, if theoretical and practical knowledge are not seen as one and the same, but rather as two *distinct* types of knowledge, then merely translating the results will not resolve the dilemma.

The gap therefore needs to be framed as a *knowledge* production *problem*. The concept of engaged scholarship has been suggested as a solution, whereby researchers and practitioners interact effectively in order to co-produce knowledge that is relevant to *both* research and practice, with academics contributing rigorously developed scientific insights alongside practitioners' understanding of the realities of the business world.[10] This approach, however, does not address the root cause of the problem.

Very often we encounter a problem of definition in research, since the research process does not begin with knowledge production but rather by *defining* the research issues and questions that should be tackled. Different forms of knowledge production or dissemination are effectively worthless if the wrong questions are being addressed.[11] Unless the research problem is framed in a relevant, mutually understood manner, there is little sense in attempting to translate research output for the benefit of management practice.

While applied research by consultants directly addresses the relevant problems of management practice, it has a tendency to be partial and short sighted. Management scholars seem to care much more about a rigorous research process leading to defensible generalizations that add to theoretical knowledge.[12] Such divergent deficiencies require a more balanced, collaborative way of conducting research that is both relevant and rigorous.

Closing the Relevance Gap

Irrespective of whether we look at McKinsey, BCG, or Booz Allan & Hamilton, the dynamics of the professional landscape serving business organizations make for a fascinating study. On the one hand, management consultancies have claimed the title of being close advisers and consultants to business executives, but still struggle to have their applied research accepted by management scholars who consider consulting methodologies as somewhat lacking in academic ambition. On the other hand, management consultancies make a point of hiring top academic talent, including the best and brightest business school graduates – while business schools struggle to motivate their top brains to pursue an academic career. At the same time, neither management consulting firms nor business schools consider it their duty to question the paradigms within which business operates, both being too occupied with gaining respect, autonomy and market share.

Let us instead imagine a world where business scholars and management consultants work together to produce relevant short- and long-term research and advice, jointly determining how companies can develop and implement sustainability strategies. Business scholars and management consultants working in tandem could become sustainability stewards, helping build a better world.

The relevance gap of management scholarship could be closed by collaboration, by defining research problems that matter, but also by finding effective means to make the resulting knowledge *useful*. A research agenda needs to be defined together with different stakeholders and disciplines (natural sciences, social sciences). Technological innovations and social media tools (video and TV, institutional and personal web pages, Twitter,

Wikis or blogs) could be integrated at both ends of the research process, which are only very rarely used by researchers.[13] Both strategies could help to reconnect scholarly output to practice and society at large. Rigorous scholarly norms do have their place in knowledge production. However, opening up business *research* to business *practice* is of decisive importance both at the beginning and at the end of the research process – areas where consultancies have traditionally excelled and where collaboration shows significant promise.

CLARIFYING COMMUNITY EXPECTATIONS

In order to broaden our understanding of the gap between current research and the types of research our community *expects* from business and management scholars, we asked our global panel of community representatives a number of pertinent questions. Note that we asked our community to focus their reflection on business schools *only*, in order to narrow their focus and improve the quality of collected feedback.

EXCERPT FROM THE 50+20 GLOBAL SURVEY (SEE APPENDIX 1 FOR DETAILS)

Our community helps us better understand the gap between what business schools focus on today, compared to what they think business schools *should* focus on in future. For starters, we have found a clear expectation that management research should become first and foremost future-oriented, and focused on developing new concepts and theories.

Table 7.1   Comparing current versus future objectives of management research

Comparing current vs future objectives of mgmt. research	*Perceived current*	*Perceived future*
1. Studying the past: explaining phenomena through historic data	60 percent	44 percent
2. Studying the present: understanding emerging phenomena and trends by developing new concepts and theories	66 percent	82 percent
3. Studying the future: addressing emerging issues by developing scenarios and alternative theories	58 percent	96 percent

---

Our community provides clear indications and preferences when asked about what management research should focus on. Resolving societal, interdisciplinary, global and trans-disciplinary issues enjoyed the highest preference amongst our respondents. Topics less favored involved pedagogy / andragogy (adult education) of developing leaders, development of business / management theory, and addressing management and business issues.

In terms of how such research should be conducted, the various approaches that scored a high response rate included interdis-ciplinary research (studying a business issue from different per-spectives), transdisciplinary research (addressing larger issues with input from non-business fields) and finally action research (being involved and interacting with a subject).

Interestingly, our community quickly clarified who should benefit from management research. The two most preferred groups of beneficiaries included business practitioners and executives (col-laborative effort accessible to wide audience), closely followed by various societal stakeholders (potentially jointly developed). By contrast, beneficiaries such as the general public (understand-able and applicable for everybody) and academic peer audiences (typically through journal publications) received few favorable responses.

Last but not least, when asked about what key *topics* need to be addressed by management research, our community again con-firms the importance of helping business to transform into a con-tributing agent to society. Specifically, most of our respondents consider how to make business responsible and sustainable an important topic, followed closely by how to develop globally responsible leaders, and the role of business and its responsibility towards consumers, society and the planet. Other topics consid-ered worthy of further investigation included new measures for economic, social and environmental effectiveness for business, as well as the role of business leaders in resolving global issues.

The feedback from our community led us to the understanding that players in the field of management education need to embrace three key enablers in order to successfully enable business organizations to serve the common good. We will discuss these enablers in the coming sections, which are:

- Research in service of society.
- Supporting companies towards stewardship.
- Accompanying leaders in their transformation.

RESEARCH IN SERVICE OF SOCIETY

Business and management research working in service of society requires a shift away from narrow, specialized research in a single discipline, in favor of research that enables business to contribute to society and the world as a larger unit. As we have established earlier, businesses are required to undergo a fundamental transformation from their short-term profit maximization doctrine to a perspective of providing sustainable value to society. While business leaders increasingly understand and seek to embrace the need to review their business strategy from a balanced sustainability perspective, many open questions remain. Clearly, this is where stakeholders in management education can play a role.

Management research must adjust its purpose to serve business in the context of global and local challenges, problems and dilemmas around environmental, societal and economic issues. Such an agenda includes a critical reflection of the deficits in existing management, financial and economic theories. Management research should concentrate on the necessary strategies and tools to bring about a sustainable economy.[14] Crucial issues concern full cost pricing, including externalized impacts and costs on ecosystems and society, the creation of inclusive indices and labels for customers, and strategies for sustainable finance and investment.

Researchers need to redefine their role primarily as developing, testing and adapting alternative research methodologies that allow for future-oriented problem solving. Management research should further engage in an ongoing dialogue with stakeholders in order to jointly identify research topics and add value by ensuring rigor with critical academic perspective. As a result, management research scholars should write for societal stakeholders rather than for their peers.

To date, business school research only rarely addresses societal issues or discusses important public policy questions, relating to issues like public health, education, poverty, demography or sustainability. While research and practice amongst professions like medicine, law or public policy have a strong code of ethics linking their contributions to the common good, business management has never succeeded in becoming a *true* profession; it has surrendered to the neoliberal utopia of free markets and follows no established code of ethics.[15] However, as highlighted above, research can and should inform society and policy and contribute to the common good

RESEARCH THROUGH THE LENS

Lengthy, jargon filled reports mean nothing to anyone outside the small academic sphere. A group of academics is working to overcome this. How? By conducting and presenting their research in video format. All the principles of academic rigor are maintained, but the end product can be accessed at the click of a mouse and understood easily because of its clear, multi-dimensional format.

 EMERGING BENCHMARKS

– and not just for the good of a few private stakeholders, as the recent financial crisis revealed.[16]

The dominance of disciplinary scholarship in business school research basically excludes contributions to some of the biggest and most pressing problems facing society, such as de-carbonizing the economic system and bringing resource consumption within the constraints of the planet. A transdisciplinary approach is required to address the problem.[17]

The emphasis on empirically derived evidence often directs the focus of research on explaining *past* events, thereby discriminating against future-oriented research which, by its very nature, cannot be based on the same kind of evidence. While highly elaborate methodologies to analyse empirical data do exist, only a few of these are used in research for future scenarios. Furthermore, past scenarios are providing less useful help in analysing and anticipating a more complex future. Perhaps John Maynard Keynes was right: "The difficulty lies not so much in developing new ideas as in escaping from old ones."

Research in a Global Context

Our proposed research agenda is defined to address existing and emerging issues in business and society worldwide. As a result, research input and focus will shift from being predominantly North American and European to a balanced global contribution, including major input from developing countries. The research definition phase will become an inclusive, open and participatory process involving all relevant stakeholders.

One of researchers' main tasks is the definition of appropriate research methodologies that enable connecting studies with broader and future-oriented topics. They also develop new processes and procedures that allow a review of their work's relevance. These measures increase the challenge and complexity for researchers to ensure rigor while guaranteeing relevant results.

To help ensure that research serves its goal, a broad range of stakeholders should be involved in evaluating research outputs. Assessments should no longer be predominantly conducted through peer review journals, but rather include:

- Engagement with organizations including businesses, NGOs and the public sector.
- Clarity of practice and policy implications of research findings.
- Whether outcomes are publicized in the media, as well as professional and academic journals.
- The impact of the research and whether it addresses real-world issues.

In the future, more research should be re-oriented towards being an enabler for long-term societal targets (such as the Millennium Development Goals or the climate change targets for 2050). Research should be conducted around issues involving a broad stakeholder base, beyond managers and entrepreneurs. Transdisciplinary research should become the norm – with the collaboratory as a platform for researchers to meet with stakeholders and others to jointly develop and test their research.

An increased interest in focusing on the social and environmental impact of proposed approaches will lead to the involvement of researchers with a wide range of backgrounds, particularly across science, social science and health science disciplines. A transdisciplinary approach is imperative in developing effective solutions to global challenges. Researchers thereby become active players in business and society, collaborating with relevant stakeholders in the process of formulating and disseminating research questions – and producing useful knowledge.

By engaging in an ongoing dialogue with a broader range of stakeholders, researchers will be able to jointly identify research topics and add value by ensuring academic rigor and a critical academic perspective. By applying a transdisciplinary approach that addresses real-world problems, research scholars will again become active players in business and society by producing truly useful knowledge.

SUPPORTING COMPANIES TOWARDS STEWARDSHIP

Many business leaders already understand that transforming the present economic system and creating a sustainable business model will serve their long-term interests. Business organizations need to embrace the role of stewardship with the implicit knowledge that they are not the real owners of the natural resources they use and occupy.

We define stewardship as an ethic that embodies responsible and sustainable management of resources. The concept of stewardship is linked to the concept of sustainability and refers to accepting *responsibility for something that belongs to someone else*. When business organizations become stewards of the resources they manage, they implicitly acknowledge that they are *not* the owners of the natural resources and land they use and occupy. They further do not own the people they employ and serve with products and services, nor the money they invest and earn as a result. Rather, business organizations are *custodians* of these resources for society and our collective future, seeking to contribute to a better world with their products and services. Achieving such a transformation is a tall order; management consultants and scholars will need to collaborate together with business leaders, embarking on a journey to unknown lands.

Enabling business organizations to create sustainable value for society requires a shift in thinking, as well as practical tools and methods to balance environmental, societal and economic demands. Some (but not all) business leaders understand that transforming the economic system and creating a sustainable business model for the future is in the best interest of business by serving its *long-term interests*. Developing organizations that can assume globally responsible leadership from an organizational

---

A NATIONAL VISION OF COMPANIES AS AGENTS OF CHANGE

A South American Business School ensures that national, regional or urban issues are integral to coursework on each degree program they offer. Corporate Social Responsibility is a fundamental criterion in all grading, and most of the final reports are considered for publication, thus ensuring they have a national impact. They are also supporting a national initiative to promote Corporate Social Responsibility.

EMERGING BENCHMARKS

perspective is a critical step that includes three core challenges: building and maintaining commitment, embedding globally responsible action into business operations, and developing an organizational culture that supports global responsibility.[18]

What kind of consulting support do business organizations need? We present some early indications of the domains in which business needs help most urgently. Note that these domains will evolve over time and include aspects that will only be uncovered once businesses have started with the transformation:

- Creating business solutions for a sustainable world: Developing shared value for business and society requires new strategies and business models. These will be developed collaboratively and address current sustainability problems.
- Developing new performance measurement systems: Organizational performance needs to be measured across all dimensions of sustainability. Whilst measuring economic performance is a well-established practice, environmental and societal performance and inherent trade-offs between these dimensions need to be defined and standardized.
- Specifying professional and ethical standards: Strategies and business solutions should be embedded into standards clarifying the specific demands on corporate and individual behavior, ranging from company standards to broader industry and global standards.

Embracing shared value requires organizations to view their business in the context of environmental, societal, economic, political, anthropological and systemic dynamics. Understanding and evaluating the potential impact of strategic choices requires a new framework for analysis and work, including the development of relevant useable and comparable measures between and within industries. A hybrid between current consulting and traditional academic research would be best suited to support organizations with simulations, crowdsourcing, research action labs, reporting and analysis beyond the existing limits and frameworks of day-to-day perspectives within existing organizations.

ACCOMPANYING LEADERS IN THEIR TRANSFORMATION

Leadership development is a life-long learning adventure following different stages of mastery, starting from awareness, actionable knowledge and guided practice, moving to independent application, and finally skilled performance. If businesses are to succeed in the transformation and become stewards of the common good, then we clearly need leadership based on a different set of values, skills and competencies. Leading a transformation while simultaneously undergoing a profound inner transformation is no simple task. Those brave enough to face the storm will need considerable and sustained support, coaching and counseling.

We need new types of support for existing leaders that are more comprehensive than anything currently offered in the field of executive and leadership training. In time, we anticipate that customized individual or group coaching and facilitation techniques will become more important than traditional off-the-shelf executive training. Guided reflection of past experiences will be one of these new supportive domains. Most leaders have not yet understood the value of internalizing an experience and integrating key lessons learned prior to embracing a new challenge.

We envision a type of *leadership sanctuary* that serves as a complementary platform for on-the-job guided reflection. A leadership sanctuary would welcome professionals for retreats, offering a powerful and safe space maintained by a variety of supportive services, such as coaches, facilitators and development workshops. The leadership sanctuary will form an integral part of the management school of the future or serve as a stand-alone operation, where managers and leaders retreat from the day-to-day demands in order to reflect on the past, crystallize lessons learned, and assess critical considerations and adaptations for the future.

NOTES

1. McKenna (2006).
2. Academy of Management Executive (2001 Vol. 15 No. 2).
3. O'Shea/Madigan (1998).
4. Argyris (2000).
5. AACSB (2008) suggests four different value propositions for business school research: value to students, value to practicing managers, and value to society, in addition to scholars.
6. Skapinker (2008).
7. Hambrick (1994).
8. Porter/McKibbin (1988); Österle (2006); Kleppel (2003).
9. Van de Ven/Johnson (2006: 802).
10. Van de Ven (2007: 3ff); Walsh et al. (2007); Rynes et al. (2001); Lorange (2008: 71).
11. Pettigrew (2001: 61, 67).
12. Dossabhoy/Berger (2002); Thomas/Tymon (1982).
13. Russell/Saunders (2011).
14. Chouinard et al. (2011).
15. Khurana (2007: 363–383).
16. Rynes/Shapiro (2005); Open Letter (2011).
17. Schneidewind (2009).
18. Quinn/van Velsor (2012).

8. Engaging in the transformation of business and the economy

> We are made wise not by the recollection of our past, but by
> the responsibility for our future.
> George Bernard Shaw

CHALLENGES IN PROVIDING STATESMANSHIP

We have reached a stage in our history where society is growing increasingly aware of global issues. More importantly, we are beginning to actively adopt various tools to discuss and resolve them. The broad scale of the envisioned transformation cannot be a self-contained effort, a quiet initiative running in the background; the crises we face are simply too pervasive, encompassing all spheres of human activity, the economy and the environment. The transformation can only be achieved by openly embracing the power of public interest and intellect within a larger societal, economic and ecological context. The future is a public affair that concerns us all – and in order to effectively raise and communicate the current problems we need more people and institutions adopting the role of the statesman.

In our understanding, the role of the statesman is an inherent part of a leadership role. Institutions in management education and individual faculty have a responsibility to assume the statesman role and strengthen their links and contribution to society. We anticipate their main contribution to cover two areas in the societal domain: (a) an active engagement in public debates, and (b) concrete and exemplary actions. In short, talking is important – but it needs some walking too.

Such links to society are typically underdeveloped as the management education institutions narrowly define their relevant markets as students, business organizations and (for research) academic peers. Even in the case of public universities, these links are usually restricted to formal exchanges related to financial and governance issues.

Business schools and international consultancies often act as centers of knowledge and expertise in areas of high relevance to the economy and to society. Not only do they develop management talent and new knowledge, but they are also home to many highly educated and qualified experts with valuable insights, relationships and networks that often span the globe. This potentially makes providers of management education a powerful resource to help support economic and societal developments in general. Furthermore, they are also needed as core *providers* of support in the context of the required transformation of business and society towards a sustainable world.

Giving a Face to the Faceless

Who in particular should adopt the role of the statesman? Among the providers of management education, business schools in particular stand out, as their activities span all fields of education and research. Another candidate might include academics, who are considered to have a high prestige because of their education, knowledge and impartiality. We could further consider institutions that enjoy public funding to have a special *public* responsibility because they are *publicly* employed and funded. However, the responsibility to engage in the transformation of business and the economy is not restricted to business schools and their faculty; it further reaches out to providers in the management education field engaged in research activities, such as consultancies, research institutes or executive education centers. If these players are not engaged in knowledge development and dissemination activities, their potential for public engagement will remain limited.

In our vision we have identified three key enablers for allowing management education to become effective contributors in the transformation of business and the economy, with particular reference to engaging in public debates and in concrete actions. These enablers are (a) open access between academia and practice, (b) faculty as public intellectuals, and (c) institutions as role models. While the role of the public intellectuals addresses individual scholars, institutions are also challenged to transform their organizations into places that can serve as *institutional role models*. Open access between academia and practice addresses both levels, creating an important precondition for the other two enablers to serve their purpose.

The best-known illustration of statesmanship is the public intellectual, who traditionally bridges the gap between academia and an educated public. American writer and poet Ralph Waldo Emerson described the intellectual as a complete person, who embodies all dimensions of human potential and actuality: the farmer, professor, engineer, priest, scholar, statesman, soldier and the artist. To Emerson, the intellectual possesses all these qualities, integrated into a reflecting and thinking individual, whose most important activity is *action*. Inaction is cowardice. Emerson's

DEVELOPING THE ENTREPRENEURIAL ECOSYSTEM IN NIGERIA

A development center in Nigeria offers business development assistance, web-based resources and customized training programs to small and medium enterprises (SMEs) in that country. Recently, the center implemented a national business planning competition for entrepreneurs which received more than 24 000 entries. They are also actively collaborating with other similar centers and openly share their business model to encourage and stimulate similar initiatives. At least 10% of their alumni base are either social entrepreneurs or operate in the social sector space.

EMERGING
BENCHMARKS

intellectual is the "world's eye", communicating ideas to the world and not just to fellow intellectuals.[1]

In some cultures, in particular in the United States, academics often participate in public debate on topics of interest to civil society. Current names in the field of economics are Paul Krugman, Paul Stiglitz, Larry Summers, or Jeffrey Sachs. In Germany, one may cite Hans Werner Sinn and Heiner Flassbeck. Apart from Peter Drucker, public intellectuals in business administration are difficult to identify. Journalists and columnists such as Thomas Friedman and George Monbiot certainly play a more important role as influencers in business than most academics (this is not to say that we necessarily agree with their opinions all the time). In some countries, such as Switzerland, public intellectuals are entirely absent, largely for cultural reasons.

History has produced a long list of intellectuals with a strong involvement in public affairs. Until the middle of the twentieth century, most intellectual activity occurred outside of academia. Since then there has been a notable shift from independent freelance status to the university. Interestingly, the shift occurred as the university sector started to expand, where greater numbers of intellectuals (previously engaged in independent careers, traveling the world and switching careers) ended up in academia. These developments led to a distinct decline in the prevalence of public intellectuals.

How can this shift be explained? The nature of modern academic life is considered as unfriendly (if not harmful) to a creative and engaged public intellectual activity. Academics play important roles in review boards, government commissions and ethics committees, but tend to shy away from public exposure. Also, the extreme specialization which academia had embarked on over the past decades has created scholars who are increasingly limited specialists or experts, unable and unwilling to consider a larger perspective or to bridge their expertise with the public interest. For scientists in particular, spending time on discourse with the general public is mostly considered a waste of time and a "dumbing down" of scholarly insights (with a few notable exceptions, such as Carl Sagan or Michiu Kaku). Addressing the public does not usually help an academic career and may even damage an academic's reputation amongst their peers. Oddly, a number of the most prominent public intellectuals are former academics, such as Henry Kissinger, Daniel Moynihan and Larry Summers, who had either departed from or interrupted their academic careers. As a result, such individuals accumulated far broader experience compared to the average academic.

TOWARDS PUBLIC ENGAGEMENT

The debate around the transformation of the economic system towards a system that serves societal progress directly involves business schools and other providers of management education. Business schools are criticized for having educated the managers who caused the crisis, and propagating theories or models that have contributed to the problems. Business schools are indirectly exposed when current and future students begin questioning their choice of study areas, or when corporate customers need support in developing new strategies and business models that embrace sustainable development. Business schools and their faculty could provide a significant contribution to initiate the transformation, but must first provide more than just new research insights and new courses. Business schools also need public engagement to help bring about the necessary changes.

Management education providers need to support business, government and other members of the community in this challenge. Not only should they participate in the process, but should also help shape and lead the agenda that will eventually reform the economic system and define a new role for business. Such reforms would include:

- **New theories and models for a sustainable world:** The financial and economic crises have demonstrated that the economic and financial systems no longer usefully serve the needs of society and require a fundamental reformation. Such discussions are commonly held in high-level political, business meetings and in the business press, yet management schools and their faculty have been mostly absent from these discussions. What we need is their active engagement, to put the underlying theories of current economic thinking to a critical test and provide support in the pragmatic search for alternatives. New theories that guide our thoughts, our actions and behavior towards a sustainable future will have to be developed, publicly discussed and tested.

- **Platforms for public debate on solutions for a better world:** New theories and models for a sustainable world cannot be developed inside academic circles alone. They can only be developed via an extended public debate, involving a range of different members of the community. Creating the relevant platforms for public debate, organizing and leading these debates is another challenging task where academic leadership and active management school involvement will be needed. We consider the collaboratory as an ideal space for such debates.

- **Sustainability incubators:** In addition to new theories and platforms for public debate, the new models will also require practical help. In order to develop sustainable solutions in practice the new models will need sustainability entrepreneurs and sustainable solutions to existing problems. Business schools have initiated business incubators in the past, providing a suitable environment and practical support for business start-ups. The same approach could be used to support the development and launch of practical sustainability startup companies and social entrepreneurship.

Three key enablers would help management education become an effective contributor in the transformation:

- Open access between academia and practice;
- Faculty as public intellectuals; and
- Institutional role models.

We will review each of them in more detail.

OPEN ACCESS BETWEEN ACADEMIA AND PRACTICE

Academic scholars tend to be strangers to the business world, typically possessing little or no personal experience in real-world problems. In much the same way, business practitioners live outside the academic world – though a small number occasionally accept limited engagements as lecturers or adjunct professors at a business school or other institutions. Some business schools have introduced professorships for management practice as a potentially attractive career choice for experienced practitioners. However, such occurrences remain a rarity.

Scholars need to become engaged in public debates by, quite simply, immersing themselves in the real world. A consequence of the extreme specialization in academia is an increasing isolation from the world and from real-life experience. The best academics today are considered individuals with the ability to methodologically conduct highly ambitious research, published in top-rated academic journals which are read and cited exclusively by other academics. Whilst academics are exceptional intellectuals with highly developed scholarly skills, they have never been encouraged to attain a greater balance, to evolve themselves into whole persons with a broad perspective above and beyond their area of expertise. Also, such experts rarely work in the professional setting, despite it being the subject of their research.

Given the predicament outlined above, it may not be a coincidence that academic publications don't reach business practice. When we consider what managers read and how they improve their practice, we find that they rarely read top-rated academic journals. Even if they did know and read such journals, they are unlikely to understand the content. More importantly, managers wouldn't know *how* they could learn something from reading such academic journals as they are unable to build a conceptual bridge that links their findings to practical applications. It should not come as a surprise that the best-selling management and leadership books[2] are written by journalists (Malcolm Gladwell), authors (Daniel Pink), consultants (Jim Collins), coaches (Anthony Robbins), novelists (Michael Lewis), independent thinkers (Tom Rath), gurus (Deepak Chopra), business leaders (Eliyahu Goldratt) and the occasional academic (Deepak Malhotra). The above list is of course debatable, but coincides with other findings.[3]

Matters don't improve when we examine how business practice is represented in academia. For one, business practitioners are generally unfamiliar with the academic world. Although some practitioners accept limited engagements as lecturers or adjunct professors at most business schools and other institutions, they are rarely offered an appointment as a regular professor. Some schools have since created professorships for management practice to make the academic route more attractive to experienced practitioners, but their numbers remain low.

Both sides would profit if the walls between academia and business practice were removed. Given the size and range of the transformation required, society at large will benefit from such a development. We need to enable open access between academia and business practice by establishing open dialogue between thought leaders (irrespective of their origin), including scholars, authors, journalists, consultants, psychologists, activists and the public. A heightened exchange of ideas and expertise can also be achieved by enriching both management education and research with real-life experiences and perspectives.

Such an exchange will enable scholars to become role models that lead co-creation in learning and education by working in tandem with business practice, NGOs, the private sector and the public. Open access between academia and practice is essential to bring about transdisciplinary collaboration, facilitating work on more future-oriented concepts; and proposing ideas and solutions that will help resolve current issues in business and management.

We need to imagine a business school or management institute quite unlike those that exist today. Imagine a place that *welcomes* business professionals as equals in debates on future-oriented concepts, ideas and solutions that help resolve current issues in business and management. Imagine an institution that willingly sends its faculty members on stints abroad, perhaps to launch an educational center in Burma, support emerging entrepreneurs in Indonesia, advise policy makers in China, or collaborate with indigenous peoples in Australia on new learning methods. Imagine an institution that is both a collaborative learning and research platform – a collaboratory – and a place of reflection and deep thought, like the leadership sanctuary we proposed earlier.

FACULTY MEMBERS AS PUBLIC INTELLECTUALS

In order for us to achieve sustained transdisciplinary and societal discourse we will need the expertise of public intellectuals – but not only because of their expert knowledge within a given field. Rather, we require their gift for *synthesizing knowledge* and coherently relating it to wider socio-political issues in a manner that makes sense to the public.

Many public intellectuals today are journalists or novelists, rather than academics. The curtailed role of academics as public intellectuals is not usually the result of a public choice, but rather by the academics' own design. Research that is addressed to other members of the scientific community helps build scholarly reputations, while contributions concerning public issues are not usually assigned the same value.

Posner defines a public intellectual as someone "who uses general ideas drawn from history, philosophy, political science, economics, law, literature, and ideas that are part of the cultural intellectual tradition of the world, to address contemporary events, usually of a political or ideological flavor and does so in the popular media, whether in the form of Op Ed pieces, television appearances, signing full-page advertisements, or writing magazine articles or books addressed to a general audience".[4] His definition excludes important intellectual figures that may be regarded as public due to their considerable influence, but who don't necessarily communicate directly to the public.

Lightman[5] introduces a useful hierarchy of involvement levels concerning the public intellectual:

- **Level 1:** Speaking and writing for the public exclusively about the chosen discipline.
- **Level 2:** Speaking and writing about the chosen discipline and how it relates to the social, cultural, and political world around it.
- **Level 3:** The intellectual is elevated to a symbol, who is asked to write and speak about a large range of public issues not necessarily directly connected to their original field of expertise. Such responsibility demands a cautious, respectful approach.

Posner[6] also points out common pitfalls of public intellectuals. He highlights how many academic intellectuals do little to shape policy or make a genuine difference, rather concentrating on gratifying the needs of a general audience. Public intellectuals may leave their area of competence and claim knowledge and insights into other disciplines. Further, universities are often wary of keeping a highly opinionated public intellectual as a prominent professor, who produces essays and books that could be considered sensationalist journalism rather than responsible academic work.

A number of guidelines are required to ensure the constructive inclusion of public intellectuals in academic fields:

1. Transparency in disclosing sources and amounts of revenues and funds received – to avoid conflicts of interest and other potentially damaging repercussions.
2. Easy access to comprehensive records of previous public statements, with particular emphasis on predictions and forecasts to clarifying changes of position and monitoring trends in previous statements.
3. Responsible behavior in terms of acceptance and delineation on subjects that are outside of their field of expertise – helping separate expressed opinion from expert advice.

4. Upfront declaration of political and ideological perspectives to ensure clarity and transparency.

Changes in business and economics need the active participation of scholars in the role of public intellectuals in order to address critical developments and provide knowledge and expertise to public debates. We believe that a regular task of all business and management faculty members of the future should be to serve as public intellectuals and to pro-actively engage in societal debates through research, teaching and public services.

'ORDINARY' PEOPLE CAN DO EXTRAORDINARY THINGS

With little guidance, encouragement and space to grow and exhibit their talent and abilities, people considered 'very ordinary' are often discarded by larger society – but such people are equally capable of doing extraordinary things. An NGO in India provides services and solutions to problems in rural communities, aiming to make them self-sufficient and sustainable. The concept has been applied from the outset where, for example, the college itself was designed and built not by urban architects and contractors, but by the locals with ample experience of building their own houses.

EMERGING
BENCHMARKS

INSTITUTIONS AS ROLE MODELS

Management schools of the future must fundamentally rethink their approach in order to become role models for a world that increasingly seeks socially, environmentally and economically just organizations. The transformation will involve changes in structure, a new generation of teachers and researchers; and new ways to measure success. Governance structures and decision processes will include concerned stakeholders who jointly define priorities and ways to measure the institution's social contribution.

We anticipate that the management school of the future will define its success by applying business theory to business *practice*. This ability needs to be measurable in order to evaluate and continuously adapt and improve the institution's strategy and implementation. We consider the following as three critical enablers:

A Structure That Serves Its Vision

The key principle in effectively organizing the future management school lies in the recognition of the contribution of each member to the core objectives of the vision. This includes educational, research and administrative staff, each facing different challenges. Many scenarios illustrate how the management school of the future can be developed. The key would be to clearly define how the institution serves one or several of the identified roles in the vision, enabling a governance structure of concerned stakeholders to jointly identify how best to measure the institution's performance in terms of contributing to society in its chosen role. More importantly, it would allow the institution to develop clear strategies for implementation and prioritization. We anticipate that the re-education of faculty members as well as the training of PhD holders is likely to be the critical enabler for most institutions concerned. Aligning reward and compensation schemes with the vision will be an effective way to drive change.

A New Generation of Teachers and Researchers

Management schools need carefully trained teaching and research collaborators who possess entirely new skills sets and competencies. A significant challenge concerns the ability to hire or re-train educational and research faculty members who can create safe and effective collaborative learning platforms. Re-training existing faculty is one of the most important levers in the successful implementation of the 50+20 vision. Given that this new generation of teachers and researchers will represent a strong majority of the faculty of the future, the development of such new capacity is a key priority. Our recommendations focus on two core activities, similar to those of the Carnegie / Ford reports of 1959 which have shaped business schools for the past 50 years (see Chapter 10 for more detail):

- The creation of an entirely new doctoral program to be created in existing business schools.
- The creation of a training organization, specializing in the transformation of existing faculty.

We envision the creation of a global faculty development and training structure that provides a comprehensive offering around the globe, with many stakeholders collaborating in its execution and sharing best practices where relevant and possible. Such training and development would need to focus on enabling existing and new faculty members to develop skills and competences in (a) coaching and facilitation, (b) transdisciplinary collaboration, (c) critical review and broadening of their individual subject specialization, and (d) broadening of existing and development of future-oriented research methodologies. Such re-training would serve to professionalize and raise the level of the current business school faculty, similarly to emerging new deans programs offered by leading business schools or accreditation organizations.

QUESTIONING WHAT WE THINK WE KNOW

Which cultural foundations and changes leave their mark on our society? How can we create optimal educational opportunities for our future leaders? A university in Germany has embraced culture, sustainability and entrepreneurship as its thematic focuses in research and teaching – helping address the future of social commitment to civil society in the twenty-first century.

EMERGING
BENCHMARKS

A New Way to Measure Success

Given that we are moving into unchartered territory, we need to be very careful with the newly adopted paradigms or levels of thinking we set to measure the success for the management school of the future. Guiding principles that evaluate to what degree a management school has implemented a designed vision includes the following considerations:

- Recognition of the responsibility to provide globally responsible leadership for a sustainable world.
- Relevant measures of the three roles of management education, namely: educating leaders, enabling companies with research and engaging in the public debate.

A critical factor will involve evaluating to what degree an institution applies its strategy in a real-world setting, requiring relevant measures for the three proposed roles of management education. These measures will be demonstrated by the degree to which the three roles are embedded in the activities of its administrative, teaching and research staff. Future curricula will be evaluated based on their content, pedagogy, actions, fieldwork, and their transdisciplinary approach to learning. The evaluation of acquired skills, competencies and attitudes of graduates requires both short- and long-term reviews. Further, collaborating with alumni and stakeholder organizations can open the pathway to establishing and monitoring an agreed-upon oath to uphold responsible leadership for the world.

We imagine the management school of the future as an organic, expanding, potentially multi-location, networking organization offering a variety of tools and techniques, including on-site, virtual, free, as well as blended learning approaches, ideally resulting from a collaboration of several engaged and contributing organizations. The underlying organizing principle is simple: *How will* your *contribution serve the vision of providing responsible leadership for a sustainable world?* The answers will vary, and the organizational structure will need to remain correspondingly flexible to adapt to new dimensions and interpretations.

NOTES

1. Emerson (1837).
2. Based on the list of bestselling business management and leadership books compiled by Amazon.com (based on book purchases), accessed in February 2012 from:http://www.amazon.com/Best-Sellers-Books-Business-Management-Leadership/zgbs/books/2675.
3. Pfeffer/Fong (2004).
4. Posner (2002).
5. Lightman (n.d.).
6. Posner (2002).

PART III

The implementation

9. Implementing the vision

> We will create educational frameworks, materials, processes and environments
> that enable effective learning experiences for responsible leadership.
> PRME Principle 3

A FUNDAMENTAL TRANSFORMATION

Good ideas are abundant. Implementing them is difficult.

An important prerequisite to realizing the 50+20 vision is to establish the conditions which enable both existing and future faculty of business and management to embrace a new approach in how we live. We believe in the potential of human beings – their unlimited capacity to change, develop and grow. A transformation of this kind is possible if an individual exhibits a willingness to change, particularly when supported by a set of favorable conditions. The most important challenge for management educators is to identify and create these conditions for change, producing an environment that motivates faculty to embrace responsible leadership for a sustainable world. The 50+20 goal is to help motivate change amongst the many stakeholders, and to convince them to accompany us in the journey of transformation.

Transforming the complex landscape of management education requires broadening the range of functions adopted by the various players in the field. We need nothing less than a fundamental transformation of management education from serving business to becoming *custodians on behalf of society*.

The Current Stalemate and Future Requirements

When comparing the current situation with future requirements we can summarise the required changes as outlined in Figure 9.1.

Implementing the vision requires understanding the challenges specific to each of these three roles discussed in Part II:

- **Educating responsible leaders** involves re-designing education in such a way to ensure that participants develop the traits, competences,

Management education for the world

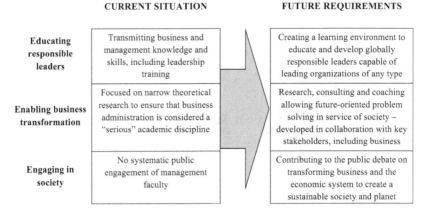

Figure 9.1   Current situation and future requirements of management education

attitudes, skills and knowledge required to embrace the emerging global issues and to collaborate with stakeholders in the pursuit of resolving them. At its core, this enabler promotes the transmission of business and management knowledge, with the aim of creating true leaders and transforming traditional lecturing into a process of co-creation.

- **Enabling business transformation** requires a redefinition of research, away from building theories about past developments. Instead, the enabler favors active players who help develop sustainability strategies for companies as part of a larger endeavor of resolving regional and global environmental, social and economic challenges.
- **Engaging in society** requires that new avenues of engagement be developed from scratch as they have not been part of the business school agenda. This enabler aims to provide society with platforms for engaged discussion and action, in order to develop solutions for existing and emerging issues.

A successful implementation of the vision involves not only players in management education but the wider community concerned with management education. In addition to faculty and students, the vision requires the active help and support of buyers, funders and influencers of management education. These include government agencies, policy makers, alumni, parents and friends of students, decision makers in business and other organizations, media (with their rating and ranking reports), and accreditation agencies.

Four Avenues of Change

There are different ways the vision can be brought about. On one hand, stakeholders may force business schools to transform. On the other hand, change can occur as a result of voluntary and pro-active changes within business school and universities. Besides these triggers, we may consider two other avenues of change that can occur: new initiatives that emerge from the collaboration of stakeholders and existing players in management education, and the creation of new types of business schools in developing and emerging regions. The resulting four avenues can be summarised as follows:

Forced change: pressures from stakeholders may force institutions involved in management education to adapt their existing models and reflect on how they can transform their often rigid structures into an organizational form that fulfills the requirements of stakeholders. Such pressures may include reduced government financing or subsidies, a shift in preferences of future students, a demand for relevant undergraduate education from parents, donations from alumni to invest in programs and projects that serve society, or new rankings based on the three roles of management education. Furthermore, new criteria from accreditation agencies that report on organizational contributions to society or market shifts from developed to emerging countries may challenge existing models, culminating in entirely new educational approaches and ideas.

Institutional transformation: some existing players in the landscape of management education may already be both able and willing to adopt the vision and engage in a fundamental transformation process within their institutions. A key ingredient includes a governance structure that allows deep change, a prerequisite that many leading business schools and management departments within universities don't yet possess. However, many business schools may well be able to initiate such deep change. The transformation at Business School Lausanne, for example, has been detailed as a case study that may serve as an example of how other schools can embrace transformational change.[1] It may also be that innovative, far-sighted consulting companies, corporate universities or executive training centers with flexible structures will seize the opportunities and initiate change themselves. Such players already possess the capacity to organize themselves around the three new roles of the vision far more quickly than traditional business schools.

New initiatives: existing or new players may set up educational programs, applied multi-stakeholder research projects, or create a variety of collaboratories addressing critical global issues. These new initiatives can be stand-alone operations or serve as experiments within existing schools, institutes and consultancies. As each element of the vision requires a collaboration and transdisciplinary approach, we anticipate such initiatives to consist of innovative new collaborations both between players in management education and with other stakeholders within the concerned community. Such collaborations might kick off as temporary projects with a relatively casual form of collaboration. In time, some of these initiatives could evolve into stronger, more formal associations or joint ventures that shape new divisions or departments by bridging existing structures with new, more collaborative and open approaches.

Creation of new management schools: forward-thinking stakeholders may create management schools of the future in regions experiencing fast growth, including developing and emerging countries like India, China, South America, or the African continent. Such new schools will help address the issues of sustainable living on our planet, working in close collaboration with each other and spearheading completely new models – like providing free online management education to those who need it.

Naturally, predicting the future is not an exact science. It is exceedingly difficult to anticipate how these options will play out, given the potential for limitless creativity when a group of players sets their mind to embrace new roles of management education. The 50+20 project does not suggest that each and every player in management education embraces the three roles. Instead, we hope that institutions consider the 50+20 vision when reviewing their strategic visions, identifying new avenues of activities that are relevant in their fields of operation, thereby enabling them to serve society more effectively.

Radical approaches are traditionally reserved for the courageous. The 50+20 vision is dedicated to those members of our community who are ready and willing to play their part in transforming management education – either as a player, a stakeholder or as a concerned citizen.

KEY IMPLEMENTATION PRIORITIES

Our collaborative process has identified six key priorities for implementing the vision. In Table 9.1 we illustrate each of these with some suggestions for action, with the aim of triggering debate amongst players in the landscape of management education and the wider community:

Table 9.1 Key priorities for implementation with suggested actions

Priorities	Suggested actions
Faculty training and development Successful implementation depends on faculty developing a passion for teaching, learning and discovery. Equally, faculty should be at ease with transdisciplinary approaches, multi-stakeholder engagements and with engaging in public discourses, which requires different types of training and development programs. See *Towards a New Breed of Faculty* (Chapter 10)	● Setting up a global faculty development program for existing business school faculty ● New doctoral training programs for upcoming young academics ● Second faculty for activities that are important for society, including political assignments ● Encouraging faculty to dedicate their sabbaticals to projects in organizations of all kind, including emerging and developing countries for deep immersion ● Pairing academic faculty with teachers of various professional backgrounds to create new student learning environments and broaden the perspective of the faculty
Creating prototypes of the vision Setting up a variety of prototypes dedicated to one or several aspects of the vision enables testing how the new roles of management education can be interpreted and translated into action. The collaboratory plays a central role in many of these prototypes, both in their creation and incubation phase – as well as in shaping new forms of education, research and platforms for public engagement	● Securing funding for a number of new management schools around the world as showcases of the vision ● Creating pop-up business schools in developing and emerging countries ● Setting up a virtual management school offering free business and management education for anybody with a thirst to learn ● Creating a range of regional collaboratories on specific critical issues (e.g. the "Africa Leads" program in November 2012) ● Creating regional or global programs involving a number of institutions
Orienting research toward the common good Encouraging the development of collaborative research centers dedicated to transdisciplinary approaches, new future-oriented research methods, as well as new incentives and measures for researchers	● Supporting inter-disciplinary and transdisciplinary research centers ● Creating a library of reflection for professionals (both online and real) ● Organizing issue-based, in-company collaboratories to review strategic progress with engaged stakeholders

Table 9.1   (cont.)

Priorities	Suggested actions
New measures for management education Implementing the vision requires different incentives and measures of success. Management education organizations require alternate evaluation and ranking tools, such as new criteria for assessing the value and impact of research, and evaluation of criteria for measuring faculty contributions to society	● Developing a student-managed tool to rank business schools according to their review ("TripAdvisor for business schools") ● Developing new criteria for assessing the contribution of research to society (e.g. rating of journals or individual contributions) ● Creating new evaluation criteria for faculty, measuring their contribution to society (including hiring, promotions, creating incentives and funding opportunities)
Celebrating excellence An important engine to drive change is to create recognition and awards for successfully living the three roles of the vision. New projects, transformation on an institutional level as well as initiatives and engagements by faculty need to be widely communicated – and praised	● Creating awards in all relevant categories of implementing the three roles of the vision, both regionally and globally ● Celebrating the social engagement of faculty
Professionalizing the management of schools Management education providers are challenged to evolve towards professional management, supported by leadership that is experienced in change management and transformative organizational processes. Many existing senior leaders have not enjoyed appropriate exposure or training to successfully lead the change needed to accomplish such a transformation	● Developing executive development for existing administrative leaders (deans, vice presidents, chancellors, directors) rather than only new deans ● Support programme directors with embedding the vision across business school offerings

Looking beyond the above-mentioned priorities, we need to embed change across the broader fields of environment of education. The cost of providing education in most societies continues to rise. Nonetheless, a number of Western governments are cutting back on educational expenditures. At the same time, governments in some developing countries (such as India) have privatized education, leading to the establishment of an education industry in the private sector. In the United States, student debt exceeds the total amount of household debt and politicians rightly fear an escalation unless youth unemployment can be dramatically reduced. Unfortunately, higher education is rapidly becoming a privilege reserved for the rich. Management education providers should therefore be mindful of the affordability of education and make efforts to provide low-cost or free options for the most deserving students – particularly those in developing regions.

Management education must become affordable for the masses by leveraging digital technologies, peer-to-peer learning, governmental and foundation support for educational ventures. Business schools and other players need to target the most deprived sectors of global society as part of their regular bursaries, grants, and scholarships. One innovative approach to providing free education is exemplified by Berea College in Kentucky, where students perform work within the institution (in the library, kitchen, physical plant, construction, landscaping, medical centre etc.) for a certain number of hours each week. Such activities also teach students the dignity of work. Other examples are the Kofi Annan School of Business[2] and the Khan Academy.[3]

In addition, management educators need to embrace new avenues to provide education for those in need in emerging and developing countries. With 2–3 billion people joining the global middle classes in the coming decades, we are in urgent need of entrepreneurs and leaders in organizations of any type who can develop and propose solutions and services that serve these new consumers and respect the limits of the planet. Getting the education right in these emerging countries is critically important. In many regions, a practical problem about business schools is that there are so few of them. This creates interesting green field opportunities which can operate as a stand-alone operation or as a collaborative group of new schools operating globally. An online platform could serve as a virtual collaboratory for these schools and organizations, providing education for those who lack the means to afford such an education or to travel to an existing business school. Several excellent examples of educational initiatives already exist, such as the Barefoot College[4] and the International Institute for Social Entrepreneurs.[5] Educating future leaders in developing regions remains an unresolved challenge, representing a key priority for all players in management education.

PROCESSES OF ENGAGEMENT FOR OUR COMMUNITY

We can't change the world with a single grandiose epiphany. A one-size-fits-all solution is dangerous and highly prone to failure. Rather, we propose a *process* of engagement which provides participants with the freedom and flexibility to begin where their organization is currently placed, leaving open how they wish to implement concrete actions. Actors in management education will undoubtedly choose different paths and produce variable approaches that depend heavily on their missions, strategies, and circumstances.

A useful starting point to implement change is to examine an institution as it exists today and bring together involved players, including students, academics, administrators, business people, NGOs and government representatives. Together, such a group can explore how to turn the vision into action. Such a process may produce any number of outcomes, such as momentum to change the institution, combining with others to change the system, or individual actions.

Society interacts with management education in several ways. Governments may fund, license and accredit, utilize the knowledge created, or send their employees on training courses. Large corporations may sponsor, endow, pay for student bursaries, buy executive education, recruit graduates, fund research, hire consultants or sell goods and services to institutes of management education. Students and their parents or friends may select a university or program, voice their demand for certain courses or competences. Accreditation bodies decide on which criteria and standards schools are measured and evaluated, while media organizations report on the industry and issue annual ratings and rankings based on criteria of their choice. Finally, we should also consider policy makers, influencers across social media, alumni, donors and investors, all of whom choose which of the players they actively support.

Depending on the region, each player within a stakeholder group will identify different solutions that are appropriate and adequate locally or regionally. We have no pretense of knowing what is right for others. We prefer to suggest a process, rather than solutions that may at best come across as presumptuous or naïve. We therefore propose a *process of engagement* that allows each stakeholder to start at the exact point where their organization is right now, leaving it open just how far a stakeholder wants to go in testing options and implementing concrete actions.

That said, we need to be careful not to get wrapped up in "bolt on" solutions that serve as quick fixes in the current system; instead, we need to focus on the deep change needed to ensure that changes are "built in".

FROM TRANSITION TOWN TO TRANSITION BUSINESS SCHOOLS

The Transition Town process[6] offers an example of how a wide range of members of a community can engage in a change process that would be too complex for any single one player or organization. The goal of the Transition Town Movement is to mobilize communities, town and cities to transition towards a low carbon future. The Movement quickly realized that the key to success lies less in providing endless lists of detailed recommendations than developing and providing a method that enables anyone to initiate such a change in their community. The goal is to ignite the desire within a community to create and act on turning the vision into action at all levels: personal, institutional and systemic.

The 50+20 vision can also be interpreted as containing three different levels of engagement in its vision (see Chapter 5):

- **Personal level:** becoming a globally responsible leader.
- **Institutional level:** enabling business organizations to serve the common good.
- **Systemic level:** engaging in the public debate to transform business and the economy.

We are searching for ways to bring together people who are willing and able to engage in these different levels in order to co-create a different future together. The Transition Town Movement supplies a simple, yet powerful process of engagement which includes five stages:

1. **Starting out:** take the initiative by moving from idea to action.
2. **Deepening:** initiative gains momentum as practical projects emerge.
3. **Connecting:** initiatives are linked to other role-players and elements, infusing a systems-wide awareness.
4. **Building:** initiatives and projects act and think on a larger scale. Projects become enterprises.
5. **Daring to dream:** taking transition thinking and action to the next level: industry, nation, global.

The key learning from this process is its pragmatic perspective on the creation aspect, providing an advanced framework to the

old "forming, storming, norming, conforming, performing" paradigm of teams that may work well in an institutional framework
but displays clear limitations in a setting that builds on voluntary engagement. Pentland[7] at MIT provides ground-breaking
insights into how patterns of communication predict the success
of teams, demystifying the chemistry of high-performing groups
and opening new perspectives on how to collaborate effectively.

We anticipate that creating built-in solutions might be as challenging for
our stakeholders as for players in the field. We invite the various players
in management education to join forces with our extended stakeholders in
order for all of us to become members in a community of co-learners, in
an adventure on a road less traveled.

Tip Toe or Deep Dive?

A useful starting point for implementing change is to examine an institution as it exists today and bring together the people involved, including
students, academics, administrators, business people, NGOs and government representatives. Such a group could explore how to turn the vision
into action. The process may result in a number of outcomes, such as
momentum to change the institution, to combine with others to change the
system, or individual actions.

Two fundamentally different approaches can enable a process of
engagement. Some institutions may opt for a "tip toe" approach: testing
the waters by encouraging engagement with some elements of the vision,
while others will opt for a "deep dive" – a full commitment by making the
vision the fundamental basis for engagement in the field of management
education. Some activities can be oriented towards removing existing
barriers to implement the vision, while others may be directed toward
encouraging the emergence of innovative solutions.

Two fundamentally different types of activities may be considered.
One the one hand, we need to remove existing barriers to implement the
vision. At the same time we need to encourage emerging innovations,
and celebrate and showcase these initiatives. For example, if we imagine
investment banks launching a new category of investment funds called
"responsible investment", we may further envision that *all* investments
will be "responsible" as the critical number of investors will have understood that it makes no sense to invest in "irresponsible" funds.

Table 9.2 summarises the two broad levels of engagement for
governments and funders.

Table 9.2   Different levels of engagement for governments and funders

Stakeholders	Level of engagement	Illustrations
Governments	Tip toe	Evaluate your current system of how you provide your licenses to operate to providers of business and management education. How does this compare to the vision? What criteria do you use to provide funding? Do you have an evaluation system in place to measure if the funds are used in accordance with the vision?
	Deep dive	Redesign your licensing system for management education to serve the purpose of the vision. For example, provide grants only to institutions that measure up to providing responsible leadership for a sustainable world. Shift from distributing funds directly to individual institutions to providing your citizens (students, participants) with study coupons of a predetermined amount, allowing them to decide which institution they want to join in their life-long learning process.
Funders	Tip toe	Channel your funding to include some of the elements of the vision, such as devoting 10–20% of your budget to support initiatives in line with institutions that are transforming towards the vision.
	Deep dive	Allocate all of your funding in the domain of management education to players who have fully implemented or needs funds to complete the implementation of the vision.

Gap Analysis – A Potential Way Forward

One way to go about implementing change is by undertaking a simple yet effective gap analysis. Using the methodology of a collaboratory, players and stakeholders can mutually support and engage with each other to suggest ideas for implementation, collaboration and engagement. The emerging learning community can develop and co-create solutions that are beyond our current level of imagination.

In order to provide a framework for institutions, we highlight the essential steps of a gap analysis, as illustrated in Figure 9.2.

Identification of future requirements	Review of current situation in view of obstacles	Definition of concrete actions and potential opportunities	Choice of engagement
Identify which parts of the vision are related to your specific operation or business model.	Review your current operations in view of answers that you have developed in Step 1.	When comparing the previous two steps, list opportunities, potential actions and activities that appear interesting and suitable for your organization.	As a result of this gap analysis, determine how your organization best embraces the opportunities connected with the three roles of management education for the world.
In what way does the vision paint a different picture from how you previously imagined your engagement or involvement with management education?	To what degree is what you currently do different to what you could be doing?	Do you see new opportunities for collaboration with current or new partners, locally, regionally or globally?	How do these opportunities and potential actions match with how your organization currently functions?
How do the three newly defined roles apply to your organization?	Which of the activities you are currently engaged in would lend themselves to be transformed in this new direction? Which don't?	Are there other means you may have to help the vision to be realized?	Can you group them into such activities that a) represent a tip toe approach and b) represent a full engagement with the vision (deep dive)?
What avenues and opportunities do they offer or inspire?	What strengths does your organization possess that could be applied to develop a new field of activities, or a new way of engaging with management education?	How do you view regional versus global opportunities?	In which area do you have more items?
Imagine the vision was already a reality: would there be new activities for you to discover and develop?	What have you heard from other stakeholders in this arena, from your own customers, suppliers, collaborators and peers?	What could you do in your area of business right now? What could be done later?	What recommendations can you formulate for your organization as a result of these reflections?
What spontaneous thoughts occur when you read the vision both for yourself and your organization?	Is there an opportunity to reduce your weaknesses and threats by embracing a new strategic direction towards the vision?		What further study would you suggest, and how would you present this to your lead team and your organization?
	Does the vision enable you to look with new eyes at your existing operations? If so, what do you see?		
	Are comparable institutions already active in moving towards such new fields?		

Figure 9.2   Different levels of engagement for governments and funders

There are, of course, newer and more innovative methods such as Theory U[8] which complements the purely intellectual exercise of a gap analysis with other emotional and spiritual levels of awareness, and competes with most hands-on prototypes that instantly test new ideas. Working with Theory U and similar methods requires professional facilitation and a certain degree of training for everybody involved. Such a learning process can propel a team into new levels of cooperation, and strengthen its cohesion and ability to implement change together. Truly innovative solutions will go beyond re-envisioning the potential contribution of a single player or stakeholder. Such new ideas will include creating new rules of the game through changes in legislation and other transformative elements that can redefine a landscape.

Such an exercise can represent a considerable challenge, depending on the current situation of a stakeholder and their proximity to management education. We suggest using the most central element of the vision, the collaboratory, as a tool to undertake the gap analysis. An organization, institution or community interested in launching the process of engagement could set up a collaboratory event in order to jointly explore these questions and work towards the answers. Utilizing the collaboratory as a method not only assures an inclusive and comprehensive approach and high levels of engagement for an organization, but also provides an excellent opportunity to test the vision and discover its potential.

By using the collaboratory, players and stakeholders can mutually support and engage with each other to suggest ideas for implementation, collaboration and engagement. The emerging learning community (a collaboratory in itself) will develop and co-create solutions that are beyond our current level of imagination. We envision further expanding this existing platform to foster and share new ideas. Ideally, this would include the set-up and creation of both real and virtual collaboratory sessions and events. We further anticipate the emergence of many new of ideas and examples of how stakeholders can go about enabling change in management education.

PRME: A Process of Engagement for Players in Management Education

More than 400 business schools have signed up to the PRME principles[9] in their committment to engage in the process of transforming their schools towards sustainable and responsible management education. The 50+20 vision serves as a lighthouse on this journey of transformation. PRME provides a path of how to implement the six PRME principles towards the three roles of management education. As such, PRME can serve as a platform to measure progress, share best practices and promote success stories, and will hopefully attract and encourage more and more of the nearly 13 000[10] business schools worldwide to join this important initiative.

Table 9.3 shows how the six PRME principles are related to the roles and enablers of the 50+20 vision. Among the six PRME principles, Principle 1 on *purpose* and Principle 2 on *values* provide the bases for the other four principles related to *action*. Principle 3 on *method* shares a close affinity with one of the three roles in 50+20 vision, namely educating and developing globally responsible leaders, and its three enablers. Both Principles 4 on *research* and 5 on *partnership* are captured by the role of enabling business organizations to serve the common good, with one of its enablers being related to research and the other two to partnership. Finally, Principle 6 and the role of engaging in the transformation of business and society go hand-in-hand. The central feature of the 50+20 vision, the collaboratory, addresses all the four PRME principles (3–6) related to action.

Given the affinity of the 50+20 vision and the PRME principles, it makes good sense to closely correlate the implementation of the 50+20 vision with the PRME Management Model which is designed to help PRME signatories to implement strategies towards becoming responsible and sustainable institutions of management education.

PRME principles are, by definition, general guidelines that underpin action. In a process of continuous improvement, the principles are repeatedly redefined based upon the progress and status of implementation. PRME signatories can further implement the PRME principles by drawing upon 50+20 as a vision of the future, providing three relevant roles to be adopted depending on each institution's unique situation.

The PRME Management Model provides a procedure for implementing the 50+20 vision and the PRME principles through an effective process of continuous improvement. The model is based on a circular rather than a linear process, a spiral of continuous and ongoing improvement. Table 9.4 provides an overview of the PRME Management Model based both on the 50+20 vision and findings of a relevant research project.[11]

The 50+20 vision, with its three roles and related enablers, can serve as an inspirational basis for institutes in management education to create their own vision. Similarly, PRME signatories can refer to the 50+20 vision as an inspiration for implementing the six PRME principles. The 10 enablers of the 50+20 vision further may help PRME signatories to consider how to address the challenges of the later stages of the PRME Management Model. The collaboratory (see Chapter 5), a learning platform where both internal and external stakeholders collaborate to conduct action learning and action research in favor of new solutions, may prove particularly helpful in achieving tangible and lasting progress.

Table 9.3   Relating the Principles for Responsible Management Education (PRME) to the 50+20 vision

50+20 (the collaboratory is the central feature of the vision and can be considered the 10th enabler)		PRME 6 principles	
3 roles	9 enablers		
Educating and developing globally responsible leaders	✓ Transformative learning ✓ Issue-centered learning ✓ Reflective practice & field work	Principle 3: Method Create educational frameworks, materials, processes and environments that enable effective learning experiences for responsible leadership.	
Enabling business organizations to serve the common good	✓ Research for the common good	Principle 4: Research Engage in conceptual and empirical research that advances our understanding about the role, dynamics, and impact of corporations in the creation of sustainable social, environmental and economic value.	Principle 1: Purpose Develop the capabilities of students to be future generators of sustainable value for business and society at large and to work for an inclusive and sustainable global economy.
	✓ Supporting companies towards stewardship ✓ Accompanying leaders in their transformation	Principle 5: Partnership Interact with managers of business corporations to extend our knowledge of their challenges in meeting social and environmental responsibilities and to explore jointly effective approaches to meeting these challenges.	Principle 2: Values Incorporate the values of global social responsibility into our academic activities and curricula, as portrayed in international initiatives such as the United Nations Global Compact.
Engaging in the transformation of business and the economy	✓ Open access between academia and practice ✓ Faculty as public intellectuals ✓ Institutions as role models	Principle 6: Dialogue Facilitate and support dialog and debate among educators, students, business, government, consumers, media, civil society organizations and other interested groups and stakeholders on critical issues related to global social responsibility and sustainability.	

Table 9.4   The PRME Management Model – a framework for implementation

---

1. Identify – Identify key stakeholders to help in the initial steps of adoption and implementation of the PRME:
✓ *Internal stakeholders: administration, faculty, students*
✓ *External stakeholders: funders, buyers and influencer of management education*

2. Create a vision – Create a vision and identify the key aspects of the organization's activities that can be changed and what must be achieved in terms of the organization's operations and services (curriculum, research and advocacy), which may include:
✓ *Using the 50+20 vision as a basis*
✓ *Developing a relatively clear but flexible vision of future developments, as well as means of achieving them by including a set of goals and objectives*
✓ *Encouraging collaborative / shared leadership, wherein members of the organization are involved in the process of change from conception to implementation*

3. Develop Requirements – Read the PRME principles and 50+20 vision. Identify which parts are related to your specific operation or business model by asking the following questions:
✓ *In what way does the 50+20 vision paint a new or different picture from how we imagined our engagement with management education?*
✓ *How do the three newly defined roles apply to us. What avenues and opportunities do they offer or inspire?*
✓ *Imagine the vision were already a reality. What new fields can we discover and develop?*
✓ *What occurs spontaneously to us when we read PRME principles and 50+20 vision for ourselves and our organization?*

4. Review – Review your current operation in view of answers that you have developed in Step 3, and further ask the following questions:
✓ *To what degree is what we currently do different from what we* could *be doing?*
✓ *Which fields of activities we are currently engaged in would lend themselves to be transformed in this new direction? Which don't?*
✓ *What strengths does our organization possess that could be applied to develop a new field of activities or a new way of engaging with management education?*
✓ *What have we heard from other stakeholders in this arena, be it our own customers, suppliers, collaborators and peers?*
✓ *Is there an opportunity to reduce our weaknesses and threats by embracing a new strategic direction towards the vision?*
✓ *Does the vision enable us to look with new eyes at our existing operations? If so, what do we see?*
✓ *Is our competition already active in moving towards such new fields?*

Table 9.4 (cont.)

---

5. Develop systems – Develop operating, accountability and reporting systems to put the vision into practice, which may include:

✓ *Securing senior administrative support in terms of value statements, resources, or administrative structures that will facilitate the change process and enable it to occur more quickly*

✓ *Establishing activities and structures that support the change efforts by, for example, hiring an individual to oversee the effort, supplying a center or a program with money or personnel, and developing policies or procedures to facilitate the change initiative*

✓ *Changing the reward and promotion structure, including financial or other types of reward, recognition for staff, faculty development, and other activities for which the individual or department can use resources, specifically to support personnel change*

✓ *Developing staff and faculty development programs that provide opportunities for members of the organization to learn certain skills or gain knowledge related to the object of change*

6. Integrate – Integrate and align efforts across the organization and in its key decision-making processes (e.g. the organization's operations, curriculum or research) by forming a multi-stakeholder, multi-disciplinary approach team. Involve administrators, faculty and students, as well as:

✓ *Encouraging persuasive and effective (either one- or two-way) communication through which positional and non-positional leaders provide written and oral reports, concept papers, and/or newsletters outlining the initiative and its implementation*

✓ *Showcasing notable action related to the change process which demonstrates to the organizational members that the change process is ongoing and important*

✓ *Creating and maintaining learning platforms (collaboratories), where both internal and external stakeholders collaborate to conduct action learning and action research*

7. Assess – Assess (within a minimum every 24 months) and share progress with all stakeholders by asking the following questions:

✓ *Do we see new opportunities for collaboration with our current or new partners locally, regionally or globally?*

✓ *By what other means can we help realize the vision?*

✓ *What could we do in our area of business right now? What can we do later?*

✓ *How do these opportunities match with what our organization currently does? Can we group them into (a) options that resemble a first test of engagement with the vision ("tip toe"), and (b) opportunities that would represent a full engagement with the vision ("deep dive")? In which areas do we have more items and how does this feel to us? Do we judge our organization to be more in the tip toe or in the deep dive mode?*

✓ *What recommendations can we formulate for our organization as a result of these reflections? What further studies would we suggest, and how would we present this to our lead team and our organization?*

COMMUNITY ENGAGEMENT: ECLECTIC IDEAS FOR ALL STAKEHOLDERS

Our recommendations have been divided into the following stakeholder groups:

- **Buyers and clients** of management education include decision-makers, leaders and managers in organizations and companies of various sizes, and individual prospective students and their immediate influencers.
- **Influencers** include a broad range of players, including international and national accreditation bodies, the media, rating and ranking agencies, and civil society organizations (including social media).
- **Funders** of management education include those who directly or indirectly control funding towards management education, such as policy makers, alumni, donor agencies, foundations or wealthy individuals. Here we also consider governments in their specific capacity as issuers of licenses to operate.
- **Providers** of management education include existing business schools and institutions, universities, leadership and executive development centers, corporate universities, professional training institutes, research institutes, think tanks and academic and professional journals.

Buyers and Clients of Management Education

> Buyers of management education include organizations, companies and governments that hire and employ students of the management education system, the students themselves along with the people and groups that most directly influence their buying decision (such as parents and teachers). This group shapes and creates the demand for management education through their individual and collective decisions and behavior.

Decision makers, leaders and managers in companies and organizations
1. Require an approach within business schools to facilitate the transition from shareholder focus to serving the common good.
2. Recruit from business schools that are able to demonstrate that they are focused on developing globally responsible leaders (such as PRME signatories which communicate on progress).

3. Be pro-active in the definition of what kind of leaders you need. Demand clear proof of how executive training goes about providing this.
4. In every business function, hire only students who show competence and values which will focus on creating value for the common good.
5. Encourage and support your employees to engage in life-long personal and professional development.
6. Allow your managers and leaders to take time off to digest and learn from their experiences, and broaden their understanding and perspectives for future challenges.
7. Require business schools to create multi-stakeholder platforms to address existing and emerging societal, economic and environmental issues – and participate in them.
8. Encourage your leaders to collaborate with transdisciplinary research teams in business schools to advance critical societal issues, and to work on how to jointly contribute to the common good.
9. Review recommendations made by multi-stakeholder initiatives to launch new forms of collaboration between management education and business (see 30 good practice case studies in university-business cooperation from Science-to-Business Marketing Research Center, 2012[12]).

Students and their influencers (parents, friends etc.)

1. Make visible your commitment to education for the common good in all dealings with your schools. Demand that the schools' administration focus on the creation of value for society.
2. Demand courses, programs and placement opportunities from school administration and faculty which demonstrate a direct focus on addressing the challenges the world faces.
3. Demand provision and publication of relevant information regarding the competences and results of providers of management education.
4. Focus your evaluation criteria for choosing management education on the institution's capacity for personal development, practical relevance and impact.
5. Assume and practice co-ownership of the educational process.
6. Ask yourself what makes a globally responsible leader. Select the institution that invests most into developing these skills and competences.
7. Bring your entire "self" to school: not only your need for professional development but your whole person. Open yourself for an inclusive process of whole-person learning.

8. Combine your political and personal engagements with your business studies.
9. Encourage your school to join national and international frameworks for responsible management education, such as the PRME initiative.

Influencers in the Management Education Ecology

Media-produced ratings, ranking agencies as well as civil society organizations such as community groups or religious organizations all influence other stakeholder groups that operate within the management education ecology.

We classify accreditation bodies under this heading too but will treat their recommendations separately.

Currently, we only have a limited set of recommendations for rating and ranking agencies, mostly covering the perspective for a different kind of a system that is user based. This field needs to be further developed, and we recommend doing so directly in collaboration with existing ranking and rating agencies.

Accreditation bodies

1. Require that business schools state their views on the kind of world we are aiming to create, identify the gaps in their contribution – and how they are going to bridge these gaps.
2. Pro-actively downgrade schools which persist in the current paradigm.
3. Reward experimentation toward a societal value goal.
4. Support faculty training and programs that develop the identified new skills of faculty (coaching, facilitation, inter- and transdisciplinary research, collaborative research approach, issue-centered learning and action research, etc.)
5. Establish standards, benchmarks and guidelines for schools to move their curriculum, faculty retention and promotion, and institutional support towards fulfilling the three new roles of management education.
6. Revise accreditation criteria around the three roles of business education and identify key measures for these roles, in collaboration with concerned stakeholders of management education.

Rating and ranking bodies (both existing and new)
1. Significantly reduce the measure of income earned by students to balance it with contributions to the common good and other relevant measures.
2. Develop metrics which track contribution types that are in favor of creating of the kind of businesses and business system we need.
3. Re-organize rating criteria around the three roles of business education and identify key measures of these roles in collaboration with concerned stakeholders of management education.
4. Consider publishing ranking tools instead of fixed ranking, allowing readers to dynamically weigh ranking criteria instead of accepting the published ranking (and its implied weighings) as the final word.
5. Establish measuring standards in accordance with the three roles of management education, enabling different players to excel either in a selected individual role – or across all three roles.
6. Include responsible management/sustainability criteria based on PRME in rating standards.
7. Work with stakeholders on how to define measuring standards for these roles.
8. Integrate a flexible measuring tool that has change and adjustments built in, as a safeguard against institutions only adapting change on a superficial level.
9. Work with future buyers of management education on relevant categories of selection, allowing a personalized rating for each user in accordance with their priorities.
10. Enable buyers to self-rate schools based on criteria that change as a matter of their choice (a management education advisor similar to TripAdvisor or wiki ratings).

Other influencers (social media and others)
1. Engage with business schools and challenge them on their contribution to the common good. Evaluate them regularly.
2. Create an association of graduates (possibly through alumni organizations) that serve to uphold the professional standard of management graduates.
3. Such an association would seek empowerment to judge on irresponsible behavior of its members and potentially determine sanctions, including the withdrawal of a provided degree or diploma (similar to other professional groups).
4. Demand continued education of all members of such an organization to ensure that their professional levels are kept up-to-date (already a standard practice in many other fields and professions).

5. Lobby governments to transform the licensing criteria for business schools to ensure they serve society first and foremost. See the ESDN Quarterly Report 26: http://www.sd-network.eu/?k=quarterly%20 reports#qr353.
6. News providers and popular media can work to expose management education's lack of critical distance, as per the recent documentary *Inside Job* (2010).

Funders of Management Education

Foundations and donors (including organizations or individuals) that donate to existing schools or enable the creation of new business schools, as well as the policy makers who determine public spending, share the ability to incentivize a new direction for management education.

We need to acknowledge the diversity of institutions that operate in the management education landscape and the various funding models (public / private / corporate), as well as government legislation that determines how funding is directed. Funding can come from the parent university, multi-lateral organizations, donations, grants, endowments, gifts, tax incentives, trusts, pension funds or be self generated. Each player needs to evaluate which levers will provide the most effective change.

Overall recommendations
1. Align funding criteria to 50+20 vision and three identified roles of management education.
2. Only donate funds to business schools that are on the leading edge of providing responsible leadership for a sustainable world.
3. Support the creation of platforms of dialogue and collaboration between academics and societal stakeholders to shape public dialogue in order to transform the economic system for business organizations to serve the global good (such as stock exchange versus social value exchange in Australia).

Government agencies and ministries of education
1. Provide broad access to low-cost business and management education for the so-called bottom of the pyramid.
2. Reconsider the concept of subsidies: (a) What institution gets what level of subsidies? (b) What are the requirements and conditions

for obtaining subsidies (linked to the three roles of management education)?, and (c) Are subsidies directly provided to educational institutions or citizens?

3. Direct funding agencies (typically acting at arm's length from government) to ensure that research grants are targeted toward research that yields an overall net positive contribution to society and that, upon publication, such research is readily available to those who may benefit from it.

4. Only donate funds to business schools that are on the leading edge of providing responsible leadership for a sustainable world.

5. Urge management education bodies such as associations of business schools and quality assurance agencies to identify ways in which the 50+20 vision can be incorporated into quality standards.

6. Distinguish between the roles as employer (who essentially consumes management education) and the policy maker / funder (who directs public spending towards management education).

7. Consider tailored programs for state-owned enterprises.

8. Train political personnel in business and management within the 50+20 vision.

9. Include responsible management / sustainability criteria based on PRME in rating standards.

Policy makers and influencers

1. Governments are urged to legislate towards management education that has a broader reach and applicability, addresses social and environmental issues as the core of its focus, and follows a collaborative approach in formulating and delivering its research and education agenda.

2. Develop standards to ensure engaged and transformative learning in business and management education.

3. Engage with civic society around the 50+20 principles and leverage CSOs as a potential channel for delivery of management education.

4. Demand the integration of service learning to link education and societal issues.

5. Integrate ethical reflection and decision making training into business education.

6. Adapt recruitment and performance evaluation systems of faculty. Provide training for junior and senior faculty to enable the development of globally responsible leaders.

7. Provide broad access to low-cost business and management education for the so-called bottom of the pyramid.

8. Develop teaching and research material addressing issues related to emerging and developing countries.
9. Reward educational projects that provide entrepreneurial education for emerging leaders at the bottom of the pyramid.
10. Promote and support research addressing societal, environmental and economic issues, both on a global and local scale.
11. Adapt measurement and reward systems for research to ensure future orientation, societal relevance and stakeholder inclusion.
12. Support the creation of platforms of dialogue and collaboration between academics and societal stakeholders to shape the public dialogue in order to transform the economic system for business organizations to serve the common good.
13. Demand and reward academics who actively play the part of public intellectuals.
14. Support ministerial and political advisors (including speech writers) in delivering ministerial statements that reflect the 50+20 vision.

Alumni, donators and investors (private, public)
1. Demand that your business school becomes a preferred meeting place for stakeholders to address societal issues. Participate in these events.
2. Donate your resources to activities and projects in business schools that serve the common good.

Providers of Management Education

The term *business school* represents multiple organization types, ranging from components of state universities through to commercial for-profit training organizations. These recommendations offer scope for any organization engaged in management teaching or research to take action without waiting for society to force change upon them.

We have not developed recommendations for universities, leadership or executive development centers, corporate universities, professional training institutes, research institutes, think tanks, and professional journals. A great deal of work remains to be done in these spheres; we recommend that these are either developed by the stakeholder groups directly through a gap analysis, or that we organize a variety of collaboratory events where such suggestions can be developed via a multi-stakeholder approach.

Existing business schools

1. Develop suitable criteria for evaluation and tenure of faculty that are mindful of their contribution to society and its challenges. Introduce new reward, recognition and promotion systems for faculty to shift current narrow subject focus in research and teaching to future-oriented, broader issue-based research serving the common good. Encourage and reward the faculty to participate in the public debate around a diverse range of societal, economic and environmental issues.

2. Provide development training to faculty to equip them with the knowledge and skills to operate in an environment of collaboration. Retrain faculty to research, teach and collaborate in multi-dimensional teams, across disciplines and nations on broader issues (see Chapter 10).

3. Open the borders between academia and business professionals to create a rich environment in which theory meets practice to resolve burning and relevant societal issues, including economic and business challenges.

4. Introduce the collaboratory as a new form of learning and research. Set up a flat central space in your school where issues can be discussed. Become an expert in open learning methodologies.

5. Shift the teaching body from academic subject experts only to a rich mix of experts, including professional entrepreneurs and innovators with first-hand experience in business and management in SMEs and MNCs in emerging, developing and developed markets and industries – as well as in other disciplines (such as philosophy, history, biology, arts). Introduce coaches and trainers as recognized equals into the teaching body in charge of developing the personal leadership aspects of future leaders.

6. Shift the focus from conveying segmented subject knowledge to encouraging and accompanying a life-long learning of interconnected, systemic entrepreneurial and action-oriented scenario thinking and doing. Recognize externally and alternatively acquired subject knowledge through validation of expertise and facilitated entry credits.

7. Challenge the underlying assumptions of every discipline and open up learning space for alternative, critical, common good-oriented approaches to every topic. Remove anything which accepts the underlying principles of the present system as inherently valid. Value and valorize pluralistic economic thinking and alternative economic systems. Turn down the hyper "free market" ideology underlying most business school curricula.

8. Replace standard subject or case-based curricula with unique issue-centered learning journeys, both on campus and in the field for all advanced courses in business, entrepreneurship and management. Develop projects that get students to engage in real-life learning opportunities that have the bottom of the pyramid concerns at their core.

9. Introduce personal development through whole-person and experimental learning as a pathway to leadership development. Replace auditorium lectures with smaller class sizes for experiential learning.

10. Elevate students from recipients of knowledge ("empty buckets") to co-learners in a mutual journey. As a result of this mind shift, stop calling these co-learners "students" – rather call them "participants" to anchor the desire of teachers, to create a powerful and safe environment where the joint learning adventure can unfold.

11. Develop new conceptual frameworks, models and theories that integrate sustainability into functional areas of finance, accounting, marketing, management, strategy and operations / decision sciences. Develop sustainability case studies, simulations and embodied learning exercises for use in classes. Redesign all subject knowledge courses to include holistic and transdisciplinary perspectives including ethics, culture and sustainability. Replace conventional and old teaching materials and content with new thinking that focuses on ethics, sustainability and social engagement.

12. Initiate platforms (such as the collaboratory) for exchange, discussion and problem solving for all concerned stakeholders (including students) of existing and emerging broader societal, economic and environmental issues. Examine relationships between traditional research topics in your area and the challenges the world needs to address to create a socially just and environmentally sustainable system.

13. Create transdisciplinary research units (diverse business subjects with arts, engineering and science) to investigate, test and propose alternative avenues for organizations to address societal, environmental and economic challenges. Adjust research definition, execution and reporting to a collaborative effort with stakeholders (corporations, government, NGO, civil society) and conduct transdisciplinary action research.

14. Join and engage in PRME and similar organizations to share best practices in relevant meetings, projects and working groups.

Academic journals
1. Include practicing managers and other societal roleplayers on editorial boards to ensure direct relevance and applicability of the research agenda to societal challenges.
2. Expand citation indexes and ranking systems to include measures for applied research.
3. Assume leadership in transforming current research into a field that serves society.
4. Embrace new forms of dissemination of knowledge and acknowledge research that gets wide acceptance through social media (measured in number of downloads, Twitter and blog discussions).

Over the past few years many of these ideas have already been established as best practice in individual fields. When looking back at half a century of changes in education, the limiting factor for change seems less about the lack of new ideas rather than the ability and will to implement them effectively. The limiting success factor is connected to the challenge of developing a faculty capable of playing the three roles that we have identified in the vision. If we want to develop responsible leaders for a sustainable world, institutes of management education must start by providing leadership.

The dilemma of requiring a different type of faculty serving as a custodian on behalf of society is similar to the problem of transforming business organizations. Corporations need different kinds of executive leaders to transform business organizations from their current short-term profit maximization focus to serving the common good. We need leaders in all organizations – both in business and in management education – who have the awareness and openness to engage in a personal as well as institutional process of transformation.

Chapters 10 and 11 analyse two critical areas of implementation: a new breed of faculty and a new type of business school. These examples provide not only further insights into the challenges of implementing the vision but also further illustrate the gap between the current status and the desired state in management education. We also highlight the PRME Management Model as a procedure for management education institutions to engage in a process of transformation towards the 50+20 vision.

NOTES

1. Kassarjian (2012).
2. www.kofiannanbusinessschool.org.
3. The Khan Academy was founded by Sal Khan and is supported by the Gates Foundation, www.khanacademy.org.

4. The Barefoot College was founded by Bunker Roy in 1972: www.barefootcollege.org.
5. The International Institute for Social Entrepreneurs is a project by Braille Without Borders: www.kanthari.org.
6. The transition town process offers a powerful process of engagement: www.transition-network.org/ingredients.
7. Pentland (2012).
8. Theory U was developed by Otto Scharmer: more information at www.presencing.com.
9. www.unprme.org.
10. AACSB (2011: 52, Table 2.3).
11. Conducted by International Centre for Corporate Social Responsibility at Nottingham University Business School.
12. European Commission (2012).

10. Towards a new breed of faculty

> Problems cannot be solved by the same level of thinking that created them.
>
> Albert Einstein

Broadening the skills, experiences and competencies of faculty represents the single biggest step in achieving the 50+20 vision. Business schools are urged to create conditions that trigger faculty's intrinsic motivation to grow and develop. Creating an environment that promotes change and an appetite for learning and development is one aspect. The next challenge lies in the creation of effective training and re-training programs for both new and existing faculty.

One of the critical levers for transforming current institutions in general and business schools in particular hinges on developing a new breed of faculty. We will follow the first three steps of the process of engagement suggested in Chapter 9, namely:

1. Identification of future requirements.
2. Review of current situation in view of obstacles.
3. Definition of concrete actions and potential opportunities.

We don't pretend to have solved this challenge. For the time being, we submit suggestions as a means of launching dialogue and debate. Many more are necessary and will need to be developed in the near future. Providing a vision is merely a first step in a long process of transformation.

IDENTIFICATION OF FUTURE REQUIREMENTS

The faculty of the future needs advanced facilitation, coaching and mentoring skills to complement traditional lecturing. We encourage an "and-and" rather than an "either-or" approach, moving beyond the currently dominant dichotomous perspective. Business schools will need to encourage exchanges and collaborations between academics and practitioners to an extent where their differences dissolve, replaced with evolved professionals who routinely cross from one role to another. In effect, the future faculty will serve as institutional role models for social entrepreneurship.

Five main areas need to be considered when creating a faculty that is ready to embrace the vision:

A Professional Commitment to Serve the Common Good

Today, professors largely pursue their own agendas, which includes furthering their research reputation, being recognized as an effective teacher, or serving the school in an administrative function. The orientation of this commitment and level of ambition are largely defined by the professor himself. A professional framework for management education must not only define the professional understanding and responsibilities of professors but include a professional commitment to serve the common good. This commitment for the common good goes beyond educating students as future leaders, consulting companies assuring their success, or assuring one's own institution's administration. Such a commitment must further include a professional commitment to educate globally responsible leaders for the world, to enable business organizations to serve the common good and to engage in the transformation of business and the economy.

A Commitment to the Mission of the School

Professors identify more closely with the network of their chosen discipline, rather than with their institution. The rigidity of these disciplines partitions both individual professors and the institution into separate fiefdoms which hinder the creation and transmission of knowledge across multiple fields. According to Gigerenzer, "one of the worst things that has happened is that people identify with a discipline or a sub-discipline in a way like members of a political movement identify with their party".[1] These narrow orientations need to be replaced with a commitment to the mission and purpose of the school as an overarching purpose. Such a re-orientation is a question professional identity, but also of school policy, structure and incentive systems.

A Passion for Teaching, Learning and Discovery

Future faculty members need to be recruited for their passion for teaching, learning and discovery. The role of a professor is to challenge the minds and imaginations of their co-learners: their students. As a result, the faculty should considers itself as a "lead-learner" rather than a holder of knowledge. Teachers of the future will be ready to innovate and experiment. For them, to teach is to be in the moment with an idea, in the presence of – and fully present with – other learners. Such a moment contains vulnerability, freedom and possibility. In effective learning environments, anything can happen and often does. We can no longer rely on traditional academics, business practitioners and coaches sitting around a table. Instead, we require a transformation of each future member of faculty in order to enlarge their own competences beyond a current domain specific specialization. We suggest that each member of faculty embraces the following competences, skills and attitudes:

- A concern for broad, up-to-date, transdisciplinary knowledge of existing and emerging environmental, social, technical and economic trends worldwide.
- Exposure to emerging practices and tools for measuring and evaluating economic, environmental and social concerns across all fields of business.
- Knowledge of applying basic management disciplines, matched with knowledge of ethics, entrepreneurship, leadership, sustainability and technology.
- Interdisciplinary business knowledge across all subject areas to ensure critical, well-balanced and relevant business thinking.
- Strong coaching competence and skills to ensure personal learning and development.
- Expertise in the methodologies of action learning and the creation of effective action learning platforms, as well as whole person learning and person-centered learning.
- Mastery of systemic thinking and risk analysis, together with other approaches which enable holistic decision making in a fast-changing environment.
- Networking capabilities to establish fieldwork projects in partnership with a broad range of stakeholders worldwide.

A Strong Interest in Issue-based Research and Action Research Methods

Management research should encourage and develop a plurality of methodologies, and accept a diversity of qualifying backgrounds (doctoral training and practical experience). The overall goal is to enable rigorous as well as relevant research. Important skills and attributes of the research faculty of the future include:

- Close contact with business leaders and societal thought leaders to ensure that research is conceived and developed in partnership with relevant stakeholders.
- An eagerness to become involved in issue-based research.

- Experience of / openness to action research methods[2] and a willingness to apply them in research projects.
- A passion for making a relevant contribution to those with and for whom one conducts research, and to publish both for an academic and a broader audience.
- The ability to use digital technology in producing and disseminating research results.
- Competency in both qualitative and quantitative research methods.
- A commitment to translating research findings into lively discussions and debates.

Diverse Experiences, Skills, Backgrounds and Interests

The faculty team of the future demonstrates diverse skills and backgrounds. Some of them have backgrounds as managers, coaches, facilitators or consultants, while others have strong academic credentials. Each team member complements and develops their knowledge, experience and capabilities in a process of life-long learning, identifying and working with other faculties from different disciplines.

Within this broad mix, some professors retain a passion in research. For others, it is teaching and learning with backgrounds as facilitators, lead learners and coaches. All members of faculty are of equal stature, working together to help participants to frame challenges associated with an issue-centered approach while embracing the broader curricula and relevant research.

To achieve this, a great deal of work must be done to identify a broad-based network of associates who may be employed on a part-time or full-time basis. The integration of part-timers in a school's culture and institutional activities represents an important challenge that requires careful study.

REVIEW OF CURRENT SITUATION IN VIEW OF OBSTACLES

A successful implementation of the vision depends crucially on the capacity of the faculty to embrace the three identified roles, namely: educating and developing globally responsible leaders, enabling business organizations to serve the common good, and engaging in the transformation of business and the economy.

When we compare the current capacity of the faculty in institutions of management education (including business schools) with the identified requirements for fulfilling the three roles of the vision, we uncover an important gap. We will examine the current situation in faculty, the requirements to embrace the three roles of management education, and concrete suggestions on how to close the gap.

Several major differences between basic types of business schools – such as governance, financing, purpose, orientation, integration, outlook, size and ownership – make it impossible to generalize the challenges in faculty management. In addition, non-academic institutions such as commercial providers, specialized institutes or corporate universities tend to define their faculty requirements quite differently to academic institutions. Such institutions are rarely tied to formal accreditation procedures, nor do they issue academic degrees. These players normally don't develop their own faculty, but rather rely on available faculty resources on the market – be it academic faculty, managers or consultants. Their higher degree of freedom shows considerable diversity with regards to their faculty structure and management, which is specifically tied to their institutional objectives.

In this chapter, we analyse the faculty of traditional business schools, as the diversity of conditions and requirements in non-academic institutions does not allow for simple generalizations. Despite wide diversity in the business school world, they do share common academic standards and rules that are subject to national or international accreditation or quality control standards. This selection is biased in favor of accredited schools, as accreditation standards spell out requirements for faculty management and development that can be generalized. We differentiate between institutional (AACSB, EQUIS) and program (ACBSP, AMBA, EPAS) accreditations, the former looking at all aspects of a school while the latter has a slightly limited perspective on the performance of different programs that favor the educational elements of faculty over a bias for research. It is important to note that only a minority of the nearly 13 000 business schools worldwide are accredited.

Our analysis of the current faculty situation focuses on the three key obstacles that prevent an easy implementation of the vision:

- A missing professional, values-based framework.
- Shortcomings in faculty training and development programs.
- Limitations of the current recruitment and promotion system.

A Missing Professional, Values-based Framework

While the question regarding the nature of the managerial profession has been a hotly contested issue since the beginning of management education over a hundred years ago,[3] the question about the nature of the profession of business school *faculty* has not really been addressed. In the meantime, consulting and auditing firms have developed into professional service firms with a clear code of conduct for their members. Why has this never happened for business school faculty or management educators in general? What if we imagine business schools as professional service firms?

When attempting to critically review the professional framework of the business school faculty that is values-based, we find that we cannot refer to any established model. Despite some attempts by professional associations to define specific codes of conducts covering professional ethics,[4] there is no accepted and shared professional framework that defines the responsibilities of business and management faculty in a broader sense of purpose and professionalism. We believe that a professional, values-based framework is of crucial importance for the future of the profession, which would address issues such as:

Defining the faculty's responsibility towards the common good and the values upon which such standards are based

Academic faculty enjoys a tremendous amount of freedom in their teaching and research, particularly after being granted tenure. This freedom ought to be bound to the common good that reaches beyond the demands and expectations of direct stakeholders such as students or companies. It further needs to include an ethical responsibility towards the general public. We need to debate where such responsibilities come from, and what values they are based upon. As an industry, we are currently missing a place to debate and define them. We require a process that allows us to implement and control responsibilities effectively, and keep them alive by updating and renewing them in ongoing discussions and debates around the underlying standards of ethics and values.

Clarifying the values upon which professional standards for effective teaching are based

We need to define how business graduates are prepared for the professional demands and challenges of twenty-first century business. As a community, we should discuss how we can get graduates prepared to perform in a multinational and multicultural environment. We further need to address current shortcomings in how graduates are prepared to perform in a public arena, given how surveys indicate that business students manifest only a weak understanding of – and even weaker concern for – the larger society in which they function.[5] Finally, we need to jointly create effective ways for the business faculty to seriously embrace its societal responsibility, as the financial and economic crises of the past five years have obviously not been used for a reform in teaching.[6]

Establishing the source of professional standards for effective research

The business academic community needs to define how researchers and professional associations can live up to their public responsibility, mitigating the fact that scholarly research is read almost exclusively only by other scholars. Next, we need to identify pathways to overcome the current situation where crucial areas for research concern the business impact on society, and how business can contribute effectively to solving societal problems, are broadly neglected. Further, we need to find means to embrace research and consulting approaches needed to contribute effective societal solutions, such as interdisciplinary and future-oriented research.

Developing professional standards for public service

If we are assuming that business faculty members should play a role as public intellectuals, we will further need to determine what that role means and how it can be performed. We as a community are challenged to ensure that this important function is no longer ignored or belittled. We should engage in discussions on how to promote the role of the public intellectual in light of the other roles which are either better controlled (teaching) or considered more personally rewarding (research).

Upgrading existing professional standards to assure a continuous update and development of the faculty

International accreditation agencies include faculty development in their standards. We need to review the effectiveness of these standards in ensuring the continuous development of faculty skills in all areas required, including areas such as leadership, facilitation and coaching, transdisciplinary collaboration, communication and information technology in order to determine better proposals and suggestions.

These issues indicate the size and challenge of the discussions and debates that must take place in order to identify, prioritize, test, implement, adapt and continuously adapt effective solutions towards the development of a meaningful, values-based professional framework of business and management faculty world-wide.

Shortcomings in Faculty Training and Development Programs

Business school faculty is trained in highly specialized doctoral programs. The higher the academic ambitions of the school and their faculty, the higher their focus on academic rigor and specialized scientific expertise. As a consequence, the programs frequently lack sufficient breadth of understanding of real-world business problems. Their graduates will not be able to understand how diverse factors and functions in real-world business situations interact to influence these problems.

Many discipline-trained scholars joining business school faculties today are not intrinsically interested in solving practical problems in business and society. Instead, they increasingly investigate theoretical and conceptual problems in the discipline of their expertise. As a consequence they view other academics – rather than practicing managers or society – as their main constituency. The goal of producing practically relevant knowledge about organizations, their management and their societal impacts has been displaced by ever narrower, specialist theories. Scholars identify with the narrow academic discipline or specialty they were trained in, very often not knowing what happens in other specialty areas, nor expressing any interest in engaging outside of their niche. This specialization process creates different academic niches for scholars, effectively separating them from each other and preventing not only broader understanding of issues, but also collaborations between different specialists.

Today, academically qualified core faculty often lacks relevant work experience and have little to no regular contact with practicing managers or public officials. Even if they were motivated to study real-world problems, they rarely have the knowledge and the experience to do so effectively. Instead, core faculty usually concentrate on the narrow technical specialties of the business function, or the topical area they were trained in. This type of faculty does not appreciate the complexities and subtleties of real business problems. How can they teach business in a relevant way without their students feeling deprived of deep insights into the business world and the practice of management? And how are they supposed to frame their research problems in a way that leads to insights that are relevant for problem solving?

The same criticisms apply to a deeper understanding and insight into societal challenges and their impact on business. These are topics and perspectives that are even further removed from traditional business faculty training. How then can faculty make practically relevant and socially useful contributions to solving current problems if they are neither aware of these issues nor trained to integrate them into their research and teaching?

A problematic aspect of business faculty training concerns the conspicuous absence of a formal training and professionalization process that goes beyond demonstrated research performance in a highly specialized field. Once on the job, they are expected to serve a highly diverse set of functions, without any real training, performing the roles of educators, coaches, leaders, project managers, communicators and public experts. We therefore need to develop new spaces and new means to train future management faculty in the basic requirements of their future job. We must introduce and engage them in the debate around professional principles and responsibilities of their task. At the same time, we must also ensure that faculty, once appointed, can keep up with the changing contexts and demands of their job. To be more precise, we must urgently discuss and debate concrete and effective solutions to very important questions that we – as a business and management faculty worldwide – are challenged to develop and implement, including:

- *Where do business faculties get their pedagogical skills?* Where do they learn to teach students, to create effective learning environments, to inspire and motivate them, and serve as role models in their personal development? Where do business faculties learn to serve as effective facilitators, coaches and mentors in their learning and development? Where do they learn how to reflect on and assess their impact in the teaching field?
- *Where do business faculties get their leadership skills?* Where do they learn to lead diverse teams and manage creative processes and projects? Where do they learn to collaborate with stakeholders, across boundaries of geographic, cultural and organizational nature, and to embrace inter- and transdisciplinary research? Where do they learn to inspire, motivate and lead young researchers and serve as coaches and mentors in their development? Where do they learn to lead assistants and administrative personnel?
- *Where do business faculties get their communication skills?* How can they learn to translate their communication skills inside business schools and within their academic and professional circles to become effective communicators in highly diverse external and public arenas? How do they learn how to become effective public intellectuals – and how are they prepared for this role?
- *Where do business faculties get their technological skills?* Information technology and social media are fundamentally transforming all activities from teaching to research, communication, administration, including the daily job and routines of faculty themselves. How will they keep up these skills during their careers? In particular, how can we ensure professors match these skills at comparable levels of their own students?
- *Where does business faculty learn to reflect on their own assumptions, activities and roles?* Business faculty finds itself in the middle of dynamic changes in every domain of their work. These changes are and will remain very challenging on a personal, professional and organizational level. At the same time, young professors are aspiring

to receive tenure, securing their jobs for a lifetime. Tenure can only preserve its useful purpose if the faculty is able to remain as dynamic on a personal level as external changes demand.

Some of these responsibilities could potentially be covered in doctoral programs or schools, but currently their focus is mostly on developing research skills. Other responsibilities may be developed by faculty advisors. Ultimately, most of the listed responsibilities rest with the individual professor – it is left to them to embrace these changes, or not. Unfortunately, the current training model continues to promote over-specialization in the research field – and a surprisingly unprofessional approach in most other functions.

Limitations of the Current Recruitment and Promotion System

More shortcomings in faculty training and development programs may be found within the current recruitment and promotion system in business schools. Several issues need to be addressed:

Redefining faculty selection and promotion procedures beyond their narrow focus on research performance
Faculty appointments at leading business schools have always depended on the research performance of the prospective faculty, a trend that has increased in importance over recent years.[7] One of the underlying drivers for this skewed focus on research is the connection of a business school's reputation, its input in particular publications and thus research performance.[8] If we want a different faculty with different skills, we must redefine faculty selection, development and promotion procedures that are closely connected to these new skills. We are challenged to find ways to create a scenario where tenured faculty from another era (and selected for different skills) are no longer sole decision-makers on the appointment and promotion of junior faculty.

Increasing the importance on teaching competences
We cannot expect research competencies to automatically translate into *teaching* competencies. Research has shown there is no correlation between research productivity and teaching effectiveness on a faculty level.[9] As a result, an institute of management education is often left with the uncomfortable choice of either investing more into its research base, or into their teaching staff. The reality of ranking-based reputation building and faculty preferences for research make it challenging for institutions to focus on improving their level of education. Indeed, as long as teaching

is looked upon as inherently inferior to research inside academia, business schools will continue to be pressured from within to over invest in expensive research, at the expense of their teaching quality.

Enhancing the importance on practical competences of faculty
While faculty is mainly trained to conduct research, daily challenges demand the ability to perform a multitude of practical roles: be it as educators, coaches, leaders, project managers, change agents, communicators and public experts. These capabilities are not systematically integrated into faculty development and promotion systems. The resulting unprofessionalism as a result of deficits in training faculty cannot be allowed to continue, but the problem persists as a result of deficits in the promotion system.

Restructuring incentive systems and reward structures for faculty away from a strong focus on research performance
The strong focus on research performance stems from the growing influence of market incentives through accreditations and rankings, which often take research as their yardstick. Research is mostly seen as a source of innovation and the core competence of a school, which is reflected in its teaching, advice to companies and public contributions. While this may be true, we often focus on the wrong kinds of research topics. Heavy investment and cross-subsidies from other areas of income into faculty research do not always achieve these goals. The general preference by faculty to conduct research may well be a major driver for this imbalance.

Overcoming life-time employment (tenure) as a potential obstacle for change
Academics undoubtedly enjoy the institution of tenure that leads to securing life-time employment – a rare privilege they share with almost no other profession. The faculty as a whole awards tenure once a candidate has fulfilled certain scholarly achievements. While tenure is awarded by public universities, many private business schools have freed themselves from the implied rigidities. Tenure is meant to guarantee the integrity of research from external infringements. It is worth asking ourselves whether lifetime employment is indeed necessary to protect scholarship, particularly if research is addressed to peers and mostly lies beyond the grasp of outside audiences! Paradoxically, tenure which is supposed to protect free inquiry may even discourage intellectual audacity among the young who often fear to leave the disciplinary mainstream as defined by their academic elders. Established faculty are tempted to recognize and appreciate this

form of loyalty among aspiring young academics, resulting in favoring intellectual conservatism. Tenure has also proven to be a main obstacle to organizational change in general, as the faculty holds considerable power to resist anything that may challenge or change their prerogatives and personal interests.[10]

CONCRETE ACTIONS, POTENTIAL OPPORTUNITIES

The real work of translating the 50+20 vision starts now: the requirements and the obstacles are clear and the challenge is tangible – yet the solutions need to be invented, tried, tested and improved in a continuous circle of improvement and daring innovation.

In-depth subject expertise across all the fields of business are likely to remain important. Such expertise are necessary but are no longer sufficient. The development and retraining of current faculty represents a significant challenge as business schools almost exclusively hire and train subject experts. These experts have traditionally shown little interest in revisiting or reframing their fields and knowledge to adapt to a new, broader context.

A central element of the successful implementation of the vision is the creation of a training and development platform for a different form of education and research. Such a platform would serve business schools in re-training their existing faculty to work as lead-learners in education and research of the management school for the future. A related challenge concerns the training and development of the next generation of faculty which could form an integral part of such a training platform. We envision such a training and development platform as either an integral part of a management school or a group of management schools – or as a separate service organization working on a regional or global level. As training both existing and new faculty represents a collective challenge, professional associations like EFMD, AACSB or academic associations like the Academy of Management could support the creation of regional or global training platforms. Collaboration with existing providers of transformational learning, leadership or coaching training could well speed up the creation of off-site training and development centers for existing and potentially new faculty.

The following ideas are provided as suggestions on how such a faculty training and development platform could look. We hope these suggestions will help spark discussion on the topic and encourage training and development providers to develop related models.

Re-training Existing Business School Faculty

Given the critical importance to include existing faculty in the transformation process, we envision a process that equips interested and open-minded faculty with the range of skills, competences and knowledge to become leaders and role models in their institutions. To get started, it would make sense to select faculty with a personal affinity, drive and curiosity in personal development.

Specifically, we recommend launching immersion programs that take place in off-campus locations around the world. The more inspiring the location, the better, be it the south of France, Italy, North Africa, India, Indonesia, Florida, California – or indeed anywhere in the world. Each faculty member would develop a transdisciplinary research project involving collaboration with other out-of-field colleagues as well as concerned stakeholders, directly experiencing how to go about creating a collaboratory and how to successfully interact in them. We offer two examples for a short-term and a longer-term training program that could easily be aligned with a summer break project or a sabbatical. There is no need to design rigidity into such a system. Learning is, after all, a very personal matter and can only be successful if and when the learner is ready for it.

Immersion programs
50+20 is currently exploring three concepts, consisting of a two-month and a six-month immersion program, as well as a new approach to PhD and DBA education. Given that training both existing and new faculty represents a collective challenge, professional associations like EFMD, AACSB or academic associations like the Academy of Management support the creation of such regional or global training initiatives and platforms. Collaboration with existing providers of transformational learning, leadership or coaching training will speed up the creation of off-site training and development centers for existing (and potentially new) faculty.

A biannual two-month immersion program could be taken during two semester breaks, creating a powerful and safe learning environment for existing and freshly appointed faculty from different regions, who join a cohort of co-learners to engage in a journey of discovery. The immersion program would consist of both common sessions for all faculty, as well as individual sessions, tailor-made to develop an identified area in personal and professional development. Each faculty member would co-create a personal developmental profile based on their strengths and weaknesses, and future ambitions with a professional coach as part of the "intake".

As learning is a process over time, a second part of the learning journey should take place a semester or a year later to deepen the learning and to reflect on the initial experiences.

We consider the following areas as critical to equip faculty with the perspective and competences to embrace the three roles of the vision:

- *Personal development:* enabling the educator and researcher to bring their whole "selves" to the table, to connect their existing inner work and state with their professional work.
- *Practice of reflective awareness:* creating the foundation to understand, reflect and transform unconscious limiting beliefs and behaviors, setting free the full potential of each participant to produce fully integral work both in the classroom and in collaborative research circles.
- *Coaching and facilitation:* understanding and applied practice help considering the other person's viewpoints, and dealing with situations in order to enable the emergence of the highest potential in that moment.
- *Creating powerful and safe learning environments:* developing the basic skills and attitudes in how to co-create (together with participants and students) effective learning environments, and how to deal with the paradigm shift of *not* needing to provide all the answers any longer.
- *Lead-learner:* experiencing the responsibility, risks and opportunities of replacing "professor" and "researcher" with lead-learning in an evolving multi-stakeholder process.
- *Critical reflection:* developing the ability to critically reflect one's preferred point of view and perspective both within one's own field – as well as across the broader business and management disciplines.
- *New research methodologies:* developing the curiosity, courage and skills to design tailor-made new research methodologies suited to develop rigorous future-oriented research approaches.
- *Effective stakeholder engagement:* practicing the required communication and collaboration skills to pro-actively engage with a wide variety of stakeholders, including those who think, behave and act very differently from traditional academics.

A comprehensive six-month international development program
The immersion program described above can be complemented with a more extensive, applied element to further develop applied and experiential learning. In addition to the developmental areas outlined above, a professor would focus on international exposure and, in particular, on

immersion into unfamiliar settings. Such exposure may be involved in emerging, developing or developed countries, depending on the origin of the faculty. The "individual in development" would meet with professors of different schools and different cultural background and, most importantly, encounter different subject specializations.

The professor is supported by tailor-made personal coaching to facilitate his personal and professional transformation process and to ensure the required degree of self-reflection. The professor would select a number of faculty development centers around the world, deepening her own research, collaborative engagement and teaching skills, working with a team of colleagues and local stakeholders on a transdisciplinary research project that addresses a relevant societal challenge. At the end of the six-month period, he/she would have completed an inter- or transdisciplinary piece of research that becomes an example of how to contribute to the common good. The applied, experiential learning environment would be designed in such a way that he/she applies her newly acquired skills in communication, stakeholder dialogue, reflective awareness, critical research analysis, probing new future-oriented research methodologies as well as inter- and transdisciplinary collaboration. This would include the coaching and mentoring of new arrived faculty in their immersion program, thereby gaining first-hand coaching and facilitation experience while being supervised and accompanied in their own learning.

A new doctoral program for the next generation of teachers and researchers
In order to develop a new generation of teachers and researchers, doctoral training needs to be revised to favor:

- Personal development;
- The pedagogy of learning, including coaching and training skills;
- Transdisciplinary thinking and problem solving, including inter-disciplinary, future-oriented, engaging and collaborative research methodologies and approaches; and
- Effective communication and collaboration skills.

The implementation of a transdisciplinary doctoral program is conceived as a contextual project, based on the knowledge, experience and personal development needs of the participants involved, including their social, cultural, political, and economical environments, as well as the scientific and cultural fields surrounding them. This contrasts with the highly disciplinary or sub-disciplinary structure and context of today's doctoral programs. The goal of such innovative doctoral studies is to bring development back to the human and local scale of the communities, allowing them to master and manage their own self-reliant development process. Three axes of development should be considered: awareness raising, conceptual clarification, and praxis:[11]

Awareness needs to be connected to a larger perspective of economic and business change. Learning that occurs during doctoral studies is conceived as a dynamic process embedded in previous learning experiences, from childhood to adulthood, related to every area of human experience. The real-life experience of the participants involved is privileged. Such doctoral studies promote alternation between formal and informal learning settings. The program further encourages transformative learning opportunities where the use of life history methodologies is particularly critical. Methods such as biographical approaches support a conception of the development of the scientific mind as a life-long process rather than the result of specific singular operations concentrated during a specific time period.

Conceptual clarification helps to put awareness into a social action perspective. The doctoral program explores the terms and languages used to position and organize different conceptions of a topic of research. The knowledge produced overcomes the fragmentation of academic disciplines and the divide between "hard sciences", "human sciences" and philosophy. Students develop systematic skepticism, which questions the scientific and ethical legitimacy of one's own teaching and research assumptions. For researchers and practitioners, a complex way of thinking involves a conception of the scientific process as an ongoing dialogue and a continuous learning source of potential transformations.[12]

Praxis remains the biggest challenge encountered in the process of reforming management education and research, as it means bridging the gap between individual and his fragmented awareness on one hand, and building sustainable communities as alternatives on the other. Sustainable initiatives should be developed through collaboration between an academic hub and local community based projects. Participatory action research stresses a practical approach to research and social change. It is grounded in a collective process of uncovering, recovering and activating endogenous knowledge that takes place within concrete and geographically rooted communities. It also implies the full and active participation of the community in problem definition, analysis and resolution.

A global and transdisciplinary doctoral program designed along these axes of development is seen as a first concrete step towards nurturing a cohort of professors that integrate their pursuit of academic excellence, in its multiple manifestations, with commitment to sustainability and responsibility.

NOTES

1. Gerd Gigerenzer is a social psychologist and director of the Max Planck Institute for Human Development. He is cited in Hacker/Dreifus (2011: 18).
2. Kurt Lewin, then a professor at MIT, first coined the term "action research" in 1944. In his 1946 paper "Action Research and Minority Problems" he described action research as "a comparative research on the conditions and effects of various forms of social action and research leading to social action" that uses "a spiral of steps, each of which is composed of a circle of planning, action, and fact-finding about the result of the action".
3. Khurana (2007); Colby et al. (2011: 18–21).
4. See for example the Academy of Management Code of Ethics (2005).
5. Colby et al. (2011: 49).
6. Colby et al. (2011: 11).
7. Bennis/O'Toole (2005).
8. O'Brien et al. (2010) however show there is a curvilinear (inverse U-shaped) relationship between the level of business school research activity and the amount of economic value created for students, which means increasing amounts of research do lead first to an increasing economic value for students, but then value decreases with further increases in research output.
9. Hattie/Marsh (1996); Marsh/Hattie (2002).
10. Hacker/Dreifus (2011, Chapter 8).
11. Finger/Asún (2001).
12. Alhadeff-Jones (2008).

11. Towards a new type of business school

> At a time of great change universities tend to be repositories of historical
> ideas, museums if you like, rather than think tanks for the future.
> Malcolm McIntosh

An effective transformation of business schools depends on the ability to create a new type of school with a broader responsibility to society. We will follow the first two steps of the process of engagement suggested in Chapter 9, namely:

1. Identification of future requirements.
2. Review of current situation in view of obstacles.

The concrete actions described in Chapter 10 focused on developing a new breed of faculty, and provide some examples of how full-scale transformation may be initiated at school level. This may go some way towards establishing a new type of business school – but ultimately we require a *process of active engagement* with the wider community of management education to come up with ideas, suggestions, to create prototypes and test alternative options in various settings.

In this chapter we share two illustrative ideas demonstrating the type of action we hope to inspire within the management education community.

We conclude with a call toward management educators to actively engage with the vision, and to collaborate beyond faculty-, school- and national boundaries on emerging of a new type of business school.

IDENTIFICATION OF FUTURE REQUIREMENTS

The successful implementation of the vision depends on the particular structure and the situation of the business school aiming to embrace the three roles identified in the 50+20 vision, namely: educating and developing globally responsible leaders, enabling business organizations to serve the common good, and engaging in the transformation of business and the economy.

When examining the nearly 13 000 business schools worldwide,[1] we find major differences between the various types of schools, making it impossible to make any effective generalization. These include research and teaching oriented schools, with the former demanding a regular stream of research output from their faculty – while the latter ask for a heavy teaching load. Private and public institutions show differences in regard to their financing, governance and market or customer orientation. Some business schools form part of a larger university structure, with many rules and regulations decided at the university level. Others are stand-alone business schools with considerably more autonomy in defining their strategies and processes. Larger schools may have many thousands of students, while the smaller schools have only a few hundred students. Such differences and approach and size have a strong influence on the context and demands on faculty. Finally, some schools have an explicit international orientation and strategy reflected in the composition and culture of the faculty, while other schools focus on close ties to their local communities.

Players in management education also include non-academic institutions of management education, such as commercial providers, specialized institutes or corporate universities which define their faculty requirements more specifically than academic institutions. These institutions are neither subject to legislation and public demands, nor do they follow academic traditions and rules. Many of these institutions are not tied to formal accreditation procedures by national or international agencies, and do not issue academic degrees. Frequently, they do not develop their own faculty but rather rely on available faculty on the market – be it academic faculty, managers or consultants. Their higher degree of freedom shows considerable diversity with regards to their faculty structure and management, which is specifically tied to their institutional objectives.

Given the differences outlined above, it is quite impossible to conduct a gap analysis comparing the current situation of a school to a situation reflecting the vision in a way that it holds for every single institution. We must therefore restrict ourselves to a generalized sample of the "industry" representing leading business schools in the West, albeit in the knowledge that they represent only a tiny – but highly visible – fraction of all business schools world-wide.

Designing the management school of the future in light of the three roles of the vision requires sweeping changes in both structures and policies within existing institutions. The three new roles are based on values that are broader than those currently practiced in the "industry". These values need to be underpinned by supportive and enabling structures, guidelines and capabilities.

We identify future requirements in three particular areas:

- Managing faculty diversity;
- New criteria for quality and success; and
- Providing leadership and change management.

Managing Faculty Diversity

Developing globally responsible leaders through education, contributing to business organizations solving sustainability issues through research and consulting, and serving as public intellectuals and role models in the transformation of business and the economy requires different capabilities and motivations on the part of the business school faculty. The redefinition of these capabilities and motivations will lead to a greater diversity among the faculty. Some professors will continue concentrating on basic research, while an increasing number of new faculty are expected to focus on applied research with a stronger orientation towards the common good. These new capabilities will also lead to greater diversity inside the faculty with regard to teaching, as new pedagogical skills in the area of experiential learning and personal development are added. Last but not least, these newly defined motivations will lead to a greater diversity with regard to public engagement, with some faculty playing an important role as public intellectuals and ambassadors, bridging the school and the wider community of stakeholders.

Managing and celebrating a highly diverse faculty culture and preserving the mutual respect between the different fractions will be a major task for business school leadership. This increase in diversity may serve as a counter trend to the current tendency of some faculty fractions feeling superior to others, creating barriers for cooperation and collaboration. One example would be the tension between basic researchers with their primary focus on their peers and theory development, and applied researchers with their primary focus on the business world and practical solutions.

Implementing the vision requires different capabilities and motivations on the part of the business school faculty. The management school of the future will need to find ways to break down existing walls and rebuild bridges between different internal faculty fractions. The core challenge, however, lies in building bridges between their faculty and the outside world. More windows in the ivory tower will not suffice. Business schools need to embrace diversity in its institutions and free movement in both directions, e.g.:

- A professor spends two years[2] working in a start-up in Somalia, or
- An entrepreneur spends a two-year executives-in-residence[3] sabbatical to digest and distill his professional experience.

Business leaders, entrepreneurs, directors of NGOs, consultants and activists will need to be invited to join the management school for one or more years to digest and reflect their experience as applied research reflecting on the work place. Business schools must embrace an open borders policy between practice and academia: a prerequisite condition to create the collaborative learning environment required for action learning and research. Moving between reflective work in a management school and applied work in business is a critical success factor in ensuring high relevance of the faculty in their role as lead-learners in the educational and research process.

It is important to note that there are different kinds of walls that need to be broken down. Those we described earlier refer mostly to institutional limitations and rules and regulations regarding the free movement of faculty and professionals in business schools and in exchange with the professional world. As the two examples above illustrate, there are already many institutions, professors and professionals who have embraced this exchange and have effectively broken down that wall. When we reflect why more professors aren't jumping on the opportunity to take radical departures from their comfort zones, we realize that we are facing different kinds of walls that need breaking down. These commonly refer to a lack of intellectual and ideological infrastructures, both on an institutional and personal level.

An effective implementation of a truly diverse and relevant faculty brings its own challenge and related key requirements, which have been identified and addressed in Chapter 11. These involve a missing professional framework, shortcomings of the faculty training and development programs, and limitations of the current recruitment and promotion system.

More than anything, the management school of the future needs a comprehensive mix of educators and researchers with a wealth of experience and backgrounds. Encouraging a sense of diversity both among the faculty and as a life-long learning goal for every person requires establishing conditions that promote the related intrinsic motivation.

New Criteria for Quality and Success

Establishing outcome-oriented measures for the three new roles of management education is a useful starting base. The related educational criteria need to evaluate to what degree graduates can face challenging issues in organizations and society. Relevant research measures must evaluate to what extent research output produces results that can be used to resolve pressing issues in business and society.

The role of engaging in the transformation of business and the economy further requires measures that assess a business school's presence in, contribution to and impact on the greater public. In addition, the school needs to implement indicators that allow measuring the progress of the school itself in terms of how the three roles are lived.

The need for greater diversity of roles for faculty must be reflected in an appropriate diversity in the criteria for measuring and rewarding the performance of faculty, as well as in recruiting new faculty. New and different criteria for success are an essential ingredient for enabling a successful transformation of the business school as a whole.

Business schools currently evaluate their success by tracking quality and success in their main areas of activity, namely education, research and services to the public. Interestingly, it is largely external forces that have imposed quality measures to business schools. Rankings and accreditations have played an important role in defining and delivering quality measures that are applied to business schools. Often, internal measures of quality and success have been modeled after these external criteria, in which some of the criteria are considered more or less relevant for a particular school. Accreditations and rankings use criteria that focus on the quality of the input (e.g. student selection, faculty qualifications and their publications, institutional infrastructures and course materials), the quality of the process (e.g. course delivery, course quality assessments and course development), and the quality of the output (e.g. satisfaction of direct "customers", namely students and participants in educational programs).

In recent years, accreditation systems have shifted to outcome measures, asking explicitly for assessments of learning (e.g. AACSB International). Outcome-oriented measures ask whether what students have learned in a class was what they were *supposed* to learn. A next step is to ask this same question with regard to the impact of research. Is research contributing to society? If so, how can this be measured?

We recommend revising current criteria to establish outcome-oriented measures for all three new roles of management education. Let us examine the criteria of quality and success with regard to the proposed newly defined three roles of management education:

Educating and developing globally responsible leaders essentially relates to the development of leadership potential. Two related actionable domains are curriculum contents (*what* do students learn?) and of pedagogy (*how* do students learn?). The related outcome criteria need to evaluate to what degree graduating students are capable and motivated to deal with challenging issues in organizations and society. Also, to what degree will graduates be effective in contributing to solving global problems? Outcome-related measures will address the degree to which graduates embrace such challenges and problems in their careers. Effective measures will require a monitoring system after graduation, which may be executed in collaboration with alumni organization.

Enabling business organizations to serve the common good is to a large degree dependent on questions asked in research and service activities, as well as on the forms of dissemination of results. Walsh's insight in his 2010 presidential speech serve as an important reminder: "Our questions set the entire research and teaching agenda and, more than anything else, determine our relevance and impact."[4] Future measures must evolve from focusing on publications in highly ranked journals or citations. Relevant measures will evaluate the degree to which questions addressed in publications and other forms of creative output produce results, and to what degree they are used to address pressing issues in business and society.

Engaging in the transformation of business and the economy will require measures that assess a business school's presence in, contribution towards and impact on the greater public. Defining measures of quality and success relates to evaluating a school's level of engagement in society both in terms of intensity and perceived success. Such public engagement ranges from local to international, and needs to be evaluated according to its public relevance, taking into account competences and potential contributions of the school.

Future measures of business schools as institutions and faculty performance will only partially correspond with measures currently used in external evaluation systems, e.g. in ratings and rankings or by the scholarly community. This discrepancy represents a challenge for business schools in the process of transition. As business schools have shown to be strongly influenced by such externally driven evaluation systems, introducing new measures may be an act of liberation from these external impositions. Independent business schools need to develop their own criteria of quality and success, based on their mission and strategy. As a result, such schools will appear differently compared to what we find in rating or ranking systems.

Translating these measures to the allocation of resources represents a further step. Research-intensive business schools have faculty and its supporting administration as a major cost position in its budget. Teaching-oriented schools will have different challenges in reviewing their cost and resource structures. Peter and Thomas remind us how limited the awareness of cost management is at a typical business school.[5] Introducing the third role of public engagement will undoubtedly help launch discussions about budget allocation with potential shifts from current research and teaching priorities.

We suggest that the business school of the future should operate a business model that is inclusive, collaborative and flexible to change. By working closely with its relevant stakeholders, the school is recognized and compensated for the value it contributes. This recognition may lead to a redefinition of sources for funding, opening potential new avenues of cooperation. Business schools of the future will be challenged to truly embrace the types of changes they envision in the world. To achieve this, the leadership of business schools needs to be experienced with relevant change management skills in order to enable the school to be measured for success that is synchronised with how the school aims to embrace the three roles of the vision. While it is impossible to predict how such measures will translate into concrete situations in different regions and national frameworks, we believe that the management school of the future will have understood that *collaboration* is much more effective than *competition*.

Providing Leadership and Change Management

Changing established institutions within higher education represents a real challenge. Such institutions were often structured to assure stability and academic freedom in the face of different external influences. As a result, faculty is equipped with significant power to resist change, even when proposed by a school's own leadership. Creating the capacity for strategic change, coupled with conditions that encourage an intrinsic motivation to change in business schools, are critical pre-conditions. Strong deans and presidents may have some success in implementing change. Unfortunately, the success stories are outnumbered by deans and presidents who are ousted by their faculty when attempting to introduce significant change.

Creating the capacity for strategic change in business schools, therefore, is a primary requirement. One way to achieve this may be to strengthen the power of the dean or president, similar to the model found in U.S. business schools. Strengthening the position of the organizational leader could be achieved by recruiting deans externally and freeing them from stringent peer control. Another way may be to reinforce the power of the governing board, e.g. by increasing the external representation of the wider community of stakeholders. The alternative to strengthening the power at the top is an inclusive strategy process, aligning a majority of the faculty behind a new vision. Whichever way works in any given institutional setting, it is of critical importance to ensure that the leader has experience in change management.

A second critical element concerns the leadership team's capacity, competence and courage to embrace their role and lead change. While this seems an obvious statement, we should remember that many current deans or presidents have academic backgrounds, with little or no previous leadership experience. Leadership is an art that is strangely underappreciated in institutions of higher learning, despite the fact that business schools teach and research the topic. Leaders in business schools have a difficult time defending and implementing their position, particularly when their actions are disputed. This may sound self-evident, but there are many examples of leaders in the context of higher education without the courage, or maybe ability, to *lead*. Instead, such leaders reduce themselves to the role of administrators and coordinators. Mobilizing internal support for realizing the vision will need both courage and a solid track record in leading change.

A third requirement is the competence to lead a business school in the context of society.[6] Business schools have of late become the object of public criticism, and are being challenged to reestablish themselves as positive contributors to society. The 50+20 vision is not designed to be a response to current criticisms, but rather argues that business schools need to embrace their responsibility towards the common good – translating this responsibility into practice. Major and sustained efforts that embrace this responsibility will be an effective response to current criticisms. Translating these new roles into concrete action will require significant new levels of competences and courage from both the members of business school management and faculty.

REVIEW OF CURRENT SITUATION IN VIEW OF OBSTACLES

The following obstacles in the landscape of management education may hinder the implementation of the vision:

- A worsening economic equation.
- Mounting public criticism.
- Challenges to leadership and professionalism.

A Worsening Economic Equation

Economically distressed governments in many parts of the world are forced to scale down their educational spending and expose universities to more autonomy and market control, creating strong public reactions from students and other parts of society. This public outcry may slow the retreat of government from financing higher education, but it is unlikely to reverse the trend. As a result, there may be a sharp increase in mergers and acquisitions between business schools or a tendency towards privatization. Any such developments are quite foreign to the higher education sector – at least thus far.

Business schools in particular will be called upon to increase their self-financing. They are considered very well placed to increase their fees, to develop their alumni base and to sell their services in the market. In return for reduced government funding, business schools will enjoy increased autonomy, allowing for more flexibility in budgeting and finances, in recruitment and compensation, and in internationalizing their activities. Reduced funding is likely to create strong pressures to professionalize cost management and operational overheads, review marketing and communication capacities, and further develop career services. As a result, we can expect an increase in the level of commercialization, which may lead to fundamental debates about the mission of business schools.

There is no denying that the economic equation is worsening, even for business education. The challenges come from very different sides. A look at the U.S. landscape may indicate future change in other regions. Two thirds of U.S. business schools with two-year residential MBA programs saw applications drop in 2011, putting middle range business schools under a degree of pressure. While tuition fees have been rising considerably, the starting salaries of MBA graduates have increased only slightly in the past five years. Suddenly, the investment value of an MBA is being brought into question.[7]

To make matters worse, student loans have become the biggest slice of overall debt, making it a perfect candidate for a next economic crisis. With starting salaries leveling and in some cases decreasing, with unemployment reaching college graduates and government being forced to reduce financial support, it is not surprising that big banks have started to get out of the student loan market. As business schools carry very high fixed costs for faculty and infrastructure, small dips in income create a significant exposure to risk. Information technology and internationalization demand fundamental changes in the strategies and operations of business schools to which many are slow to respond. At the same time, private for-profit institutions have increased their market share in the U.S. from 3.5 percent in 2000 to 11.8 percent in 2009,[8] rapidly eating into the low-end market with large-scale, IT-supported, teaching-only programs. Such institutions often offer significantly more flexibility and better services to their student customers than traditional business schools.

Changes are also coming from a very different angle. As China and India are investing heavily in their own business education programs. Demand from international students for all but the well-established brand names is unlikely to remain as high as it is today.

Mounting Public Criticism

In 2010, Walsh stated in his presidential address to the Academy of Management that "This really should be our golden age".[9] Business has emerged as a central feature of life in contemporary society, rivaling that of the church and the state. Management, according to Peter Drucker, has become the most important societal function. Business as a field of study is attracting more students than any other field, amounting to one in five undergraduates and one in four graduate students. U.S.-based business school professors are among the best paid academics.

And yet, this is no golden age at all. President after president of the Academy of Management has bemoaned the discipline's irrelevance. Hambrick started in 1993, by asking "what if the Academy really mattered?", while Hitt demanded in 1997 to make basic research more easily accessible and usable for managers. Van den Ven remarked in 2001 that the gulf between the science and practice of management is widening. Pearce realized in 2003 that classrooms existed virtually independently from the results of scholarship. Rousseau repeated in 2005 that all parties needed to put greater emphasis on learning how to translate research findings into *solutions*. Cummings in 2006 was fed up with the perennial talk of mattering more and felt the time had come to put up or shut up. Smith suggested in 2007 to be passionate about ideas, but creative and somewhat pragmatic in presenting them to the market. Finally, de Nisi repeated in 2009 that researchers must do a better job of connecting research to the world around them.[10]

The emerging picture, reflected by leading representatives of the academy themselves, is one of a highly successful professional business school showing great difficulties in having a significant impact through its research on management practice and in connecting to society in general. Also, students may still be flooding into business schools, but it is not clear if they are more attracted by the quality of placement offices or by what they learn in the classrooms.

Business schools ranking "league-tables" have become very popular in recent years, signaling a clear need by varied audiences to better understand and assess the value and performance of different business schools. The outside world does not yet know how to appraise the value of the schools' contributions and therefore resort to rankings. Students and their parents, participants of continuous and executive education programs, as well as sponsors and politicians, are looking for guidance in evaluating the quality of different business schools. Indeed, the schools themselves have welcomed rankings as a marketing tool to communicate their performance and build their reputation. Business schools have embarked on managing these rankings for better performance, concentrating mostly on marketing and communications. Now, the consequences have started to become real and problematic.

Rankings suggest simplicity in the evaluation of educational and scientific performance, as if schools were football teams in a league. Although things are not so simple and the various methodologies used in different rankings are hotly debated, the influence of these rankings is striking. Within a short decade, they have become an unavoidable part of academic life, for better or worse. Adapting to ranking criteria leads to expensive window dressing with big investments made to create top-quality executive centers, serving company recruiters and students' happiness quotients. The strong concentration of most rankings on salary levels of graduates increases the commercial focus and further distracts attention from the educational impact of learning and the relevance of research. It also encourages a frenzy of mindless publishing with tenure, and promotion and reward systems that are increasingly built around narrow, technocratic research.[11]

An unexpected wave of public criticism reached business schools after the banking and financial crisis brought not only financial markets but whole countries and economies to their knees, destroying enormous values and savings of many families around the world. The smartest graduates of the best business schools did not only earn the highest salaries and huge bonuses, but they *helped* in creating a financial system that primarily benefitted financial service firms themselves – while creating enormous risks for everybody else. No wonder the wave of criticism has reached the business schools for having produced the kinds of graduates that showed this highly self-interested and unethical behavior. In Podolny's words: "the fact is, so deep and widespread are the problems afflicting management education that some people have come to believe that business schools are harmful to society, fostering self-interested, unethical, and even illegal behavior among their graduates."[12] Podolny is only reiterating what had been said before by Mitroff[13] in his angry open letter to the deans and faculty of American business schools, and by

Ghoshal, who stated that "bad management theories are destroying good management practices".[14]

Although this criticism is not completely new for business schools and their leadership, it nonetheless came as a big surprise to many other. Various business schools have taken concrete action to seriously integrate issues of responsibility and sustainability into their educational and research activities.[15] But such efforts remain for the most part marginal, leaving core subjects in economics and finance untouched and in its dominant position. Management education has become an industry serving students perceived as customers, who increasingly base their choice on media rankings and starting salaries. In doing so, business schools have not only undermined their competitive position vis-à-vis commercial providers, but they have virtually abandoned any idea of a social purpose. When the legitimacy crisis hit the corporate world, business schools were found in the same boat, having provided the agents, the tools and the theories that supported investor capitalism and greed.

Challenges to Leadership and Professionalism

Business school management has only recently started a process of professionalization. Similar to other institutions and domains that put high value on specialist knowledge and skills (e.g. hospitals or law firms), academia has traditionally been an area of self administration. Business school management has become a true challenge in the context of increasing market orientation and competition between business schools, but also as a consequence of increasingly internationalized and diversified activities (e.g. in the executive education field). Business school management increasingly needs professional leadership and management at the top, as well as in additional functions. However, existing structures and the typical context of business schools are not conducive to such changes.

Although the practices and regulations in this field are varied, deans are often elected from the pool of professors on a temporary basis. After serving their time deans return to their function as an ordinary professor. Usually, deans undergo no preparation or training for such appointments, while elected faculty are hesitant or unskilled to bring about change "against" their fellow professors. A market for deans is only slowly emerging. The same holds true for program managers in business schools. Support and training for new deans and managers is scarce, with only a few such programs offered by professional associations. In addition, new responsibilities and functions have been added to business school management which requires specialized functional management in areas like marketing, communication, alumni relations, public relations and career services.

Governance structures within business schools often prevent any attempts at change or transformation. Tenured faculty holds a very strong position, based on their independence and job security. As a result, change can only be achieved *with* their support, but not against them. As tenured faculty is typically risk averse, business schools face a huge obstacle when implementing change. Professional managers rarely succeed in such settings of collective decision making within a strongly decentralized power structure – no wonder then they don't find such jobs very appealing. In addition to these internal challenges, positioning the school externally in the business world, in politics and in the public arena, demands competences and capabilities that are rarely combined in a single individual. As a consequence, leadership may be urgently needed in business schools, but is rarely realized.

The story is similar for traditional universities. Inflexible structures, strong traditions and a strong faculty defending their autonomy set clear limits to strategic change and leadership. As has been observed by a former dean and chief technology officer in a major computer company in the U.S.: "no other modern enterprise has been as untouched by changes in markets, demographics and economies as the American institution of higher learning".[16] And, "in the view of many, higher education is out of touch with changing realities and suffers from many of the same structural flaws that have harmed the healthcare system".[17] It is high time to "awaken the academy" and introduce new leadership.[18]

FURTHER ILLUSTRATIONS AND IDEAS

We would like to share two noteworthy ideas developed during the 50+20 vision creation process as a means of illustrating the type of action we hope to inspire within the management education community.

The first proposal on question-based learning seeks to illustrate the paradigm shift we experience with new educational formats. Embedding learning in a felt-sense physical experience fundamentally shifts learning, opening new doors with a level of integration far beyond traditional learning techniques.

The second is a drafted proposal for an undergraduate program that fulfills the vision, and integrates notions of transformative learning, issue-centered learning and reflected practice and field work. As many of us struggle to imagine what such a program could look like – or if it is even possible to educate in accordance with our enablers on an undergraduate level – we provide draft idea that hopefully serves to launch a broader debate on the topic.

Question-based Learning

The secret to uncover solutions that leap-frog above and beyond current practices involves the ability to ask pertinent questions. Enabling students to ask insightful questions is the higher purpose of teaching and represents an essential factor of successfully educating leaders to embrace problems we don't yet know, and determining solutions that do not yet exist based on technologies that have not yet been invented.

An intended side-effect of question-based learning is an increase in a student's ability to hold the tension of *not* knowing answers, as well as and the ability to live with half-truths or partial answers without shying away from courageously taking a step in what appears to be the right direction, given the information that is known at that time. Acting, reflecting, correcting and acting again will be the future dance of our leaders – otherwise known as "elegantly stumbling forward" as we progress towards meaningful engagement with ourselves and the world.

The key benefit to question-based learning is the development of liberal learning and critical thinking. This is achieved by (a) analytical thinking, (b) multiple framing, (c) reflective exploration of meaning, and (d) practical reasoning. Uncovering assumptions that shape the way we view the world is a critical step toward forming one's own opinion about what feels right. Another element of this approach is the inherent possibility to render conscious the many undeclared assumptions of oppressive economic thinking, thereby opening the opportunity to discuss alternative avenues.

One step further: asking questions that demand visualization of future answers

Asking questions that allow students and participants to imagine answers is an experimental approach towards a future-oriented learning pedagogy. The process of asking questions is three-fold:

1. Ensuring students/participants are really "present" (in body, spirit and mind).
2. Asking questions that trigger images ("What image comes up when you think of the global financial system?", "How do you imagine an ideal financial system for the world and its citizens?").
3. Connecting these images to physical sensations by asking: "Where do you feel this in your body? What is your body's reaction to this?"

Step 3 connects the theoretical question with a physical sensation, establishing an internal resonance with the external world from an energetic perspective. This technique empowers a powerful embodiment of such a future-oriented question which seek answers we don't know as yet. These steps further ensure a learning process that reaches beyond a purely mental exercise.

The all-important action that connects a question to a physical experience enables a step that is otherwise nearly impossible to take by removing an individual out of their known/learned sphere and taking them to a place where they may connect with deeper knowledge,[19] values and potential that is usually difficult to access. As such, it represents an important addition to more established processes[20] as it anchors an individual visioning experience with the potential of the world.

We hope to stimulate further online debate around the sample provided, and invite schools and institutions to contribute further benchmarks.

A Proposal for an Undergraduate Program

The proposal for an undergraduate management education serves as an illustration of how safe and powerful learning environments can be developed for students with limited to no prior professional experience. Clearly, the purpose here is not to suggest a one-size-fits-all approach but rather to provide a suggestion of how to rethink undergraduate education that may serve to stimulate discussions and debates for a review in the context a particular school operates in.

Year one – contextual studies through personal learning agendas

The first year after graduating from high school is dedicated to broaden the mind of our youngest students. The objective of the year is to ensure that students have a clear understanding of the global issues in the past, present and are likely to emerge in the future. Subjects are presented from a transdisciplinary perspective, requiring students to develop basic applied research and systemic thinking skills. Students are introduced to the adventure of learning and self-study, choosing from which angle and with what focus they would like to understand the world in which they live. They will successfully pass their first year upon learning to assume responsibility for their studies and demonstrating how their approach has enabled them to develop an understanding for the context in which business operates.

The first semester focuses on studying global issues and key innovations

Global issues: water, energy, climate, migration, technology, hunger, health, religions, poverty, pollution, demographic shifts, regional and trans-regional conflicts – from a historic, present and future perspective.

Innovations and trends: nanotechnology, neuroscience, organic food, biotechnology, alternative energy, globalization, longevity medicine, emerging technologies, the potential of the human being, positive psychology, emerging trends in leadership.

1. *Overview Phase*

    Experts present an overview of the global challenges, innovations and trends, outlining the learning approach over several weeks. Students are free to select which group they wish to participate in and which topic they select.

    Study groups (approximately 20 students) are formed around these topics. Students are tasked to independently prepare an overview of a number of these topics and present them to their study groups. Facilitators ask critical questions to identify gaps and ensure a comprehensive understanding of a topic.

    Once further research is completed, study groups split into teams to prepare an interactive learning journey on the various topics that have been investigated.

    Facilitators and experts evaluate the work of the various study groups and select the best proposals of the various study groups. Selected teams present their topics in a full day experience to the larger cohort, applying what they have learned about the pedagogy of learning.

2. *Learning journey phase*

    Experts introduce systemic thinking and the learning journey for the next weeks. Students select a region in the world they are interested in understanding better. Groups are formed by region.

    Newly formed study groups divide into sub-groups which examine the connections between two to three global issues by studying the history, the present and the anticipated future of a specific world region.

    Teams investigate the interconnectivity of chosen topics in a given region, complementing desk research with personal interviews of relevant stakeholders about the selected challenges using modern technology and tools, in order to integrate different perspectives on complex issues.

    Facilitators help study groups determine key lessons learned from all projects (both from the perspective of content as well as team dynamics) and select the most relevant challenge to be presented to a larger cohort. The entire study groups prepares an experience day around this challenge (interactive, using current tools and pedagogy).

3. *Reflection and feedback phase*

    Each student submits a paper describing questions of a select number of global issues, innovations and trends they didn't study, presenting personal reflection regarding the key dynamics influencing these issues in the coming decades. Each student also submits a personal learning journal based on the experiences in the various groups and teams.

Experts and facilitators provide relevant feedback to each individual and summarize issues, potential gaps and key learning with the cohort in a plenary session.

The second semester focuses on strategic implications for society and business

Students focus on three key activities:

1. ### *Earning money*
   Each student or small student group finds employment or an activity for which they are remunerated. A facilitator guides them in this process without offering any concrete support. The entire cohort competes. Winners are evaluated according to pre-established criteria: adding most value (as perceived by the client), working most hours, earning most money.

2. ### *Designing the Wanderjahr (see Year 2 below)*
   In their second year of study, each student embarks on a personal year of adventure and learning. The second semester of the first year is reserved to clarify goals for the second year, develop contacts and create a concrete plan for how to achieve these goals.

3. ### *Understanding strategic implications of global issues, innovations and trends*
   Students work individually and in small teams to understand and subsequently summarize opinions of experts, thought leaders and stakeholders relative to the strategic implications of the global issues, innovations and trends identified in the first semester. They are coached by facilitators and supported by experts.

   Teams of four to five students prepare a presentation (media form open) on their learnings to the entire cohort. The cohort ranks the winning teams according to pre-determined (variable) criteria. The best five presentations are shown to the entire school (all students, experts and facilitators present on campus) in the year-end immersion week.

Year two – the Wanderjahr (the wander year)

The purpose of the second year is to provide young students with life and work experience, while successfully entering the adult world by assuming responsibility for their life and learning journeys. The *Wanderjahr* is an ancient Western European ritual by which young adults set out on foot to learn their trade in different parts of Europe, returning home as responsible adults enriched carrying a wealth of personal experience and exposure to different cultures, customs and trades. Stakeholders clearly indicate that it is impossible to teach the "trade of business" without students possessing prior work (and life) experience.

In our age and time we believe it is essential for students in developed countries to be exposed to the realities of developing or emerging countries, or of different social realities in their own country or region. As such, the literal distance traveled is not necessarily a good indicator of the figurative distance traveled in a personal learning journal. A *Wanderjahr* may include:

- Setting out to travel the world, finding local work to finance further travels.
- Finding an NGO to dedicate their time and energy adding to value to a local initiative.
- Starting up a company offering a relevant service to a group of consumers in need.
- Learning a new language, writing a book or shooting a movie.
- Helping a relative on a farm.
- Forming a traveling group with fellow students to discover foreign cultures.
- Finding a job locally to gain work experience.

Each second year student can rely on the coaching and mentoring support of a fourth-year bachelor student, who in turn gains exposure to the challenges of coaching and mentoring. Facilitators work with groups of students to ensure that they are equipped with appropriate tools and methods, ensuring that they can not only experience but also reflect on their experiences. Each student keeps a personal learning diary that they periodically share with their mentor and group via the facilitator. The support structure is structured in such a way, that "failing" this year is highly unlikely (failure is often an essential ingredient for transformational learning).

At the beginning of the third year, returning students will present their *Wanderjahr* in a major exhibition for the entire school, inspiring most particularly new first-year students who get a first taste of what they might want to embark on in their own second year of studies. The exhibition is followed by accounts of facilitators who include feedback from the mentors.

Years three and four – management studies and specialization
The objective of the second part of a business bachelor is to ensure immersion in the topics of business and management. Studying the various

subjects of business (marketing, finance, HR, accounting, strategy, operations, supply chain, sales, management, leadership) will allow different, more holistic approaches to various topics – but only after having obtained a background of the context of global issues, innovations and trends, a learning-oriented education, as well as personal experience in this world.

The learning experience will have to be carefully crafted to ensure that students remain responsible for their learning, carefully balancing expert intervention with applying learning in an appropriate context (experiential learning). Next to learning concrete business content, these students will continue to build the bridge from the larger context to business making a contribution to society and the world. Third-year students will conduct study projects translating strategic issues of global challenges to business, creating a business plan around a relevant contribution to society. They will experiment with emerging business performance measures that exceed profit maximization, focusing on adding value to society and the planet (triple bottom line). Fourth-year students will apply what they have learned in a domain of their choice (specialization) and coach second-year students on their Wanderjahr.

Of course, some (or all) of our ideas may prove to be obsolete or otherwise deemed unsuitable well before any attempts at implementation of such programs are attempted, given how new and improved initiatives will undoubtedly develop the moment we embrace the transformation in management education. More than anything, our hope is that these preliminary ideas will spark a wider debate amongst the players in management education and the wider community.

HEEDING THE CALL

As tempting as it was to include a 'shopping list' of ideas or step-by-step suggestions for creating a new type of business school, that is not the ultimate purpose of this book or this vision.

At the third PRME Global Forum meeting held during RIO+20 in June 2012, we were reminded of the fact that our work in management education is a *calling*. During the event, which saw the launch of the 50+20 Agenda, participants were treated to a moving rendition of a sixteenth century poem by George Herbert titled *The Call* which challenges truth and life to triumph over death.

Similarly, we would like to think of 50+20 as a *calling*: to management educators and those concerned with the role management eduction plays in creating our collective future. This work is a *call* to actively engage with the 50+20 vision, finding ways to implement it, share it with others and find out how we can transform management education to serve the common good.

Many of us are already aware that radical action is required. We know that *this* is our junction in the road. *This* is our calling to create a world worth living in – and we hope to see you on the journey.

NOTES

1. AACSB International (2011).
2. Kennedy School of Government, Harvard University.
3. IMD, Lausanne.
4. Walsh (2011: 224).
5. Peters / Thomas (2011).
6. Walsh (2011: 226, 228) speaks of "The courage to lead in the university" and "The courage to lead the university in society."
7. *The Economist* (2011).
8. Olian (2011).
9. Walsh (2011: 215).
10. Cited in Walsh (2011: 216–217).
11. Adler/Harzing (2009); Khurana (2007).
12. Podolny (2009: 63).
13. Mitroff (2004: 185).
14. Ghoshal (2005: 86).
15. The CEMS schools have reacted by publishing a book on business schools and their contribution to society: Morsing/SauquetRovira (2011).
16. DeMillo (2011: 93).
17. Immerwahr et al. (2008).
18. Willms/Zell (2002).
19. There is an abundance of literature on the quantum field, its potential and how human beings can connect to it. See for example: McTaggert (2008).
20. Scharmer (2009).

Conclusion

The 50+20 vision is intended for both organizations and individuals who hold a deep awareness and understanding of the upcoming global challenges, who share a sense of urgency to bring about change – and embrace the idea that we all own the responsibility to transform society.

We will always be a species on the move, a bigger tribe inhabiting a smaller world – but now it's time to take a different path. In order to survive, we need nothing less than an evolution in thought and cooperation, a transition into becoming a responsible society. We are, after all, working towards a more human future, leaving behind centuries of expansion and rampant consumption.

If nothing else, we urge our readers to imagine how business, the economy and the world will look if we think and act inclusively in a long-term setting. Picture our world – say, a century from now – where traditional economic growth has reconnected to human and ecological goals, supporting a diverse society with wholly redefined definitions of prosperity, the basis of profit, loss, progress and value creation. This society is visibly more stable, healthier and happier as it works towards a sustainable future.

In this future, business will be celebrated for its contribution to society. Thoughtful leadership and sustained collaboration are commonplace not only within organizations, but also actively address the (notably fewer) remaining regional and global problems.

Business scholars and management consultants are respected as sustainability stewards, helping build a better world through research and advice, jointly determining how organizations can develop and implement real sustainability strategies. Similarly, governments, corporations, NGOs, activists, citizens, parents and educators all contribute their knowledge on a regular basis without regard to tenure, reputation, qualifications or social standing. The best solutions, as everybody knows, are those reached by adopting a transdisciplinary approach, across all fields of expertise, age groups and cultural backgrounds.

This future world includes education and research organizations which positively influence the development of society as a whole. Places of knowledge sharing are deeply embedded in the midst of communities (much like the prototype collaboratories from the early twenty-first century). These nodes are the heart of the new society: dynamic meeting spaces where ideas are born, where participants and contributors can freely express their views and share knowledge in an open environment.

We may picture a world where risk-taking is encouraged, a place that is intensely alive with mutual respect, friendship, vibrant thought, insightful questions, where creativity blooms across all generations. Such a renewed, living world enables lifestyles that offer different levels of immersion between work and learning within a new and more open society.

Environmental disruption has been virtually eliminated. Once more, the world has wide tracts of untouched, high-biodiversity wilderness. The human population is finally stable. People are content, unified – but also more diverse. Its citizens are determined, passionate, argumentative but ultimately cooperative, a well-organized civilization working towards the singular goal of sustainability.

This is a world worth living in. Let us begin creating it.

Epilogue

Vera Sanchez – Rio de Janeiro – PreSnap (Prefrontal Snapture) –
(June 18–24) – AD 2032

I've been doing this too long.

After three days of uncomfortable conference halls, endless presentations, interminable speeches, accusations and counter accusations,
reluctant handshakes, air-conditioned hotel lobbies, pamphlets, police
and protests I was close to giving up. Apart from the faster bandwidth
and the explosion of microdrones cluttering the smoggy sky it seemed
as if little had changed since Rio 2012: the world is a conflagration of
ecological destruction, a stuttering economy, and interminable politics. Of
course, many people were trying to resolve some of the problems through
the old channels – but their efforts seemed futile when set against the
overwhelming crises we face.

*People don't change. This is how we've always done things, by slash and
burn, a euphoric, non-stop carnival of mass suicide. Why stop now? Why
bother trying?*

I woke up disoriented, having fallen asleep during one of the last of the
seminars in the Windsor Barra Hotel. I looked around the low-ceilinged,
deserted conference room, littered with discarded menus, presentation
printouts, napkins, business cards: the unhappy debris of yet another
failed seminar. I rolled up my slate, gathered my things and shuffled out
of the conference room. The facilities were almost deserted; only a few of
the catering and cleaning staff lingered about, quietly talking amongst
themselves (funny how robots simply seem incapable of handling the
complexities of the most menial human tasks, I thought).

I had given myself six days in Rio: three for the Rio+40 Sustainability
Conference, another three to consolidate my notes, catch up with friends,
perhaps interview a few stragglers. I felt my cynicism bleeding through
again, a dull pessimism layered on physical exhaustion.

But it's not professional, damn it! I tried to recall whether I had thought
any differently in 2012. Nope, can't remember. The intervening twenty
years had been defined by extensive travel, the magazine launch, taxes,

unplanned motherhood, marriage, bankruptcy, failure to re-renter the job market, night classes, freelancing, divorce, relocation – along with all the drudgery and minutiae of life that pile up like rock strata, threatening to crush any passion, any sense of real *purpose* of the self.

Growing increasingly sour, I pushed open the heavy glass doors and emerged into typically Brazilian heat, along with the polluted air, the noise of traffic, and the humanity where everybody seems to be jostling for something better, a respite from the pressures, blithely shouldering aside their neighbours in order to secure the slightest advantage to their lives. People are like that, and I suppose I am no different.

I guess that was my low point.

But then I came across something unexpected, something new.

The first time I heard about the Idea was on a sultry evening, the day after the end of the Sustainability Conference. I found myself near a beach outside the Windsor Barra, where several people, Brazilians and foreigners, were clustered around a small, open air restaurant. Somebody had lit a fire nearby, fuelled with driftwood and conference programmes. The people looked oddly out of place, somehow too *random* in their backgrounds. It's not every day you get to see a gathering of races and cultures like that, the old and the young, tortoise-shell spectacles alongside writhing anima-tattoos, glossy spider-silk suits mingling with dreadlocks that still smelled faintly of tear gas and spray paint. Some of the people were standing. Others were seated on a series of curiously wrought benches arranged in a rough circle.

My first impression was that they had been arguing amongst each other, but as I cautiously approached them a few turned to me. They were smiling, their illuminated faces flushed. I felt the heat of the flames on my face. I discreetly plugged in my translation software and listened.

"Economic growth will be decoupled from the ecosystem destruction *and* material consumption. The economy will progress in parallel with the well-being of society which has replaced GDP as the key global indicator of wealth. Families, communities, villages, even cities are creating a global alliance"

"That's the ultimate goal, but let's start at the beginning," said another man, some kind of professor, an old-school academic. "The first question has been answered, I think: that the current model provided us with very little intrinsic *value*. It's made a real mess of everything, so we need to change how business is conducted and taught. Remember, the key is thinking *long term*: encouraging responsibility, leadership, enabling business to serve the common good and accelerating the transformation of business and the economy. We're in the middle of species-wide sanity check – and not a moment too soon!"

A woman stepped forward, picking her teeth with a splinter of wood. "Well, he's right about leadership. But the priority is not to scream out solutions or recommendations, but rather engagement with others. People are working together now, at last. The collaboratory helps create that space by . . ."

The discussions grew increasingly animated over the course of the evening. Several more people strolled in and out of the group. Even a few of the tanned Brazilian locals joined in, curious about the noise. I retreated a little way towards the beach, settling near the fire. I laid down in the sand, suddenly numb with fatigue, and fell asleep.

I woke with a snort and opened my eyes. It was daybreak.

"Rise up and shine, lady," said a girl beside me, wrapped in a blanket. She was Asian and looked no older than eighteen. She seemed energetic, nervous. Activist type, probably. "You can cut off the leaves, but the roots remain," she said, exhaling pungent smoke from a self-rolled cigarette.

"Okay. Wait – *what?*" I asked dully, brushing sand and ash off my blouse.

"Grass roots, localized nodes of action. The foundation stirs: you, me everybody. Haven't you seen? It's started. Things different: no more lies, only work. No choice – not anymore. Now we *fix-fix-fix.*"

The girl grinned as I crept away from the dying embers of the fire. Truthfully, I didn't care what she thought. At that moment I was craving a hot shower, shampoo in tiny little bottles, breakfast, the Internet. I staggered back to the guesthouse a few blocks away.

My dreams that night were a series of shallow explorations, skipping over memories that did not even qualify as REM sleep. I recalled a student trip to the deep Tunisian hinterland over twenty years ago, the shredded trash flying through the cold winter breeze like colourful snow, the well-educated, over-qualified and utterly unemployable men and women selling homemade snacks on the street corners. Well, the Tunisians had certainly done something about *that*.

I opened my eyes. *When things are really bad, everybody gets involved*, I distantly thought.

Later that morning I made arrangements to meet up with Alfons Prieto: a tough, middle-aged Venezuelan-born activist and writer on societal issues in South America. He'd moved to Brazil after getting booted out the CAU (Central American Union) for his critical editorials on the ruling oligarchy. We agreed to meet for lunch, where I half intended to pick out a few souvenirs for the kids back home.

I found Alfons loitering outside a large, makeshift marquee. After exchanging greetings he tilted his head toward the noise coming from within.

"Hey Vera, you seen this yet?" he asked, gesturing at the open tent flap. "This is the fifth gathering of the kind I've found today. The police don't know what to make of it. Hell, a few of them have even joined in. I feel like we should be celebrating."

I looked around nervously, half expecting to hear the pop and hiss of a tear gas grenade, the snarl of police dogs and the whine of drones armed with sonic weapons. After Berlin I swore I'd never get involved in another confrontation of that kind (which had left me half deaf in one ear).

Alfons saw my unease and smiled. "Don't worry, girl. Something else is going on here, nothing like the conference, or the protests. I just don't understand. The people in that tent are from all over the world. Other meetings had community leaders, local officials, students – even street kids, for God's sake. The conversations are spontaneous but *structured*. I've been in this city for years and have never seen anything like it."

I nodded and told Alfons about what I had heard on the beach.

"Then you've seen it too," he replied, "Funny how people just get together and solve problems themselves."

"Yes. Usually, when they're angry," I said, peering through the flap and watching the group of some twenty people gathered in a circle. Many of them were sitting on benches.

"Hm, not these," Alfons said, "They're talking about the future, change – an *Idea*. I've already called a sociologist friend to look into it."

"I shouldn't have bothered," I said, turning away. "It's probably just another meme, a fad. Like pictures of cats, wearing monocles."

"Perhaps, perhaps not. Somebody once explained to me that an Idea evolves, matures. It's just *ready*, a necessary development that takes root amongst small groups before expanding exponentially, independent of technology, culture or politics. I've been listening: they're figuring out what it means to be happy, what works in today's world and what doesn't. They're solving problems. And you know what? They really believe they *can do it*. Hell, *I* almost believe it!"

"Sounds like the conference all over again," I said sourly.

"Hah! At the conference people were just recycling dogma, pretending to justify their tenure and permanent salaries. But over the past few weeks I heard of multiple initiatives around Rio and elsewhere on the continent. Most are very small, local – often little more than five or ten people. The *favelas* are in an uproar, but in a *good* way, I think. Now governments, colleges, universities, schools are joining in too. Even businesses are involved, thank goodness. They know something is wrong. Maybe some of them are actually looking beyond their quarterly reports."

I didn't smile at the joke. "I don't get it, Alfons. What are all these people doing that's so special?"

Alfons considered the question for a few moments. "They're *cooperating*, Vera. It seems they really listen to each other. No, don't give me that look," he said gently, "I've seen what they do. Everybody gets a say in there. Everybody has a job to do. The locals are calling these gatherings *collaboratores*."

"The collaboratory," I said distantly, recalling what I had heard on the beach.

"Something like that. Maybe this *isn't* twenty twelve all over again. Waddaya think?"

I peeked through the tent flap again, warily watching the boisterous group inside.

"I think it's good. It's about time *everybody* did something about this mess we're in," I said, turning to Alfons, "Listen. Does a cynic who comes full circle become an optimist again – or just a worse cynic?"

Alfons regarded me; his eyes narrow in the hard light. "Anybody ever tell you you've been doing this kind of thing too long?" he asked.

This time I laughed. I let Alfons guide me away from the marquee and into a small market where I bought a miniature bench – a tiny thing that fitted neatly in the palm of my hand, a dainty, gaily painted toy of varnished matchsticks. It would make a charming (analogue) addition to my daughter's AI-controlled doll house.

We sat on a bench and conversed a while longer, eating frozen yoghurt while watching the *Rainbow Warrior* dirigible dispense clouds of smog scrubbers over our heads like confetti.

Later that afternoon I returned to my hotel room without bothering to arrange more interviews. Nobody was answering their slates anyway and the heat, sweat and noise of central Rio had left me drained. At the same time I also wanted to find out whether there was anything else to what Alfons has said to me earlier.

To my surprise, I found that the world's vlogs and hive feeds were literally abuzz with activity. The forums groaned under the strain of comments, suggestions and arguments, though with noticeably less of the customary bickering I was used to seeing on the political feeds. I hurriedly scrolled through hundreds of trending topics with mystifying titles such as *Colab_712_HK_submissions, CLB 2nite NAIRB, 3E-Academia, ExecMonLocations?*, or *Pop-up BuS (Ougadougou)*. One of the more animated discussions was nested under the heading *Fix-This-Shit*, seemingly initiated by a loose group of social workers, schools, small business owners and squatters in Diepsloot Township near Johannesburg.

I pushed away the slate, my head spinning from the avalanche of information.

My last two days in Rio were no different. Alfons was right: people were changing, listening, working together with an enthusiasm and efficiency that seemed frankly impossible a few weeks ago. A little more digging had revealed that the Idea had started well before Rio+40 amongst an informal group, just a bunch of semi-random people who shared a vision, deciding they'd had enough and that the time had come to start again.

I came to Rio believing I'd find our society making little or no progress on problems as old as humanity itself. I was wrong. I had found something else, perhaps something better and more lasting than the endless circular dialogue I had come to expect from such political and money-tainted gatherings. For the first time I thought I saw direction, a consensus that people – *all* people – can do something about the ridiculous, self-manufactured disasters our species has landed itself in.

To be honest, those three days after the conference had scared me a little. From what I've seen during my career, the human race is not naturally inclined to cooperate, but that was what I saw in Rio. It's what I'm seeing all around the world right now: a real desire to resolve problems, a willingness to talk, listen, admit mistakes – a common urge to *create something truly good*. Maybe Alfons was right; maybe things will be *different* now.

Either way, I'll help them. It's time to try something else.

Appendix 1   50+20 Global Survey of Management Education

DEMOGRAPHICS

A balanced group of 145 respondents completed the survey, representing 37 countries around the world:

46% Western Europe
17% North America
12% India, Pakistan and
   Bangladesh
 6% South America
 6% Africa

6% Australia and New Zealand
6% Russia
6% Eastern Europe
1% Middle East
1% Asia (China and Singapore)

Generational perspective:
21% below 30 years
36% 30–45 years
27% 45–60 years
16% above 60 years

Note: To ensure a balanced geo perspective, Spain is represented only by people below 30 years, NGO and not-for-profit employees.

Professional background:
21% business professionals /
   executives
20% business or management
   scholars
16% students or graduates of
   business schools
16% NGO or not-for-profit
   employees
11% consultants
10% pedagogical / educational
   coaches
 6% concerned citizens, futurists,
   artists

SUMMARY CONCLUSIONS

The Future of Business Schools (b-schools)

Eighty percent of respondents demand that business schools focus in the future on developing leaders that drive global problem solving with all stakeholders, rather than "simply" training skilled professionals for business. A surprising 57% of respondents demand that business schools should focus on the bottom 4 billion of the pyramid (i.e. developing and emerging countries), a perspective that is largely ignored today. Entrepreneurs (62%), SMEs (small and medium-sized enterprises) (47%), organizations of all types (NGOs, start-ups, MNCs, SMEs, not-for-profit, government organizations) and the individual student and her needs are stated the other top stakeholder groups business school should focus on.

When asked how the success of business schools should be measured, the salary increase of graduates as well as the ranking of the school are considered largely irrelevant (70% and 65% respectively). Research is not selected as a measure at all, contrary to all leading ranking that put important value on research publications as a relevant measure. Respondents measure the success of a business school solely by the competences, abilities and skills of graduates, namely: "the ability to adopt different perspectives and understanding the larger picture" (81%), "holistic decision-making skills, including societal and environmental factors" (78%), "entrepreneurial skills" (56%) and "leadership skills" (51%). While it may be a bit of a challenge to determine how to measure these competences of graduates, one may wonder why these factors are mostly absent from ratings and rankings today.

The Future of Management Education

Developing leadership skills ranks as the clear number one priority when looking at future educational priorities: for young students it is defined as "ethics, values and developing the person" (81%), and for professionals / executives as "responsible, sustainable and ethical behavior" (84%). Executives are also expected to "understand the larger context of business, societal and environmental issues" (83%). Leadership competences to be developed most are "deeply engrained ethics and a responsible behavior" (80%), "critical reasoning and holistic decision-making" (70%) as well as "reflective skills" (66%).

When asked how such leaders can be developed, the respondents favor state-of-the-art pedagogical approaches: "creating experimental learning situations for personal leadership skills" and "hands-on learning situations" (both 56%), "embodied and experimental learning" (49%), "values-based learning" (45%) and "co-creating the curriculum with students" (37%).

The Future of Management Research

New priorities for management research emerge: resolving societal and global issues (53% and 50% respectively), inter-disciplinary issues in business (51%) and transdisciplinary issues of business and other sectors (47%). Topics to be addressed are: "how to make business responsible and sustainable" (70%), "how to develop globally responsible leaders" (66%), "the role of business and its responsibility towards consumers, society and the planet" (63%) and "new measures for economic, social and environmental effectiveness of business" (57%).

There is clear consensus that future research should be conducted in an inter-disciplinary way (84%), as action research (81%) and transdisciplinary addressing larger issues with input from non-business fields (80%). There is an overwhelming request that research objectives address emerging issues of the future (96%) rather than studying current and past phenomena. Respondents believe that management research should be conducted for business practitioners (62%) and various societal stakeholders (61%) rather than for an academic peer audience (15%).

UNDERSTANDING PRIORITIES, MEASURES AND FUTURE FOCUS OF BUSINESS SCHOOLS

What business schools are perceived to focus on today (4)

1. Train skilled professionals for business (51%)
2. Ensure literacy in managing skills (37%)

Criterion: yes – very much (30% + above)

What b-schools should focus on in future (5)

1. Develop leaders that drive global problem solving with all stakeholders (80%)
2. Develop managers/leaders for all types of organizations (64%)
3. Train skilled professionals for business (51%)
4. Ensure literacy in comprehensive managing skills (42%)

Direct quotes from respondents:

- I am doing research in this field: knowledge and some skills to get a job.
- Most schools, particularly in less developed economies, are just doing a little more than producing degrees.

- Managers must have a broader social and political as well as philosophical framework to have the right thinking framework – management skills can be easily taught later 'on the job'.

In future, which stakeholders should b-schools focus on most (6)

1. Entrepreneurs (62%)
2. The bottom 4 billion of the pyramid: developing and emerging countries (57%)
3. Small and medium-sized businesses (47%)
4. Organizations of all types: NGOs, start-ups, MNCs, SMEs, not-for-profit, government organizations (40%)
5. The individual student who wants an education (40%)
6. Non-government and not-for-profit organizations (33%)
7. Government organizations (29%)
8. Large multinational corporations (28%)
9. Bankers and financial institutions (26%)
10. Anybody who wants to learn about business and management: providing quality education for free online (24%)

Criterion: very important (all)

Direct quotes from respondents:

- Really depends on the country and cannot be answered in general. Business schools for emerging markets are really different animals (or should be) than business schools for mature markets.
- Schools and students need to understand the linkages between Public, Private and NGO/Third sector.

How should the success of b-schools be measured (7)

Very important	*Irrelevant + I am indifferent*
1. Graduates' ability to adopt different perspectives / understand the larger picture (81%)	1. The salary increase of graduates (70%)
2. Graduates' holistic decision-making skills, including societal and environmental factors (78%)	2. The ranking of the school (65%)
3. Graduates' entrepreneurial skills (56%)	
4. Graduates' leadership skills (51%)	*Criterion for both: 50% + above*

Direct quotes from respondents:

- Also the long-term contribution in the society say in 5 or 10 years
- Re ranking: the criteria for rankings should change.

UNDERSTANDING EDUCATIONAL PRIORITIES OF THE FUTURE

Future educational priorities

Young students (8)	**Professionals and executives (9)**
1. Developing leadership skills: ethics, values, developing the person (81%)	1. Developing leadership skills: responsible, sustainable and ethical behavior (84%)
2. Creating an awareness of future emerging business, societal and environmental issues (72%)	2. Understanding the larger context of business, societal and environmental issues (83%)
3. Creating real-life exposure to the world, business and work (69%)	3. Creating hands-on exposure to global issues (project work) (56%)
4. Providing contextual insight of the role of business in the world (society, planet, historic) (59%)	4. Testing business models serving society, the planet and making money (51%)
Criterion: very important (50% + above)	*Note:* "Providing a general management education: applying theories to business" (19%) scored lowest.

Direct quotes from respondents:

- Education must be connected to practice – not a repetition of early years class room pedagogy.
- Definitely needs to be applied and systemic. They need a felt experience of their choices and actions on others and the environment in which they work.

- Efforts must "mesh" the role of business (public and private) as well as government, NGOs, church, relation and spirituality, education, law enforcement, health care into systemic and integrated efforts.

Importance of work experience (10)

- Very important: Managers / leaders cannot be developed without work experience (60%).
- Quite important: Work experience helps students understand business concepts (34%).
- Not very important: Management education can be provided at all levels (6%).

Direct quotes from respondents:

- Ideally the German model of apprenticeship should be the role model for the business school. The business school should not only focus on theory but also on the deliberate development of skills to develop talents.
- An oxymoron. You can't teach management to someone who hasn't managed. Biology is a subject. Management is an art and an activity that has to be continually honed.

What should a leader look like (11)

1. An innovator able to create long-term sustainable value (73%)
2. A leader working with various stakeholders towards a better society and world (66%)
3. A person connecting deeper values to the organizational context (51%)

Criterion: very important (50% + above)

Leadership competences to be strengthened most (12)

1. Deeply engrained ethics and a responsible behavior (80%)
2. Critical reasoning and holistic decision-making (70%)
3. Reflective skills: personal development and self-knowledge (66%)
4. Collaborative skills (62%)
5. Strategic thinking (56%)

Direct quotes from respondents:

- The new social contract for the twenty-first century is business in service of society in a much more sophisticated way than today where the assumption is deliver growth and obey the law and we all benefit.

- Courage is a competency? Would like to see a bit more of it in some of the companies I know. And hypocrisy is a competency that has been refined among many leaders I see (should be avoided).

How can such leaders be developed (13)

1. Creating experimental learning situations for personal leadership skills (56%)
2. Hands-on learning situations, projects (53%)
3. Embodied and experimental learning experiences (45%)
4. Values-based learning (49%)
5. Cross-creating the curriculum with students: sharing the responsibility of learning (37%)
6. Issue-centered learning that is facilitated: joint learning (34%)
7. Teaching functional skills: marketing, finance, HRM, strategy (10%)

Criterion: very important (all)

> **Direct quotes from respondents:**
>
> ● Co-creation of the curriculum is the key to the future – the choice to decide what to learn and how led by great facilitators.

UNDERSTANDING RESEARCH PRIORITIES OF THE FUTURE

What should mgmt. research focus on (14)

1. Resolving societal issues (53%)
2. Inter-disciplinary issues in business (51%)
3. Resolving global issues (50%)
4. Transdisciplinary issues of business and beyond (47%)
5. Pedagogy / andragogy of develop. leaders (28%)
6. Addressing mgmt. issues (22%)
7. Addressing specific business issues (20%)
8. Development of bus/mgmt. theory (17%)

Criterion: very important (all)

How should mgmt. research be conducted (15)

1. Inter-disciplinary research: studying a business issue from different perspectives (84%)
2. Transdisciplinary research: addressing larger issues with input from non-business fields (80%)
3. Action research: being involved and interacting with subject (81%)

Criterion: very important (50% + above)

Direct quotes from respondents:

- Should be "active research", not only passive.
- I think our understanding of today's reality is very fragmented. We need to think our-of-the-box. We need to innovate theory. We need new models.

- The how is less important than the what should be researched. We need to design a business system that delivers social justice and environmental sustainability – there is almost zero knowledge on how to implement such a system. This is the research agenda for ALL business schools to focus on so society can benefit from the resources we apply to these institutions and they may then stand a chance to be useful to the future.
- Developing solutions for real issues.

Comparing current versus future objectives of management research	*Perceived current*	*Perceived future*
1. Studying the past: explaining phenomena through historic data	60 %	44 %
2. Studying the present: understanding emerging phenomena and trends by developing new concepts and theories	66 %	82 %
3. Studying the future: addressing emerging issues by developing scenarios and alternative theories	58 %	96 %

Direct quotes from respondents:

- Management research today is academic self satisfaction.
- Current research is becoming focused on turning the practical academics of management into a pure academics field. This is a dead end.

- Done collaboratively with practitioners!
- Looking at business issues in the context of society and the next generations.

Who should management research be done for (18)

1. Various societal stakeholder: potentially jointly developed (61%)
2. Business practitioners and executives: collaborative effort accessible to wide audience (62%)
3. General public: understandable and applicable for everybody (25%)
4. An academic peer audience: typically through journal publications (15%)

Criterion: very important (all)

Key topics to be addressed by management research (20)

1. How to make business responsible and sustainable (70%)
2. How to develop globally responsible leaders (66%)
3. The role of business and its responsibility towards consumers, society and the planet (63%)
4. New measures for economic, social and environmental effectiveness of business (57%)
5. The role of business leaders in resolving global issues (44%)

Direct quotes from respondents:

- The use of business potential/power to solve real (social) issues.
- The new measure cannot be merely quantitative – we need to value more again qualitative evaluations.

Source: Developed at Business School Lausanne.

Appendix 2 Authorship, contributors, participants, reviewers, editors

SPONSORING CO-AUTHORS

The following institutions generously provided financial assistance to 50+20 and are formally recognized as sponsors and co-authors of the 50+20 Agenda:

ACKNOWLEDGEMENTS

This book, *Management Education for the World: A Vision for Business Schools Serving People and Planet* has been written to capture and present in depth the work of the 50+20 Project. This project was inspired by a growing number of business schools and societal roleplayers critically questioning the role of business and economics. It was initiated by three "founding partners" namely the Globally Responsible Leadership Initiative (www.grli.org), the World Business School Council for Sustainable Business (www.wbscsb.org) and the secretariat of the United Nations Global Compact's Principles for Responsible Management Education (www.unprme.org). Financial assistance was received from 16 institutions already listed. They are recognized as official co-authors of The 50+20 Agenda. That document was launched at Rio+20 (the United Nations Conference on Sustainable Development) on 15 June 2012 at the occasion of the 3rd Global Forum for Responsible Management Education.

The book was created by an authoring-editorial team on behalf of the 50+20 Project who collectively both wrote original work, melded in the contributions from across the project and incorporated the wisdom contained in the plethora of prior writings on the subject. These author-editors are: Dr. Katrin Muff, Dean of Business School Lausanne, who lead with passion, energy, conceptual thinking and many weeks of writing and re-writing and was an inspiration to her co-editors; Professor Thomas Dyllick, Director of the Institute for Economy and the Environment at the University of St. Gallen, who partnered Dr. Muff in writing and re-writing, conceptualization and foundation in the academic literature; Mark Drewell, who as CEO of the GRLI combines a rare mix of thought leadership and business and NGO practice; John North, who brought a substantial writing contribution alongside his role as project manager and master of the deliverable; Professor Paul Shrivastava, Director of the David O'Brien Center for Sustainable Enterprise, John Molson School of Business, Concordia University who made a critical contribution to raising the bar whenever the work appeared to become too comfortable; and Jonas Haertle who as head of the PRME Secretariat provided an important link to the broader incremental agenda of PRME. Outside the author-editor team, Professor Derick de Jongh, Director of the Albert Luthuli Centre for Responsible Leadership at the University of Pretoria merits special recognition for his contribution as a member of the 50+20 Steering group.

Of course, a comprehensive work like this always stands on the shoulders of intellectual giants whose ideas infuse it in many different ways. A number of specific contributions are acknowledged within the document. Our thanks go to these people – and our apologies to anyone we may have inadvertently overlooked. In terms of extensive writing, conceptual thinking and contribution to this work, the core team would like to specifically acknowledge and thank (in alphabetical order):

Anders Aspling (GRLI Foundation, BE)
Antonin Pujos (Zermatt Summit Foundation, CH/FR)
Caroline Rennie (Business School Lausanne, CH)
Chris Taylor (OASIS, GB)
Claire Maxwell (OASIS, GB)
Eddie Blass (Swinburne University of Technology, AU)
Fernando D'Alessio (Centrum Catolica, PE)
Henri-Claude de Bettignies (China Europe International Business School, CN)
John Cimino (Creative Leaps International, US)
John Ryan (Center for Creative Leadership, US)
Jonathan Smith (Anglia Ruskin University, GB)
Josep Lozano (ESADE, ES)
Madelon Evers (Business School Lausanne, CH)
Mark Rice (Worcester Polytechnic Institute, US)
Michel Alhadeff-Jones (Teachers College, Columbia University, US)
Peggy Cunningham (Dalhousie University, CA)
Peter Jonker (4N6 Factory, CH)
Philippe de Woot (GRLI Foundation, BE)
Regina Eckert (Center for Creative Leadership, BE)
Ruben Guevara (Centrum Catolica, PE)
Uwe Steinwender (Daimler Corporate Academy, DE)

In addition, more than 100 thought leaders from five continents and many institutions contributed to the work by commenting on the drafts or by adding their vital perspectives to the vision during the various workshops and retreats, as well as on the GRLI's SB21 project which was merged into the 50+20 work.

These contributors are (in alphabetical order):
Ahmad Al-Mughrabi (Business School Lausanne, CH)
Aileen Somers (IMD, CH)
Alain Irwin (Copenhagen Business School, GB)
Alex Barkawi (oikos Foundation, CH)
Alfons Sauquet (ESADE, ES)
Altaf Muhammad Saleem (Shakarganj Mills Limited)

Amanda Gudmundsson (Queensland University of Technology, AU)
Ana Magyar (Petrobras, BR)
Anncathrin Scheider (Business School Lausanne, CH)
Anne Tsui (Arizona State University, US)
Armi Temmes (Aalto University, FI)
Arnold Smit (University of Stellenbosch, ZA)
Birgit Kleymann (IESEG School of Management, FR)
Bjorn Larson (The Foresight Group, SE)
Carol Adams (La Trobe University, AU)
Cathy Neligan (Oasis, GB)
Charles Savage (Knowledge Era Enterprises, DE)
Chris Taylor (Oasis, GB)
Chris Turner (WBCSD, CH)
Christina Trott (Daimler Corporate Academy, DE)
Christoph Badelt (Vienna University of Economics and Business, AT)
Christopher Wasserman (Zermatt Foundation, CH/FR)
Chukwunonye Emenalo (Lagos Business School, NG)
Cláudio Boechat (Fundação Dom Cabral, BR)
David Grayson (Cranfield School of Management, GB)
Dennis Hanno (Babson College, US)
Don Ritter (KOR)
Doug Gilbert (University of Phoenix, US)
Edson Cunha (Petrobras, BR)
Eline Loux (GRLI Foundation, BE)
Ellen van Velsor (Center for Creative Leadership, US
Enase Okonedo (Lagos Business School, NI)
Eric Cornuel (EFMD, BE)
Frederik Landman (University of Stellenbosch, ZA)
Geoff Tudhope (Merryck & Co, UK)
George Kohlrieser (IMD, CH)
Giselle Weybrecht (Independent, BE)
Gustaf Delin (The Foresight Group, SE)
Hamid Bouchikhi (ESSEC, FR)
Harald Heinrichs (Leuphana University , DE)
Harriet Jackson (oikos International, CH)
Heidi Newton-King (Yellow Woods)
Howard Gardner (Harvard Graduate School of Education, US)
Howard Thomas (Singapore Management University, SG)
Ivo Matser (TSM Business School, NL)
Jean-Christophe Carteron (Euromed, FR)
Jeanie Forray (Western New England University, US)
Jerôme Caby (ICN Business School, FR)

JingJing Wang (Daimler Corporate Academy, DE)
John Alexander (Leadership Horizons, US)
John Mooney (Pepperdine University, US)
John Ryan (Center for Creative Leadership, US)
Jonathan Cook (University of Pretoria, ZA)
Jonathan Gosling (Exeter Business School, GB)
Jost Hamschmidt (oikos Foundation, CH)
Julia Christensen Hughes (University of Guelph, CA)
Kai Hockerts (Copenhagen Business School, DK)
Kim Poldner (oikos International, CH)
Kristina Henriksson (Simon Fraser University, CA)
Lene Mette Sørensen (Copenhagen Bus. School, DK)
Leticia Greyling (Rhodes University, ZA)
Liliana Petrella (EFMD, BE)
Lisle Ferreira (PRME, US)
Lloyd Williams (ITTL Doctoral Research Center & University, US)
Louis Klein (Systemic Excellence Group, DE)
Maja Göpel (World Future Council, BE)
Malcolm McIntosh (Griffith University, AU)
Marielle Heijltjes (Maastricht University , NL)
Marion McGowan (Middlesex University Business School, GB)
Mark Esposito (Grenoble Ecole de Management, FR)
Mary Gentile (Babson College, Boston)
Mary Godfrey (Bettys & Taylors of Harrogate)
Mary Watson (The New School, US)
Mathias Falkenstein (EFMD, BE)
Matt Statler (NYU Stern School of Business, US)
Matthew Wood (EFMD, BE)
Michael Hanson (Columbia University, US)
Michael Jensen (Harvard Business School, US)
Michael Powell (Griffith University, AU)
Mike Donnelly (Swinburne University of Technology, AU)
Nick Ellerby (Oasis, GB)
Nick Main (Deloitte Touche Tohmatsu, GB)
Nidhi Srinivas (The New School, US)
Nigel Roome (Vlerick Leuven, BE)
Otto Scharmer (MIT, US)
Paul Hopkinson (University of Gloucestershire, GB)
Paulo Resende (Fundacao Dom Cabral, BR)
Percy Marquina (Centrum Catolica , PE)
Peter Little (Queensland University of Technology, AU)
Philippe Du Pasquier (Business School Lausanne, CH)

Pierre Tapie (ESSEC, FR)
Ralph Meima (Marlboro College, US)
Richard Barrett (Barrett Values Centre, US)
Rishab Thakrar (Business School Lausanne, CH)
Sandra Waddock (Boston College, US)
Sanjay Sharma (University of Vermont, US)
Sanjeeb Kakoty (Rajiv Gandhi Indian Institute of Management, IN)
Sascha Spoun (Leuphana University, DE)
Sauli Sohlo (Oulu Business School, FN)
Sevanna Kassarjian (POAL, US)
Susan Jackson (Rutgers University, US)
Suzanne Feinmann (WBCSD, CH)
Thomas Bieger (University of St. Gallen, CH)
Thomas Sattelberger (Deutsche Telekom, DE)
Tobias Hagenau (Northern Institute of Technology Management, DE)
Vyacheslav Gordeyev (Moscow International Higher Business School, RU)
Walter Baets (University of Cape Town, ZA)
Walter Fust (Kofi Annan Foundation, CH)
Yuriy Blagov (St.Petersburg University, RU)

Our thanks go to Jürgen Zimmermann (ZA) for his editorial input – with particular emphasis on his work on the Agenda and writing the manuscript epilogue. Appreciation and thanks are also given to Gay Haskins (UK) and Rosie Boscawen (UK) for their support in editing, copywriting and copyediting. Our thanks to Ilka Franzmann (DE) for her tireless work in directing the 50+20 film and documentary and Claudius Bensch (DE) for his art direction for the benchmark installation and benches – and thanks to both Claudius and Ilka for conceptualizing the benchmark campaign. Christopher Rowe (DE) deserves thanks in his role as cameraman along with Nic Grobler (ZA) who also designed the 50+20 identity, prepared the layout of the 50+20 Agenda and the cover of this book. Our thanks also go to Jacqueline Fouché (ZA) for supporting website development. Photography of the New York and St. Gallen retreats was managed by Jon Reznick (US) and the Brussels retreat by Emilie Derville (BE). Many thanks to Jan Kees van der Wild and his team at Volcafé for enabling and sponsoring the transportation of the benches to the Rio launch of the 50+20 Agenda.

This truly was a collaborative effort. Thank you all.

GLOBALLY RESPONSIBLE LEADERSHIP INITIATIVE

The Globally Responsible Leadership Initiative is a worldwide partnership of over 74 companies, business schools and learning organizations working together to develop a generation of globally responsible leaders. Founded by EFMD and UNGC in 2004 it published "A Call for Engagement" in 2005. This and subsequent work in catalytic projects, new learning practices, advocacy and thought leadership is focused on a deep transformation in management education beyond incremental changes. In 2009 the GRLI began creating a blueprint of the business school of the twenty-first century. This work has been incorporated into the 50+20 vision. The GRLI is also making the 50+20 vision the central platform of its work and will continue to act as holding space from which 50+20 can expand its impact.
www.grli.org

WORLD BUSINESS SCHOOL COUNCIL FOR SUSTAINABLE BUSINESS

The World Business School Council for Sustainable Business (WBSCSB) was founded in August 2010 at a pre-conference to the Academy of Management Annual Meeting, organized by Paul Shrivastava of the O'Brien Center at Concordia University in Montreal. A small number of deans and directors from around the world agreed that it was high time for the community of business schools to engage in the public dialogue on sustainability

and how management education could contribute to resolving global challenges. In 2012 the WBSCSB announced that it will integrate with the GRLI to enable the work of deep transformation in management education to proceed efficiently.
www.wbscsb.com

PRME Principles for Responsible Management Education

PRINCIPLES FOR RESPONSIBLE MANAGEMENT EDUCATION

The Principles for Responsible Management Education (PRME) is a UN Global Compact sponsored initiative with the mission to inspire and champion responsible management education, research and thought leadership globally. The Principles seek to establish a process of continuous improvement among management-related academic institutions to develop a new generation of business leaders capable of managing the complex challenges faced by business and society. Over 450 academic institutions in 80 countries have signed up. PRME's Steering Committee includes AACSB International, EFMD, AMBA, GMAC, the Association of African Business Schools and Association of Asia-Pacific Business Schools, CEEMAN, Latin American Council of Management Schools, EABIS, GRLI, and Net Impact.
www.unprme.org

Bibliography

AACSB International (2011): *Globalization of Management Education.* Tampa: AACSB International.

AACSB International (2008): Final report of the AACSB International Impact of Research task force. Tampa: AACSB International.

Adler, N.J./Harzing, A.-W. (2009): "When knowledge wins: transcending the sense and nonsense of academic rankings". *Academy of Management Learning and Education*, Vol. 8, No. 1, 72–95.

Alhadeff-Jones, M. (2008): "Promoting scientific dialogue as a lifelong learning process". In: Darbellay, F./Cockell, M./Billotte, J./Waldvogel, F. (eds). *A Vision of Transdisciplinarity.Laying Foundations for a World Knowledge Dialogue*. Lausanne, Switzerland: Swiss Federal Institute of Technology Press & CPC Press, 94–102.

Argyris, C. (2000): *Flawed Advice and the Management Trap. How Managers can Know When They're Getting Good Advice and When They're Not*. Oxford/New York: Oxford University Press.

Barton, D. (2011): "Capitalism for the long term". *Harvard Business Review*, March, 85–91.

Beck, D.E./Cowan, C.C. (2005): *Spiral Dynamics: Mastering Values, Leadership and Change*. Wiley-Blackwell.

Bennis, W.G./O'Toole, J. (2005): "How business schools lost their way". *Harvard Business Review*, May–June, 96–104.

Bieger , T. (2011): "Business schools – from career training centers towards enablers of CSR: A new vision for teaching at business schools". Morsing/Sauquet (eds), 104–113.

Carroll, A./Buchholtz, A.K. (2011): *Business and Society: Ethics, Sustainability, and Stakeholder Management*, 8th edn. Mason, OH: South-Western Cengage Learning.

Chin, G., Jr./Lansing, C.S. (2004). "Capturing and supporting contexts for scientific data sharing via the biological sciences collaboratory". *Proceedings of the 2004 ACM conference on computer supported cooperative work*, 409–418, New York: ACM Press.

Chouinard, Y./Ellison, J./Ridgeway, R. (2011): "The sustainable economy". *Harvard Business Review*, Vol. 89, October, 52–62.

Coetzee, J. (2012): *The Social Contract with Business: Beyond the Quest for Global Sustainability*. London: Xlibris Publishers.

Cogburn, D.L. (2003): "HCI in the so-called developing world". *Interactions*, 10: 80.

Colby, A./Ehrlich, T./Sullivan, W.M./Dolle, J.R. (2011): "Rethinking undergraduate business education: Liberal learning for the profession". A report by the Carnegie Foundation for the Advancement of Teaching. San Francisco: Jossey-Bass.

Cooperrider, D.L./Whitney, D. (2005): *Appreciative Inquiry: A Positive Revolution in Change*. San Francisco: Berrett-Koehler Publishers.

Datar, S.M./Garvin, D.A./Cullen, P.G. (2010): *Rethinking the MBA. Business Education at the Crossroads*. Boston, MA: Harvard Business Press.

De Jesus, P./de Souza, F./Teixera-Dias, J.J.C./Watts, M. (2005): "Organising the chemistry of question based learning". *Research and Science in Technological Education*, Vol. 23, No. 2.

Denning S. (2011): "Why 'shared value' can't fix capitalism". *Forbes*, 20 December.

DeMillo, R.A. (2011): *Abelard to Apple. The Fate of the American Colleges and Universities*. Cambridge, MA: MIT Press.

Domegan, C./Bringle, R. (2010): "Charting social marketing's implications for service-learning". *Journal of Nonprofit & Public Sector Marketing*, Vol. 22, 198–215.

Dossabhoy, N.S/Berger, P.D. (2002): "Business school research. Bridging the gap between producers and consumers". *Omega*, Vol. 30, 301–314.

Drucker, P. (1979): *Management* (an abridged and revised version of *Management: Tasks, Responsibilities, Practices*). London: Pan Books (first published 1977).

Economist, The (2011): "Trouble in the middle". *The Economist*, 15 October, 71–72.

Emerson, J. (2003): "The blended value proposition. Integrating social and financial returns". *California Management Review*, Vol. 45, No. 4, Summer.

Emerson, R.W. (1837): "The American scholar". A speech given at Cambridge, MA, 31 August, accessed at 1837.http://www.emerson central.com/amscholar.htm.

Erhard, W.H./Jensen, M.C./Granger, K.L. (2012): "Creating leaders: an ontological/phenomenological model". In: Snook, S.A./Nohria, N.N./ Khurana, R. (eds): *The Handbook for Teaching Leadership*. Thousand Oaks: Sage Publications, 245–261.

Ernst, C./Chrobot-Mason, D. (2011): *Boundary Spanning Leadership. Six*

Practices for Solving Problems, Driving Innovation, and Transforming Organizations. New York: McGraw-Hill.

European Commission (2012): *30 Good Practice Case Studies in University-Business Cooperation*. Münster, Germany: Science-to-Business Marketing Research Centre.

Finger, M./Asún, J.M. (2001): *Adult Education at the Crossroads. Learning Our Way Out*. New York: Zed Books.

Friedman, M. (1970): "The social responsibility of business is to increase its profits". In: *The New York Times Magazine*, 13 September.

Gardner, H. (2011): *Leading Minds. An Anatomy of Leadership*. New York: Basic Books.

Gentile, M.C. (2010): *Giving Voice to Values*. New Haven: Yale University Press.

Ghemawat, P. (2011): *World 3.0 – Global Prosperity and how to Achieve It*. Boston, MA: Harvard Business Review Press.

Ghoshal, S. (2005): "Bad management theories are destroying good management practices". *Academy of Management Learning and Education*, Vol. 4, No. 1, 75–91.

Gibbons, M./Limoges, C./Nowotny, H./Schwartzman, S./Trow, M. (1994): *The New Production of Knowledge*. London: Sage.

Gilding, P. (2011): *The Great Disruption: How the Climate Crisis will Change Everything (for the better)*. New York: Bloomsbury Press.

Gladwell, M. (2011): "The order of things. What college rankings really tell us", *The New Yorker*, 14 and 21 February.

Globally Responsible Leadership Initiative (GRLI) (2008): "Globally Responsible Leadership. A call for action", accessed at http://www.grli.org/images/stories/grli/documents/Manifesto_GLOBAL.pdf.

Globally Responsible Leadership Initiative (GRLI) (2005): "Globally Responsible Leadership. A call for engagement", accessed at http://www.grli.org/images/stories/grli/documents/globally_responsible_leadership_report.pdf.

Gordon, R.A./Howell, J.E. (1959): *Higher Education for Business*. New York: Columbia University Press (Carnegie Foundation Report).

Gore, A./Blood, D. (2011): "A manifesto for sustainable capitalism. How businesses can embrace environmental, social and governance metrics". *The Wall Street Journal*, 14 December.

Graves, C.W. (2005): "The never ending quest". In Cowan, C./Todorovic, N. (eds). Santa Barbara, CA: ECLET Publishing.

Hacker, A./Dreifus, C. (2011): *Higher Education? How Colleges are Wasting Our Money and Failing our Kids – and What We Can Do About It*. New York: St.Martin's Griffin.

Hambrick, D.C. (1994): "What if the academy really mattered?" *Academy of Management Review*, Vol. 19, No.1, 11–16.

Hart, S.L. (2005): *Capitalism at the Crossroads: Aligning Business, Earth, and Humanity*. Upper Saddle River: Pearson.

Hattie, J./Marsh, H.W. (1996): "The relationship between research and teaching. A meta-analysis". *Review of Educational Research*, 66, 507–542.

Hay, M. (2008): "Business schools: A new sense of purpose". *Journal of Management Development*, Vol. 27, No. 4, 371–378.

Immerwahr, J./Johnson, J./Gasbarra, P. (2008): "The iron triangle: College presidents talk about costs, access, and quality". San Jose: National Center for Public Policy and Higher Education, cited in: DiMello (2011: 121).

Jackson, T. (2011): *Prosperity Without Growth. Economics for a Finite Planet.*London: Earthscan.

Jennings, C. (2012): "The rise of workplace learning. Introduction". A *Global Focus* Special Supplement .Vol. 6., No. 01.Brussels: EFMD.

Johnson, I. (2011): "Sustainability under scrutiny". Discussion Paper 01/11. Winterthur: The Club of Rome. www.clubofrome.org.

Jullien, F. (2009): *Les Transformations Silencieuses*. Paris: Editions Grasset & Fasquelle.

Jung, C. (2010): *Synchronicity: An Acausal Connecting Principle*. (From Vol. 8. of the Collected Works of C. G. Jung.) Princeton, NJ: Princeton University Press.

Kassarjian, J.B.M. (2013): "Business School Lausanne – a business school in transition". Case study. www.eech.com.

Khurana, R. (2007): *From Higher Aims to Hired Hands*. Princeton, NJ: Princeton University Press.

Khurana, R./Penrice, D. (2011): "Business education: The American trajectory". In: Morsing/Sauquet (eds), 3–15.

Kleppel, C. (2003): "Binnenwahrnehmung vs. Image – Zur Praxisrelevanz der deutschen Betriebswirtschaftslehre". *Die Betriebswirtschaft*, Vol. 63, No. 5, 581–585.

Kolb, D. (1984): *Experiential Learning: Experience as the Source of Learning and Development*. Englewood Cliffs: Prentice Hall.

Kolb, A.Y./Kolb, D.A. (2005): "Learning styles and learning spaces: Enhancing experiential learning in higher education". *Academy of Management Learning and Education*, Vol. 4, No. 2, 193–212.

Kuh, G.D. (2008): *High-impact Educational Practices. What They Are, Who has Access to Them, and Why They Matter*. Washington, DC: Association of American Colleges and Universities.

Lightman, A. (n.d.): "The role of the public intellectual". MIT

Communications Forum, accessed at http://web.mit.edu/comm-forum/papers/lightman.html (accessed 9 March 2012).

Lorange, P. (2008): *Thought Leadership Meets Business. How Business Schools can Become more Successful.* Cambridge: Cambridge University Press.

Marsh, H.W./Hattie, J. (2002): "The relation between research productivity and teaching effectiveness: complementary. antagonistic, or independent constructs?" *The Journal of Higher Education*, Vol. 73, No. 5, 603–641.

Martin, R.L. (2007): *The Opposable Mind: How Successful Leaders Win Through Integrative Thinking.* Boston, MA: Harvard Business School Press.

Marx, K. (1848): *The Communist Manifesto*, Brussels.

McCall, M. (2010): "The experience conundrum". In: Nohria, N./Khurana, R. (eds) (2010): *Handbook of Leadership Theory and Practice.* Harvard Business School centennial colloquium. Boston, MA: Harvard Business Press, 679–707.

McKenna, C. (2006): *The World's Newest Profession: Management Consulting in the 20th Century.* Cambridge: Cambridge University Press.

McTaggert, L. (2008): *The Field: The Quest for the Secret Force of the Universe.* New York: Harper Collins.

Meadows, D./Meadows, D./Randers, J./Behrens, W. (1972): *The Limits to Growth. A Report to the Club of Rome.* New York: Universe Books.

Mezirow, J. & Associates (2000): *Learning as Transformation: Critical Perspectives on a Theory in Progress.* San Francisco: Jossey-Bass.

Mintzberg, H. (2004): *Managers not MBAs: A Hard Look at the Soft Practice of Managing and Management Development.* San Francisco: Berret Koehler.

Mirvis, P.H./de Jongh, D. (2010): "Responsible leadership emerging – individual, organizational and collective frontiers". Center for Responsible Leadership Research Report.University of Pretoria, South Africa.

Mitroff, I. (2004): "An open letter to the deans and faculties of American business schools". *Journal of Business Ethics*, Vol. 54, 185–189.

Morgan, G. (2006): *Images of Organizations.* Thousand Oaks: Sage Publications.

Morsing, M./SauquetRovira, A. (eds) (2011): *Business Schools and their Contribution to Society.* London: Sage.

Muff, K. (2006): White paper on soul leadership. www.yupango.ch.

Muff, K. (2012): "Are business schools doing their job?" *Journal of Management Development*, Vol. 31 (7), 648–662.

Muff, K. (2012): "The collaboratory method and approach". Discussion Paper for 50+20, www.50plus20.org.

Nidumolu, R./Prahalad, C.K./Rangaswami, M.R. (2009): "Why sustainability is now the key driver of innovation". *Harvard Business Review*, September, Vol. 87, 57–64.

Nohria, N./Khurana, R. (2010): "Advancing leadership theory and practice". In: Nohria, N./Khurana, R. (eds), *Handbook of Leadership Theory and Practice*. Harvard Business School centennial colloquium. Boston, MA: Harvard Business Press, 3–25.

O'Brien, J.P./Drnewich, P.L./Crook, T.R./Armstrong, C.E. (2010): "Does business school research add economic value for students?" *Academy of Management Learning and Education*, December, Vol. 9, No. 4, 638–651.

OECD (2012): Education at a glance. Indicators for 2011.http://www.oecd.org/dataoecd/61/2/48631582.pdf.

Olian, J. (2011): "Business schools: A look back, a look ahead". In: BizEd, Tampa, FL: AACSB, November/December, 24–25.

Open Letter to Jose Manuel Barroso, President of the European Commission, et al. (2011): Public research should benefit society, not big business. Signed by nearly 100 NGOs from 22 European countries. Health and Environment Alliance: www.env-health.org/spip.php?article1232.

O'Shea, J./Madigan, C. (1998): *Dangerous Company: The Consulting Powerhouses and the Businesses they Save and Ruin*. New York: Penguin Books.

Österle, M.J. (2006): "Wahrnehmung betriebswirtschaftlicher Fachzeitschriften durch Praktiker". *Die Betriebswirtschaft*, Vol. 66, No. 3, 307–325.

Peck, M.S. (1994): *A World Waiting to be Born: Civility Rediscovered*. New York: Bantam Books.

Pedler, M. (ed.) (1991): *Action Learning in Practice*, 2nd edn. Brookfield, VT: Gower Publishers.

Pentland A. (2012): "The new science of building great teams". *Harvard Business Review*. April, 61–70.

Peters, K./Thomas, H. (2011): "A sustainable model for business schools?" *EFMD Global Focus*, Vol. 5, No. 2, 24–27.

Pettigrew, A. (2001): "Management research after modernism". *British Journal of Management*, Vol. 12, Special Issue, S61–S70.

Pfeffer, J./Fong, C.T. (2004): "The end of business schools? Less success than meets the eye". *Academy of Management Learning and Education*, Vol. 1, No. 1, 78–95.

Pierson, F.C. (1959): *The Education of American Businessmen*. New York: McGraw-Hill (Ford Foundation Report).

Pink, D.H. (2002): *Free Agent Nation: The Future of Working for Yourself*. New York: Warner Business Books.

Pless, N.M./Maak, T. (2011): "Responsible leadership: Pathways to the future". *Journal of Business Ethics*, 98, 3–13.

Podolny, J.M. (2009): "The buck stops (and starts) at business schools". *Harvard Business Review*, June, 62–67.

Popli, S. (2012): "Trends in business education – a perspective from India". Presentation at EFMD Deans & Directors Conference, Nottingham, January.

Porter, L./McKibbin, L. (1988): *Management Education and Development: Drift or Thrust into the 21st Century?* New York: McGraw-Hill.

Porter, M.E./Kramer, M.R. (2011): "Creating shared value". *Harvard Business Review*, January–February, 62–77.

Posner, R. (2002): *Public Intellectuals – a Study of Decline.* Cambridge, MA: Harvard University Press.

Prahalad, C.K. (2005): *The Fortune at the Bottom of the Pyramid: Eradicating Poverty through Profits.* New Delhi: Pearson Education/ Wharton School Publishing.

Quinn, L./van Velsor, E. (2012): "What it takes to get it right". *Leadership in Action*, January–February, Vol. 29, No. 6.

Quinn, L./van Velsor, E. (2009): "Globally responsible leadership: A leading edge conversation". Center For Creative Leadership Whitepaper. Greensboro, NC: Center For Creative Leadership.

Quinn, R.E. (2004): *Building the Bridge As You Walk On It: A Guide for Leading Change.* San Francisco: Jossey-Bass.

Rappaport, A. (1986): *Creating Shareholder Value: The New Standard for Business Performance.* New York: Free Press and London: Collier Macmillan.

Rappaport, A. (2011): *Saving Capitalism from Short-Termism : How to Build Long-term Value and Take Back our Financial Future.* New York: McGraw-Hill.

Ray, P.H./Sherry, R.A. (2000): *The Cultural Creatives: How 50 Million People are Changing the World* (illustrated edn), New York: Harmony Books.

Rayment, J./Smith, J. (2010): "The current and future role of business schools". Research report. Anglia Ruskin University: Cambridge and Chelmsford, UK.

Revans, R.W. (1982): *The Origin and Growth of Action Learning.* London: ChartwellBratt.

Rockström J. et al. (2010): "A safe operating space for humanity". *Nature*, 461, 24 September 2009, 472–475.

Rogers, C./Freiberg, H.J. (1994; first published 1969): *Freedom to Learn.* 3rd edn. Upper Saddle River: Prentice Hall.

Russell, B./Saunders, M. (2011): "How could business school research be perceived in 2025?", slides from presentation at EFMD conference. Brussels, 7 June.

Rynes, S.L./Shapiro, D.L. (2005): "Public policy and the public interest: what if we mattered more?" Editors Forum. *Academy of Management Journal*, Vol. 48, No. 6, 925–927.

Rynes, S.L./Bartunek, J.M./Daft, R.L. (2001): "Across the great divide: Knowledge creation and transfer between practitioners and academics". *Academy of Management Journal*, Vol. 44, No. 2, 340–355.

Scharmer, O. (2009): *Theory U. Leading from the Future as it Emerges.* San Francisco: Berret-Koehler.

Schneidewind, U. (2009): *Nachhaltige Wissenschaft. Plädoyer für einen Klimawandel im deutschen Wissenschafts- und Hochschulsystem.* Marburg: Metropolis-Verlag.

Senge, P./Scharmer, O. et al (2008): *Presence: Human Purpose and the Field of the Future.* New York: Currency Doubleday.

Shapiro, D.L./Kirkman, B.L./Courtney, H. (2007): "Perceived causes and solutions of the translation problem in management research". *Academy of Management Journal*, Vol. 50, No. 2, 249–266.

Shrivastava P. (2010): "Pedagogy of passion for sustainability". *Academy of Management Learning and Education*, Vol. 9, No. 3, 443–455.

Simon, H.A. (1967): "The business school: A problem in organizational design". *Journal of Management Studies*, Vol. 4, No.1, 1–16.

Skapinker, M. (2011): "Why business still ignores business schools". *The Financial Times*, 24 January.

Skapinker, M. (2008): "Why business ignores the business schools", *The Financial Times*, 7 January.

Sonnenwald, D.H./Whitton, M.C./Maglaughlin, K.L. (2003): "Scientific collaboratories: evaluating their potential". *Interactions*, Vol. 10, No. 4, 9–10.

Starkey, K./Tempest, S. (2008): "A clear sense of purpose? The evolving role of the business school". *Journal of Management Development*, Vol. 27, No. 4, 379–390.

Starkey, K./Hatchuel, A./Tempest, S. (2004): "Rethinking the business school". *Journal of Management Studies*, Vol. 41, No. 8, 1521–1531.

Starkey, K./Madan, P. (2001): "Bridging the relevance gap: Aligning stakeholders in the future of management research". *British Journal of Management*, Vol. 12, Special Issue, S3–S26.

Swaen, V./de Woot, Ph./de Callataÿ, D. (2011): "The business school of the twenty-first century: Educating citizens to address the new world challenges". In: Morsing/Sauquet (eds), 175–192.

Thomas, K.W./Tymon, W.G. (1982): "Necessary properties of relevant research: lessons from recent criticisms of the organizational sciences". *Academy of Management Review*, Vol. 7, No. 3, 345–352.

UN Secretary-General's high-level panel on global sustainability (2012): "Resilient people, resilient planet. A future worth choosing", accessed at http://www.un.org/gsp/.

Van de Ven, A. (2007): *Engaged Scholarship*. Oxford: Oxford University Press.

Van de Ven, A./Johnson, P. (2006): "Knowledge for theory and practice". *Academy of Management Review*, Vol. 31, No.4, 802–821.

Van Velsor, E./McCauley, C.D./Ruderman, M.N. (eds) (2010): *The Center for Creative Leadership Handbook of Leadership Development*, 3rd edn, San Francisco: Jossey Bass/Wiley.

Walsh, J.P. (2011): "Embracing the sacred in our secular world". 2010 presidential address. *Academy of Management Review*, Vol. 36, No. 2, 215–234.

Walsh, J.P./Tushman, M.L./Kimberly, J.R./Starbuck, B./Ashford, S. (2007): "On the relationship between research and practice: debate and reflections". *Journal of Management Inquiry*, Vol. 16, No.2, 128–154.

Willms, W.W./Zell, D.Z. (2002): *Awakening the Academy. A Time for New Leadership*. Boston, MA: Anker Publishing.

Wood, J.D. (2010): ."Building responsible leaders". *Viewpoint*. 21 June. Original version accessed at: http://www.businessweek.com/bschools/content/jun2010/bs20100621_879379.htm.

World Business Council for Sustainable Business (WBCSD) (2010): "Vision for 2050. The new agenda for business". Geneva: WBCSD.

World Economic Forum (2012): *Global Risks 2012*, 7th edn, www.weforum.org/issues/global-risks.

Wulf, W. (1993): "The collaboratory opportunity". *Science*, 261, 854–855.

WWF et al. (2010): "Living Planet Report 2010: Biodiversity, biocapacity and development". www.footprintnetwork.org.

Glossary

Collaboratory. An emerging approach and philosophy on management education that is central to the three roles envisaged in the 50+20 vision. The collaboratory may be defined as a facilitated circular space (physical or conceptual) created around any issue of relevance where members of a community (stakeholders, elders, students, researchers, parents, thought leaders across disciplines) meet on equal terms to develop viable solutions to our current challenges. The term was first used in computer sciences to describe virtual research centres and was later used to describe emerging networked organizational forms associated with unique collaboration, communication and governing principles.

Common good. The greatest possible good for the greatest number of individuals: a world where all citizens live well and within the limits of the planet.

Creating shared value. The principle of creating shared value involves building economic value in a way that also creates value for society by addressing its needs and challenges. The concept was popularized by a 2011 article in Harvard Business Review written by Michael Porter and Mark Kramer.

Emerging Benchmarks. Standards and examples against which to measure and promote collaborative "best for the world" management education initiatives and approaches that are relevant and sensitive to the challenge of developing responsible leadership for a sustainable world. This stands in contrast to the traditional and prevalent view of benchmarking as a process in a competitive "best in the world" context. In the 50+20 vision "emerging benchmarks" refers to a collection of emerging innovations and practices by management educators around the globe that are attempting to pioneer "best for the world" management education.

Engaged scholarship. Researchers and practitioners interacting effectively to co-produce knowledge that is relevant to both research and practice, with academics contributing rigorously developed scientific insights alongside practitioners' understanding of the realities of the business world.

Experiential learning. A pragmatic, intellectual approach to learning, focusing on the analytical interpretation of an experience. Current practices such as internships, field trips and business simulations are examples for experiential learning.

Experimental learning. Learning that differentiates between affective, imaginative, conceptual, and practical modes of psyche and focuses on what occurs within the learner. Experimental learning offers more ways of understanding and integrating an experience than experiential learning, thereby enriching the learning experience.

Globally responsible leadership. A response to existing gaps in leadership theory and practical challenges facing leaders. It is defined by the Globally Responsible Leadership Initiative (GRLI) as "the global exercise of ethical, values-based leadership in the pursuit of economic and societal progress and sustainable development. It is based on a fundamental understanding of the interconnectedness of the world and a recognition of the need for economic and societal and environmental advancement."

Perspective transformation. The process of enabling individuals to revise their beliefs and modify their behavior. Used in the context of transformative learning.

Reflective awareness. An evolved level of consciousness and personal awareness within an individual that is reflected in the way he/she relates to him/herself, their environment and various aspects of the world. It is developed through the capacity of self reflection and seen as a fundamental, non-negotiable foundation of a globally responsible leader.

Stewardship. An ethic that embodies responsible and sustainable management of resources. The concept of stewardship is linked to the concept of sustainability and refers to accepting responsibility for something that belongs to someone else.

Third person perspective. Assessing leadership from a distance, usually by discussing how other leaders have performed rather than actually experiencing the leadership role personally.

Transdisciplinarity. Used mostly in the context of research, transdisciplinarity goes beyond multi- and interdisciplinarity with the goal of intertwining the process of research with the process of problem solving in the real world. It systematically connects research and practice.

Whole person learning. Embracing all aspects of what it means to be human: feelings, senses, intuition, connection to others and the broader cosmic environment, as well as the mind and intellect, combining both experiential and experimental learning.

Index